Computer Corpora and Open Source Software for Language Learning:

Emerging Research and Opportunities

Kristina Posavec
University of Zagreb, Croatia

A volume in the Advances in Educational Technologies and Instructional Design (AETID) Book Series

IGI Global
PUBLISHER of TIMELY KNOWLEDGE

Published in the United States of America by
IGI Global
Information Science Reference (an imprint of IGI Global)
701 E. Chocolate Avenue
Hershey PA, USA 17033
Tel: 717-533-8845
Fax: 717-533-8661
E-mail: cust@igi-global.com
Web site: http://www.igi-global.com

Library of Congress Cataloging-in-Publication Data

Names: Posavec, Kristina, 1984- author.
Title: Computer corpora and open source software for language learning : emerging research and opportunities / Kristina Posavec.
Description: Hershey : Information Science Reference, 2020. | Includes bibliographical references and index. | Summary: "This book explores the use of free open source software (NoSketch Engine) for learning the Croatian, English, and German languages in Croatian primary and secondary schools"-- Provided by publisher.
Identifiers: LCCN 2019057530 | ISBN 9781799836803 (hardcover) | ISBN 9781799836810 (paperback) | ISBN 9781799836827 (ebook)
Subjects: LCSH: Language and languages--Computer-assisted instruction. | Language and languages--Computer-assisted instruction--Research. | Computational linguistics. | Croatian language--Computer assisted instruction. | English language--Computer-assisted instruction for foreign speakers. | German language--Computer-assisted instruction for foreign speakers. | Language arts--Croatia--Computer assisted instruction.
Classification: LCC P53.28 .P6727 2020 | DDC 418.0078/5--dc23
LC record available at https://lccn.loc.gov/2019057530

This book is published in the IGI Global book series Advances in Educational Technologies and Instructional Design (AETID) (ISSN: 2326-8905; eISSN: 2326-8913)

British Cataloguing in Publication Data
A Cataloguing in Publication record for this book is available from the British Library.

All work contributed to this book is new, previously-unpublished material.
The views expressed in this book are those of the authors, but not necessarily of the publisher.

For electronic access to this publication, please contact: eresources@igi-global.com.

Advances in Educational Technologies and Instructional Design (AETID) Book Series

ISSN:2326-8905
EISSN:2326-8913

Editor-in-Chief: Lawrence A. Tomei, Robert Morris University, USA

MISSION

Education has undergone, and continues to undergo, immense changes in the way it is enacted and distributed to both child and adult learners. In modern education, the traditional classroom learning experience has evolved to include technological resources and to provide online classroom opportunities to students of all ages regardless of their geographical locations. From distance education, Massive-Open-Online-Courses (MOOCs), and electronic tablets in the classroom, technology is now an integral part of learning and is also affecting the way educators communicate information to students.

The **Advances in Educational Technologies & Instructional Design (AETID) Book Series** explores new research and theories for facilitating learning and improving educational performance utilizing technological processes and resources. The series examines technologies that can be integrated into K-12 classrooms to improve skills and learning abilities in all subjects including STEM education and language learning. Additionally, it studies the emergence of fully online classrooms for young and adult learners alike, and the communication and accountability challenges that can arise. Trending topics that are covered include adaptive learning, game-based learning, virtual school environments, and social media effects. School administrators, educators, academicians, researchers, and students will find this series to be an excellent resource for the effective design and implementation of learning technologies in their classes.

COVERAGE

- Curriculum Development
- Bring-Your-Own-Device
- Adaptive Learning
- Hybrid Learning
- Educational Telecommunications
- K-12 Educational Technologies
- Classroom Response Systems
- Collaboration Tools
- Game-Based Learning
- Instructional Design Models

IGI Global is currently accepting manuscripts for publication within this series. To submit a proposal for a volume in this series, please contact our Acquisition Editors at Acquisitions@igi-global.com or visit: http://www.igi-global.com/publish/.

The Advances in Educational Technologies and Instructional Design (AETID) Book Series (ISSN 2326-8905) is published by IGI Global, 701 E. Chocolate Avenue, Hershey, PA 17033-1240, USA, www.igi-global.com. This series is composed of titles available for purchase individually; each title is edited to be contextually exclusive from any other title within the series. For pricing and ordering information please visit http://www.igi-global.com/book-series/advances-educational-technologies-instructional-design/73678. Postmaster: Send all address changes to above address.

Titles in this Series

For a list of additional titles in this series, please visit:
http://www.igi-global.com/book-series/advances-educational-technologies-instructional-design/73678

New Technological Applications for Foreign and Second Language Learning and Teaching
Mariusz Kruk (University of Zielona Góra, Poland) and Mark Peterson (Kyoto University, Japan)
Information Science Reference • © 2020 • 300pp • H/C (ISBN: 9781799825913) • US $195.00

Teaching Language and Literature On and Off-Canon
José Manuel Correoso-Rodenas (Univesidad de Castilla-La Mancha, Spain)
Information Science Reference • © 2020 • 300pp • H/C (ISBN: 9781799833796) • US $195.00

Examining the Roles of Teachers and Students in Mastering New Technologies
Eva Podovšovnik (University of Primorska, Slovenia)
Information Science Reference • © 2020 • 330pp • H/C (ISBN: 9781799821045) • US $195.00

Methodologies and Outcomes of Engineering and Technological Pedagogy
Kaushik Kumar (Birla Institute of Technology, Mesra, India) and J. Paulo Davim (University of Aveiro, Portugal)
Engineering Science Reference • © 2020 • 364pp • H/C (ISBN: 9781799822455) • US $195.00

Enriching Teaching and Learning Environments With Contemporary Technologies
Mehmet Durnali (Ereğli Faculty of Education, Zonguldak Bülent Ecevit University, Turkey) and İbrahim Limon (Ministry of National Education, Turkey)
Information Science Reference • © 2020 • 329pp • H/C (ISBN: 9781799833833) • US $195.00

For an entire list of titles in this series, please visit:
http://www.igi-global.com/book-series/advances-educational-technologies-instructional-design/73678

IGI Global
PUBLISHER of TIMELY KNOWLEDGE

701 East Chocolate Avenue, Hershey, PA 17033, USA
Tel: 717-533-8845 x100 • Fax: 717-533-8661
E-Mail: cust@igi-global.com • www.igi-global.com

Table of Contents

Preface

This book examines corpus-based teaching of Croatian as first and English and German as second and foreign language in Croatia's primary and secondary schools.

This research relays on analyse of teachers needs when it comes to corpus tools in the context of everyday demands language classes have. The book provides conclusions concerning the teachers opinions on teaching innovations in the form of corpus-based methodology of language teaching. The examination and analysis of the attitudes, needs, knowledge and perceptions of the teachers who participated in this research determined the advantages and disadvantages of corpora and corpus tools in corpus-based teaching of language classes in primary and secondary schools.

Main questions of this research were directed to investigate and determine the teachers needs and attitudes about:

- Use of free ICT tool (computer corpora) for preparing teaching materials for their students
- Perception and attitude towards using computer corpora and corpus tools for teaching language classes in primary and secondary schools
- Use of corpus tools directly in classroom with students (DDL approach)
- Education and knowledge about what corpora and corpus tools are for teachers in primary and secondary schools
- Functionalities and possibilities of computer corpora and corpus tools in the field of language education at primary and secondary education level

Factors within the research have emerged regarding the implications of computer corpora in language teaching, e.g. fear of changes, time limitations, finance situation of schools, motivation for indirect or direct use of corpora, etc. Additionally, book provides explanation of functionalities of NoSketch

Engine (online corpora) which was used during this research. On one hand this book contains practical knowledge on how to use, search and analyse corpus results in a term of concordances, KWIC, collocations, wordlists, frequency of words, sorting results, etc. It is a handbook for language teachers to learn how to use corpus tools but it is also a research which provides insight into teachers and students perceptions and motivation to use corpora for language learning and teaching L1 and L2 languages.

THE CHALLENGES

Main challenge during this research was to find teachers who were willing to participate in the research. Many of teachers declined participation and the minority who accepted were reluctant to conduct experiment with their students directly in the classroom. Because of that qualitative analysis was conducted in a form of in-depth interviews which gave deeper understanding of teachers' attitudes and perception about use of computer corpora for teaching language subjects in primary and secondary schools. Another challenge was to present results so it could be applied to any language not just Croatian. Therefor results of in-depth interviews with teachers are describing their thoughts and suggestions how they interpret corpora, how they seen their use in primary and secondary education and what needs to be done for corpora to find their place in classrooms.

SEARCHING FOR A SOLUTION

The research was conducted in the second half of school year 2018/2019 (from February till June) with four language teachers. Two teachers are working in secondary school where one teacher is teaching Croatian as first language and second teacher is teaching English and German as second language. Other two teacher are working in primary schools (higher level of primary school) where one teacher is teaching Croatian as first language and second teacher is teaching English as second language. With all four teachers were conducted in-depth interviews to get insight into their perceptions, attitudes and needs about use of computer corpora and corpus tools for preparing teaching materials and classes for their students. Based on their answers, attitudes and knowledge about teaching and working with students in primary and secondary schools, conclusions were formed with additional insight information about use of corpus-based language teaching. Implication of corpora use for teaching language subjects emerged during this research and gave information about what needs to be done regarding school infrastructure, finance, education, national curriculum and teachers training so that corpora and it tools could be incorporated into primary and secondary education for teaching language subjects. Although the research was conducted in Croatia, conclusion could be applied for other language because the aim of research was to investigate how language teachers see use of computer corpora in primary and secondary regardless of language they teach.

ORGANIZATION OF THE BOOK

The book is organized into eight chapters. A brief description of each of the chapters follows:

Introduction

The chapter will provide an introduction into topics and explanation of main goals which will be researched and examined in this book. It will give an overview of the research areas and provide a theoretical background of computer corpora and its possibilities for education propose in learning first and the second language in primary and secondary schools in Croatia. It will explain the role of computer corpora and its tools in the language learning process, conducting linguistic research and analysis for Croatian as a first language, English and German as a second language.

Chapter 1: Characteristics and Typologies Types of Computer Corpora

This chapter will give insight to available corpus tools which are free for end users and have open language databases with different types of texts. Main corpus tool which will be presented is NoSketch Engine, online interface for searching, creating and analyzing corpus data. The chapter will provide information about available corpora in NoSketch Engine and additional corpus tool which are available to users for conducting language analyzes, preparing teaching materials, exploring and learning the language.

Chapter 2: Corpus Tools and Technology

This chapter will give insight to available corpus tools which are free for end users and have open language databases with different types of texts. Main corpus tool which will be presented is NoSketch Engine, online interface for searching, creating and analyzing corpus data. The chapter will provide information about available corpora in NoSketch Engine and additional corpus tool which are available to users for conducting language analyzes, preparing teaching materials, exploring and learning the language.

Chapter 3: Searching Methods for Corpora in NoSketch Engine

In this chapter readers will get insight to free online system for creating and searching corpora, No Sketch Engine and its abilities. The chapter will provide valuable information about all corpus tools and functionality which users can use for conducting linguistic research, preparing teaching materials, exams or exercise for their students. In detailed will be explained the basic syntax for querying corpus, a corpus query language (CQL). Along with that, the chapter will provide examples of CQL syntax so that users can easier comprehend the basics for searching and exploring large language databases in different languages.

Chapter 4: Methodology and Research

This chapter describes used methodology approaches used in this research and how research was organized and conducted with involved participants.

Chapter 5: Using Computer Corpora in Primary School

This chapter will provide information and data about primary schools and their teachers who participated in the research. The chapter will show in-depth interviews with teachers from two primary schools in Croatia. The purpose of the in-depth interview is to research and analyze teachers needs, opinions, attitudes, values and knowledge about computer corpora in general. The second goal is to explore in which way teachers in primary schools would use computer corpora for creating teaching materials, exams or language exercise. The aim of this chapter is to investigate can computer corpora be implemented in primary schools for teaching language subjects, in which why and for what students/ grades it would be most eligible.

Chapter 6: Using Computer Corpora in Secondary School

This chapter will provide information and data about secondary schools and its teachers which are included in the research. The chapter will show in-depth interviews with teachers from secondary schools. The purpose of the in-depth interview is to research teacher needs, opinions, attitudes, values and knowledge about computer corpora in general. The second goal is to explore in which way teachers in secondary schools would use computer corpora for creating teaching materials, exams or language exercise. The aim of this chapter is to investigate can computer corpora be implemented in secondary schools for teaching language subjects, in which why and for what students/grade it would be most eligible.

Chapter 7: Implications of Using Corpus Tools in Primary and Secondary Education

This chapter will give a comparison of using computer corpora in primary and in secondary schools. It will compare information which will be collected from primary school teachers and secondary school teacher about using computer corpora for language subjects on primary and secondary educational level. Based on the given information chapter will provide an explanation of the advantages and disadvantages of using computer corpora in language learning on those two educational levels. The chapter will explore which educational level have more possibilities for incorporating computer corpora in their teaching activities and can it be used in the classroom with students.

Chapter 8: Conclusion and Further Research

This chapter will give an overview of full research with its conclusions and implications of creating teaching materials, exercises, and exams with the use of computer corpora. It will explore future possibilities of using corpus and its tools in learning language subjects. The chapter will show research conclusions based on teachers experience working with computer corpora and its tools to prepare their teaching units for language learning. This chapter will try to give an answer to the question does computer corpora have its future in language learning subjects in primary and secondary educational levels. Additionally, this chapter will present ideas for further research and existing limitations of this research.

Appendix A

Appendix A contains list of all questions which were included in the in-depth interviews with teachers from primary and secondary schools in Croatia. Results of Appendix A are shown and interpreted in Chapter 6 and 7.

Appendix B

Appendix B shows survey which was given to students from primary school who participated in this research and who were using DDL approach and corpus-based materials during the school lesson. Results of Appendix B are shown and interpreted in Chapter 6.

Appendix C

Appendix C shows teacher's AP corpus-based teaching unite (materials) which he prepared during this research for his students for learning Croatian as first language in primary school. Results of Appendix C are shown and interpreted in Chapter 6.

Kristina Posavec
University of Zagreb, Croatia

Acknowledgment

The editor would like to acknowledge the help of all the people involved in this project and, more specifically, the teachers who participated in the research and gave valuable insights and contributions, and reviewers that took part in the review process. Without their support, this book would not have become a reality.

First, the editor would like to thank each one of the teachers for their contributions. Our sincere gratitude goes to the teachers who contributed their time and expertise for creating corpus-based materials and conducted DLL approach in their classrooms.

Second, the editor wishes to acknowledge the valuable contributions of the reviewers regarding the improvement of quality, coherence, and content presentation of chapters.

Kristina Posavec
University of Zagreb, Croatia

Introduction

One of the advantages of corpus linguistics approach lies in its empirical nature which makes language analysis objective (McEnery, Wilson, 2001). Corpora are now used intensively in almost all branches and fields of linguistics, including lexicography, contrastive linguistics studies, translation studies, semantics, pragmatics, stylistics, sociolinguistics, discourse analysis, forensic linguistics and language pedagogy.

Use of computer corpora when using for language learning (primary, secondary, university, adult education) can be considered as part of computer-assisted language learning (CALL) and technology-enhanced language learning (TELL).

Davies (2016) defines computer-assisted language learning (CALL) as "an approach to language teaching and learning in which the computer is used as an aid to the presentation, reinforcement and assessment of material to be learned, usually including a substantial interactive element" (p. 1). This could be applied to preparation process of teaching materials, which will be used in the classroom for language teaching, or to present students with language materials, which are produced by teacher using computer corpora.

Kranthi (2017) defines technology-enhanced language as "learning refers to the use of computer as a technological innovation to display multimedia as a means of complementing a teaching method language teacher" (p. 31). Additionally, Kranthi (2017) emphasis the difference between CALL and TELL stating that "in CALL, the computer assisted learning, and in TELL, the computer supports learning" (p. 30). TELL can be applied to direct use of corpora in classroom with students where teacher is using corpora to teach certain language unit and students can individually or in groups work with corpora to gain new knowledge.

These definitions of CALL and TELL are putting use of computer corpora on the both sides of this approaches. Role of computer corpora in language learning can be seen both as CALL and TELL depending on teachers approach and use of technology in his or her classroom. Corpora can be CALL if teacher is using it preparing teaching materials for classroom but also it can be part of TELL when teacher is using corpora directly in the classroom where students use it to gain new knowledge in specific part of language or for investigation of some language issues. Some of participants in this research conducted both, preparing teaching materials and using corpora directly in classroom with their students.

In the previous decade, many scientific studies (Gavioli, Aston, 2001; Hunston, 2002; Boulton, 2010) focused on examining the role of corpora in language teaching and learning, emphasizing corpus data analysis, which allows students to become experts in observing language by raising their grammar awareness and creating generalization when it comes to learning native and other languages. Römer (2008) states that corpus linguistics and language teaching have a dynamic relationship in which language teaching benefits from the resources, studies and methodology provided by corpus linguistics, whereas the demands and needs of language teaching motivate and entice further research in the field of corpus linguistics because it wants to find an adequate solution for the demand in the field of teaching foreign languages.

Leech (1997) noticed that language learning (teaching) and corpora have three contact points: indirect use of corpora when it comes to teaching (reference sources, teaching materials and language examinations), direct use of corpora in teaching ("teaching about", "teaching to exploit" and "exploiting to teach") and the development of corpora with the purpose of teaching (learner corpora).

Bennett (2010) describes different ways in which corpora can be included in language classes: corpus-based teaching materials (by using patterns and frequencies extracted from a corpus), corpus-based reference materials (dictionaries, textbooks and grammars) and corpus-based teaching activities where the student works with real data.

Direct use of corpora in language pedagogy is limited by certain factors: time, the lecturer's knowledge and skills needed to analyse the corpus and to mediate pedagogically, access to sources such as computers and appropriate computer tools or a combination of these factors (Gabrielatos, 2005; McEnery, Xiao, 2011).

The biggest advantage of using corpora in lexicography is that they are machine-sensible. This allows lexicographers to extract all typical examples of a lexeme's usage from a large corpus of text in a matter of seconds. Another advantage of the corpus-based approach is the frequency of information and quantification of collocations, which can be provided by the corpus. The frequency of data has an even bigger and more important role in the so-called frequency dictionaries, which define the basic vocabulary in order to help students of different foreign languages learn the basics of that language, e.g. Davies (2005) for Spanish or Xiao, Rayson and McEnery (2009) for Chinese.

Some scientists have used data from corpora directly in order to evaluate existing materials for teaching English as a foreign language. Mindt (1996) discovered that the usage of grammatical structures in textbooks for learning English as a foreign language significantly deviates from their use in English as a mother tongue. This is why students often struggle with communicating with native speakers of a language. A simple yet important role of using corpora in language teaching is introducing more realistic examples of language use which reflect the complexity and nuances of a natural language. Mindt (1996) claims that a syllabus for language teaching should be based on empirical evidence, not on tradition and intuition, with the frequency of use acting as a guide for determining teaching priorities.

The focus of the lexical approach to language pedagogy is teaching collocations (i.e. the usual co-occurrences of lexical units), as well as the concept of phrasemes related to it. There is a consensus that the knowledge of collocations is necessary for developing skills concerning both the mother tongue and foreign languages (Bahns, 1993; Hoey, 2004; Nesselhauf, 2003). This knowledge points to how frequently a lexical unit appears next to others and what their relationship in a sentence is.

Corpora are not used just because collocations can be measured quantitatively but because seeing tokens and their context in the corpus - KWIC (*key word in context*) - exposes students to a large amount of authentic and structured data. Kennedy (2003) discussed the connections between corpus data and the nature of language learning. The author claims that learning a second or a foreign language is a process of consciously adopting explicit knowledge which demands exposure to linguistic data.

Another field of language pedagogy which is starting to use the corpus-based approach is language examinations. Coniam (1997) shows how to use word frequency from a corpus when automatically creating tests where students have to fill in the blanks. Kaszubski and Wojnowska (2003) presented a computer program, TestBuilder, based on a corpus, for creating ELT (English Language Teaching) exercises based on sentences.

Corpora are used today for archiving examination scripts, developing examination materials, optimizing examination procedures, improving the quality of grading, and examination validation and standardization (McEnery,

Xiao, 2011). Corpora are also used for educating foreign language lecturers (Conrad, 1999; Seidlhofer, 2000; O'Keeffe, Farr, 2003). O'Keeffe and Farr (2003) claim that corpus linguistics should be included into lecturers' initial education in order to improve their research skills and language awareness.

And while indirect corpus use, such as syllabus design and material development, is closely related to what is being taught, corpora also provide a valuable insight into teaching methods. From Leech's (1997) three contact points, direct corpus use includes "teaching about", "teaching to exploit" and "exploiting to teach". "Teaching about" concerns teaching corpus linguistics as an academic subject, like other sub-disciplines, such as syntax and pragmatics. "Teaching to exploit" means providing students with practical knowledge, as emphasized by McEnery, Xiao and Tono (2006), so that the students can search a corpus themselves and thus meet their own needs. "Exploiting to teach" implies using the corpus-based approach to replace language teaching methods which are not corpus-based.

Many scientists (Sinclair, 2004; McEnery, Wilson, 2001) describe ways in which computer corpora can be used in language teaching. As a matter of fact, both early and modern-day studies point to the field's importance by enumerating examples of practical use of computer corpora when it comes to language teaching.

Corpora, unlike traditional textbooks, offer a large number of examples. In other words, they provide students with "a large selection of situations that show how different lexical terms are used, depending on the context in which they appear." (Dash, 2011)

The advantages of using corpora instead of textbook materials in teaching foreign languages are numerous. It is important to emphasize that we are not talking about getting rid of textbooks altogether here, but about integrating corpora into the language teaching process. This can be applied to preparing teaching materials for classes or to integration of corpora into the teaching process itself, which would make teachers intermediaries between students and corpora and consequently improve the efficiency of the teaching process. Corpus analysis is an "ideal tool for reevaluating the order of presentation of linguistic features from textbooks and for making principled decisions about which parts of the textbook should be presented" (Barbieri, Eckhardt, 2007, p. 322). Lawson (2001) mentions four fields of language teaching in which the use of a corpus can provide better understanding of language structures and grammar. He states that a corpus provides information about the frequency of tokens in the authentic language. To put it differently, it gives us an insight into the most commonly used words or phrases in everyday language, whereas textbooks often contain artificially created. The second point Lawson (2001) makes is that a corpus provides information about the difference in use of special linguistic features in a certain context or situation. The third point is about the information a corpus provides about the linguistic features of language use, and the last one talks about information on discourse properties of certain linguistic features such as collocations, lexical-grammatical association etc.

The use of corpora can provide us with qualitative and quantitative analyses (McCarten, 2007), with the latter meaning statistical representation of information, like for example the frequency of tokens, while the former stands for the ability to display the large number of texts the corpus contains, texts which allow students and lecturers to show the context in which a certain token, i.e. a word or a phrase, appears and how it is used in different contexts.

Corpus linguistics can help with preparing language teaching materials because it allows lecturers to notice recurring patterns in a language. It can identify linguistic patterns by using the representation of frequency of a certain term, word or phrase used in everyday conversation. Still, even with all the advantages of corpus use in language teaching, the key to a successful corpus-based approach is in the appropriate level of the lecturer's guidance or pedagogical mediation which depends on the student's age, experience and prior knowledge. It is therefore very important that lecturers be equipped with the necessary knowledge and educated for using and analyzing corpora on a daily basis.

REFERENCES

Bahns, J. (1993). Lexical collocations: A contrastive view. *ELT Journal*, *47*(1), 56–63. doi:10.1093/elt/47.1.56

Barbieri, F., & Eckhardt, S. E. (2007). Applying corpus-based findings to form-focused instruction: The case of reported speech. *Language Teaching Research*, *11*(3), 319–346. doi:10.1177/1362168807077563

Bennett, G. R. (2010). *Using corpora in the language learning classroom: Corpus linguistics for teachers*. University of Michigan Press. doi:10.3998/mpub.371534

Boulton, A. (2010). Data-driven learning: Taking the computer out of the Equation. *Language Learning*, *60*(3), 534–572. doi:10.1111/j.1467-9922.2010.00566.x

Coniam, D. (1997). A preliminary inquiry into using corpus word frequency data in the automatic generation of English language cloze tests. *CALICO Journal*, *§§§*, 15–33.

Conrad, S. (1999). The importance of corpus-based research for language teachers. *System*, *27*, 1–18.

Conrad, S. (1999). The importance of corpus-based research for language teachers. *System*, *27*(1), 1–18. doi:10.1016/S0346-251X(98)00046-3

Dash, N. S. (2011). *Corpus-Based English Language Teaching: A New Method.* Available at: https://www.academia.edu/3563414/Corpus-Based_English_Language_Teaching_A_New_Method

Davies, G. (2016). *CALL (computer assisted language learning).* http://www. llas. ac. uk/resources/gpg/61

Davies, M. (2005). *A Frequency Dictionary of Spanish*. London: Routledge.

Gabrielatos, C. (2005). Corpora and Language Teaching: Just a Fling or Wedding Bells? *Tesl-Ej*, *8*(4), n4.

Gavioli, L., & Aston, G. (2001). Enriching reality: Language corpora in language pedagogy. *ELT Journal*, *55*(3), 238–246. doi:10.1093/elt/55.3.238

Hoey, M. (2004). Lexical priming and the properties of text. In A. Partington, J. Morley, & L. Haarman (Eds.), *Corpora and Discourse* (pp. 385–412). Bern: Peter Lang.

Hunston, S. (2002). *Corpora in applied linguistics*. Ernst Klett Sprachen. doi:10.1017/CBO9781139524773

Kaszubski, P., & Wojnowska, A. (2003). Corpus-informed exercises for learners of English: the TestBuilder program. *Research and Scholarship in Integration Processes: Poland-USA–EU*, 337-354.

Kennedy, G. (2003). Amplifier collocations in the British National Corpus: Implications for English language teaching. *TESOL Quarterly*, *37*(3), 467–487. doi:10.2307/3588400

Kranthi, K. (2017). Technology Enhanced Language Learning (TELL). *International Journal of Business and Management Invention*, *6*(2), 30–33.

Lawson, A. (2001). Rethinking French grammar for pedagogy: The contribution of French corpora. In *Corpus linguistics in North America. Selections from the 1999 Symposium*. Ann Arbor, MI: The University of Michigan Press.

Leech, G. (1997). Teaching and language corpora: a convergence. In A. Wichmann, S. Fligelstone, T. McEnery, & G. Knowles (Eds.), Teaching and Language Corpora, (pp. 1-23). Academic Press.

McCarten, J. (2007). *Teaching vocabulary*. Lessons from the Corpus, Lessons for the Classroom.

McEnery, T., & Wilson, A. (2001). *Corpus Linguistics*. Edinburgh: Edinburgh University Press.

McEnery, T., & Xiao, R. (2011). What corpora can offer in language teaching and learning. Handbook of research in second language teaching and learning, 2, 364-380.

McEnery, T., Xiao, R., & Tono, Y. (2006). *Corpus-Based Language Studies: An Advanced Resource Book*. London: Routledge.

Mindt, D. (1996). English corpus linguistics and the foreign language teaching syllabus. *Using corpora for language research*, 232-247.

Nesselhauf, N. (2003). The use of collocations by advanced learners of English and some implications for teaching. *Applied Linguistics*, *24*(2), 223–242. doi:10.1093/applin/24.2.223

O'Keeffe, A., & Farr, F. (2003). Using language corpora in initial teacher education: Pedagogic issues and practical applications. *TESOL Quarterly*, *37*(3), 389–418. doi:10.2307/3588397

Römer, U. (2008). Corpora and language teaching. In A. Lüdeling & M. Kytö (Eds.), *Corpus Linguistics. An International Handbook* (Vol. 1, pp. 112–130). Berlin: Mouton de Gruyter.

Seidlhofer, B. (2000). Operationalizing intertextuality: Using learner corpora for learning. In L. Burnard & T. McEnery (Eds.), *Rethinking Language Pedagogy from Corpus Perspective* (pp. 207–223). Frankfurt: Peter Lang.

Sinclair, J. (1991). *Corpus, Concordance, Collocation*. Oxford: Oxford University Press.

Sinclair, J. M. (Ed.). (2004). *How to use corpora in language teaching* (Vol. 12). John Benjamins Publishing. doi:10.1075cl.12

Xiao, R., Rayson, P., & McEnery, T. (2009). *A Frequency Dictionary of Mandarin Chinese*. London: Routledge.

Chapter 1
Types of Computer Corpora

ABSTRACT

This chapter will give an overview of different types of corpora and explain their differences. It will provide readers with different examples of computer corpora that are available to users and for which language analysis can be used. Based on differences of existing corpora, the chapter will show in which way users (language teachers) can use these corpora for creating teaching materials for their students. It will explain why certain types of corpora can be and are open educational resources that provide teachers with a large number of language examples. Additionally, the chapter will examine open source technology (e.g., available tools and programs for creating computer corpora).

INTRODUCTION

Definitions

One of the methods by which a language can be analysed and studied is corpus linguistics, which "in its broadest sense encompasses corpus-based language research" (Utvić, 2013), i.e. use of corpus to analyze language. A corpus is a collection of texts, written or spoken, stored in a computer (O'Keefee, McCarthy, Carter, 2007), online in the cloud[1], on web or in books, so it can be defined as a systematized collection of a natural language (Nesselhauf, 2005; Reppen, 2011). The Glossary of Language Technologies[2] defines a corpus as a "written or spoken language resource collected and annotated with

DOI: 10.4018/978-1-7998-3680-3.ch001

the purpose of: analyzing a language to determine its properties, analyzing human behavior (in the sphere of language use) in certain situations, training the system to adapt its behavior to specific language circumstances, empirical testing of a language theory, creating a test for a language-engineering technique or an application of the technique to see how it functions in practice." The same glossary also gives a definition of computer corpora for which it claims that they are "encoded in a standard and consistent way with the intention of keeping them open for computer searches." Information and communication technology plays a key role in development of corpora because "the creation of computer technology has made corpus research possible, as the computer is able to store, code, categorize, and retrieve massive amounts of information" (Durand, 2018, p. 132).

The term originates from the Latin word "*corpus, corporis* meaning a body, a whole, totality, a set, an almanac" (Utvić, 2013, p. 1). The term "corpus linguistics" was created in the 1980s (Leech, 1992) and it is was first mentioned by Aarts and Mejia in 1982 in the paper "Grammars and Intuitions in Corpus Linguistics", and it appeared again in 1984 in the book "Corpus Linguistics I: Recent Developments in the Use of Computer Corpora". In 1991, on an international symposium of British, Dutch, Swedish and Norwegian linguists, a new group of researchers under the name corpus linguists was formed. From 1996, they have also been publishing their own journal - *The International Journal of Corpus Linguistics* (Leech, 1992; Utvić, 2013). Utvić (2013) thinks that the authors of the definitions of corpus linguistics are stating their opinions about corpus linguistics and based on that treat it as a tool, method, methodology, methodological approach, discipline, theory, theoretical approach, theoretical or methodological paradigm or a combination of all of the above. He also claims that corpus linguistics is today considered to be primarily a methodology or a group of methodologies, not a separate theoretical discipline in the field of linguistics and also wonders whether or not corpus linguistics represents something more than mere methodology (Utvić, 2013). More detailed overview of definition and discussion on what corpus linguistics is can be found in Taylor (2008) "What is corpus linguistics? What the data says" where author states that "corpus linguistics is a tool, a method, a methodology, a methodological approach, a discipline, a theory, a theoretical approach, a paradigm (theoretical or methodological), or a combination of these" (Taylor, 2008, p. 180).

Corpus linguistics, apart from analyzing language with the use of corpora in its studies, wants to answer two important questions: "Which specific patterns are connected to lexical and grammatical features? and How do those patterns differ inside different corpora?" (Bennett, 2010)

As one of the leading figures during the rise of corpus linguistics, Leech (1992) states that computer corpora are not random collections of texts (p. 107). They are usually collected with a certain goal in mind and should be considered representative of certain types of text. According to Sinclair (2004), a corpus is "a corpus is a collection of pieces of language text in electronic form, selected according to external criteria to represent, as far as possible, a language or language variety as a source of data for linguistic research" (p. 16). Taking into consideration all of these definitions of a corpus, McEnery and Wilson (2001) conclude that a corpus should possess four main characteristics: sampling and representativeness, size, machine sensibility and standard reference.

In the book "Using corpora in the language classroom", Reppen (2011) claims that a corpus is a large compilation of texts in a natural language stored in some type of electronic form, e.g. online or on computer. Author separately considers and explains the definition by claiming that the term "natural language" denotes a language in real everyday use, such as newspaper articles, letters, books, conversations etc. The part of the definition stating that a corpus is a coherent collection of texts refers to corpus design. For example, if the subject is a described language, then the corpus should contain different categories like fiction, academic prose, personal letters, memoirs, literature etc.

Characteristics

Computers and computer programs are used for corpus creation because they allow a faster and simpler use, creation and search. Since corpora are composed of a large number of texts and words, computers simplify the process of finding and analysing the language. A corpus can never represent a language in its entirety, but it can offer its users, for example, "information on frequency, word registry and how the language is used" (Bennett, 2010). The corpus in and of itself represents a huge database of documents and texts stored on a computer, but without an appropriate software it cannot be searched and used. Therefore, computer programs "bring to life" the corpus' content and allow us to conduct a language analysis. Most often, these are corpus tools that, with the help of appropriate software, "process corpus data by showing frequency, phraseology and collocations." (Hunston, 2005, p. 3)

Technological advancement has provided multiple options when it comes to creating language corpora on a computer. Corpora can contain written texts which are input into a computer program designed for work with corpora directly, i.e. typed in, scanned, inserted as an electronic document (e.g. .pdf, .csv, .txt, etc.), copied directly from the internet, converting print files, images or PDF files to text files using Optical Character Recognition[3] (OCR) software which allows user to convert printed materials, images or PDF files to editable text files that are supported most commonly with widespread programs like, Microsoft Word, Excel, Notepad, etc. Another way of filling out a corpus is recording and inputting texts and words by spoken word or speech. The speaker's voice is recorded as they read the texts which are then input into the computer system for corpus creation. Wynne (2005) elaborates process of developing spoken corpora which consist out of four main stages which includes data collections, transcriptions, markup and annotation and access. He describes every stage providing detailed information and steps. Stage of data collection refers to process of recording speech and storing it on media storage device (e.g. computer, web, USB drive, etc.), transcription refers to process of placing transcription[4] on recordings, markup and annotation refers to process of POS tagging the audio materials in corpora and access refers to publishing materials (spoken corpora) and its transcriptions to the wider community (Wynne, 2005).

Apart from that, corpora can contain images and video materials which complement the text. Language analysis with the help of corpora is described through four characteristics which Bennett (2010) defined as follows: the first characteristic is the empirical analysis used to examine real patterns of language use in original, i.e. authentic texts, the second includes the large collection of original texts which are taken to be the primary basis for conducting the analysis, the third characteristic is using computers and computer programs to conduct the analysis, whereas the fourth encompasses qualitative and quantitative analytical methods. As he was contemplating the possibilities and expectations regarding the influence of corpora in the language teaching process, Tucker (2009) concluded that a corpus can be considered "a synchronic equivalent or a record of the speaker's diachronic language experience in the sense that existing phrases can be tested and their frequency can be measured, given that all the texts in which they are used are stored in an electronic form".

In their book *From corpus to classrooms*, authors O'Keeffe, McCarthy and Carter (2007) mention two types of analyses which can be used in language analysis thanks to corpora: quantitative and qualitative language analysis.

Quantitative analysis, for example, can determine the frequency of occurrence of a certain word in different contexts, while the qualitative analysis is all about studying the way a word, term or a phrase is used in the corpus; in this case, the frequency is not relevant.

The way corpora can be used and their purpose vary a lot. It can be used for creating learner dictionaries which are "based on both quantitative and qualitative data such as frequency, collocation, phraseology, and lexis in grammar; they also aim to provide definitions at the level of language that learners can understand, along with illustrative examples extracted from corpora; corpus an serve as a source of evidence that complements both the intuitions of teachers who speak English as a first or additional language, and the notions of learners about the ways speakers and writers actually use the language (Huang, 2017 p. 4). Apart from being the basic tool in corpus linguistics, where they are used to analyze language, they can also be used as something that helps with teaching second or foreign language. In addition, they can be used for translating texts and documents from one language to another or for "examining cultural stances which are expressed through language" (Hunston, 2005). When it comes to using corpora in teaching and the changes their use in this field has brought, scientific literature often emphasizes the advantages. Hunston (2002) condenses in terms of the importance of frequency, collocations and phraseology, variations, grammar lexemes and language authenticity.

It is important for learner/student (e.g. especially for second language learners) to be emerged into real language because "it increases the meaningful input for learners, as they get familiar with real authentic language (Girgin, 2019, p. 3). Additionally, despite the significant role of authentic language another advantage of using corpora in the language classroom is a role which student adopts during the learning process, as Boulton (2017) and Johnes (1991) claims learners/students are becoming researchers because they are working with real data and teacher is there to guide them and help them with process of discovering language. One of the aims of DLL approach is to motivate students to learn and explore language, "DDL hands students the same research tools as academic researchers, sets them tasks and encourages them to explore the data, this approach has proved effective in intermediate-to-advanced translation studies for idiomatic expressions" (Wallis, Cushing, Aarts, 2019, p. 2). In this type of learning "the learner plays an active role, the process is supported by teachers or peers, and the pedagogical materials reflect the learner's emerging needs" (Huang, 2017 p. 3).

But apart from positive features, computer corpora have some flaws, which are discussed by Susan Hunston (2002) as she lists four main problems. Before using corpora, the user has to be aware of their potential flaws if they are to use them properly. The first problem, Hunston (2002) states, is the fact that a corpus does not provide info about what is possible and what is not but only about what is frequent and what isn't. Furthermore, a corpus displays only its own content, not language as a whole, which is why the conclusions made about the language shouldn't be treated as hard facts. The third flaw is the fact that a corpus does not provide information, only evidence, which means that it can provide a large number of language use examples which can be interpreted by using intuition and additional language knowledge. The last flaw is expressed in the claim that a corpus presents a language outside of its context, meaning that it cannot completely transfer the non-verbal parts of language communication, such as body language, vocalization, accents, tone of voice and other paralinguistic information unless the corpora are spoken and the user has the option of listening to a certain language.

Computer corpora can be used for working "on language for specific purposes, frequency lists and learner corpora, error-correction and contrastive analysis, to corpus uses in syllabus design, materials and resources, testing and translation, as well as fields from lexis to acquisition studies and more general language learning theory" (Boulton, 2017, p. 484). Main characteristics of corpora use in language learning is regarding autonomy, individualization, self-assessment, correction and translation but in the center is the teacher who guides their students during the learning process (Boulton, 2017; Johnes, 1991; McEnery, Wilson, 2001). It can be assumed that "skills in corpus methods, that is, certain techniques to analyse the data, are also a requirement, as is, finally, knowledge of how to interpret the information, so it seems that a range of skills are needed from teachers as well as from learners if they want to benefit from corpora" (Jantunen, 2016, p. 98).

Typologies

There is no universal corpus that can satisfy the needs of all users. Rather, there are several separate types of corpora which differ in their functionality. Depending on the needs of the research, motivation, language analysis, language learning, language teaching etc., different corpora will be used. Also, no single corpus can contain an overview of the whole language but should "collect a part of the language as an example that should be made as representative as possible" (Gabrielatos, 2005) for analysis and use. In the field of language teaching and application of corpora and corpus tools in class and for preparation of teaching materials, corpora are divided into four basic categories: "Corpora on a CD-ROM, online corpora, concordance program packages and corpus-based works and teaching materials" (Römer, 2006). Corpora on portable media such as CDs or DVDs often have a fee attached to them and cannot be upgraded, plus the user has to install them on their computer in order to search them. Most widespread and most often used corpora are those that are available online. In most cases, the user has free access to the corpus database and no additional installation onto the user's computer is required. This type of corpus is upgradeable and is constantly updated with new content, with the functionality of corpus searches and tools inside the program systems constantly being perfected for example British National Corpus, Corpus of Contemporary American English, Sketch Engine, etc. Concordance program packages include pre-made searchable text databases which can be analyzed and are most commonly found on portable media with some sort of fee attached to them, whereas corpus-based works and teaching materials include all types of scientific literature and cover the field of corpus linguistics with their structure, no matter if the subject is theoretical aspects or if we're talking about handbooks on how to use corpora and corpus tools. When it comes to dividing corpora, the division into eight main categories is the most common one in the scientific literature concerning corpus linguistics. Hunston (2002, 2005) in book "Corpora in Applied Linguistics" mentions and elaborates in great detail eight corpus types:

1. Specialized corpora refers to corpus which contains language data sets specified for certain filed, e.g. medicine, technology, engineering, news, etc.
2. General or corpora refers to corpus which contains language data sets which presents certain language (e.g. British National Coprus).
3. Comparative corpora refers to corpus which contains two or more corpora in different languages.
4. Parallel corpora refers to corpus which contains of at least two different language data sets (e.g. Italian and English language) which data/texts are exact by their content.
5. Learner corpora refers to corpus which contains language data sets created by students or learners during their foreign language classes.
6. Pedagogical corpora refers to corpus which contains language data sets which are used in the classroom.

7. Historical corpora refers to corpus which contains language data sets from certain period of time (e.g. Romanticism, Baroque, Medieval, etc.)
8. Monitor corpora refers to corpus which contains language data sets which monitor/track changes which are made in certain language (e.g. new words, phrases, idiom, etc.)

Each of them will be detailed explained and elaborated on in the later chapters of this text.

The same division, only in a more condensed version, is given by Bennett (2010), where author brings an overview and description of four main corpora - general, specialized, learner and pedagogical - which she claims are most commonly used when teaching second or foreign language.

Nesselhauf (2005) in her work "Corpus Linguistics: A Practical Introduction" divides corpora into two main groups based on the type of texts they contain and the analysis that is conducted on the texts in the corpus. The former division, the one based on the type of texts that are included in the corpus, includes:

- General and specialized corpora whose goal is to present language as a whole and which contain written word, but can also contain spoken word.
- Historical corpora and modern language corpora whose goal is to present the historical development of a language and give an overview of modern-day language in use.
- Regional corpora with the goal of presenting regional features of a certain language.
- Learner corpora whose goal is to present a language as a product of the students studying it.
- Multilingual and monolingual corpora whose goal is to present at least two different languages containing the same text so that a contrastive language analysis can be conducted.
- Speech and written corpora whose goal is to present spoken language, i.e. spoken word, whereas the written ones only have content in textual form.

The second type of division of corpora mentioned by the author is based on the way the text in the corpus is treated. In other words, the way this text is observed and analyzed is examined, not the type of text in the corpus. Author makes a distinction between annotated and unannotated corpora and claims that the tagged ones have undergone an appropriate analysis of the texts, such as sentence analysis or word classification.

Corpus linguistics dictionary[5] composed at the Department of Linguistics of the Faculty of Humanities and Social Sciences in Zagreb mentions several types of corpora. These are:

- Monitor corpus is the type of corpus not limited by standard corpus parameters (primarily its final size and the time span covered by the texts in the corpus).
- Untagged corpus is the type of corpus composed of texts which have no additional information. The texts forming the corpus are plain ASCII texts and contain no additional tags.
- Tagged corpus, on the other hand, contains various types of structural (title, paragraph, sentence etc.) and linguistic (grammatical categories, syntactic structure etc.) information.
- Parallel corpus is a corpus that contains texts in more than one language, with the texts being translations of each other.
- Reference corpus is a very large corpus used for determining basic characteristics of a language.

Gabrielatos (2005) and Miangah (2012) discuss several types and division of corpora. When it comes to corpus design, two main types of corpora are mentioned - reference corpora, which have a fixed size and do not grow larger, i.e. the number of their tokens is a constant, and monitor corpora which, unlike reference corpora, can grow, be upgraded and their number of tokens is constantly rising. In addition, Miangah (2012) states that there is a difference between corpora with complete texts and those that contain only samples of a text which have a certain length. The same author proceeds then to divide corpora according to their content, i.e. context, and speaks of general and specialized corpora which differ in that specialized corpora apply to a specific group of users and content, while the general ones are meant for wider use. The last division the author provides is based on language representation in a corpus and includes monolingual corpora (texts in only one language) and multilingual corpora, which contain texts translated into and represented in several languages, with parallel corpora being considered a subtype of multilingual corpora.

Learner corpus is composed of a group of texts created by students or learners during their foreign language classes. It can also be defined as a "systematic computer collection of texts created by students" (Nesselhauf,

2004). The purpose of this corpus is to notice the differences that appear between students of a foreign language and native speakers in order to see how big those differences are. For this type of research, a comparative corpus containing texts by native speakers is needed (Hunston, 2002). One of the advantages of using learner corpora is the possibility to improve the creation of pedagogical (teaching) materials because their use can "discover inherent issues of a certain group of students, which is especially important for higher levels of language learning whose issues are more subtle and which cannot be observed in a non-systematic way" (Nesselhauf, 2004). Apart from improving the construction and quality of teaching materials, learner corpora can be used for directly teaching students in order to show them the mistakes they make during their language practice and how to identify those mistakes so that they can acquire the necessary language skills and knowledge more efficiently.

One of the most famous corpora of this kind is the International Corpus of Learner English[6] (ICLE), which is composed of academic essays created as part of learning English as a second language by students of intermediate and advanced levels who are on their third or fourth year of their undergraduate programs. 16 language groups are represented in the ICLE, i.e. the native languages are: Bulgarian, Chinese, Czech, Dutch, Finnish, French, German, Italian, Japanese, Norwegian, Polish, Russian, Spanish, Swedish, Turkish and Tswana[7], a language spoken in regions of southern Africa. The first version of the ICLE was created in 2002, was available on a CD and contained 2.5 million words (Granger, Dagneaux, Meunier, 2002). The second, upgraded version was created in 2009, contains 3.7 million words and has "improved design of the interface through which the corpus is searched, the option to create concordances and the option to parse search results" (Granger, Dagneaux, Meunier, Paquot, 2009) according to profile information of the students whose essays are in the corpus.

Learner corpora are in most cases "tagged and can be explored in order to determine the most common mistakes students make" (Bennett, 2010). In the process of building and creating learner corpora, it is important to meet certain criteria, which is why this type of corpora is systematized. Nesselhauf (2004) enumerates the basic criteria that have to be set when selecting the content of learner corpora. These apply to the language level the students are learning, their first (native) language, type of language acquisition and the surrounding in which the language practice created as a part of the class is conducted and executed, while the included texts have to be representative and balanced. The learner corpus of students who are studying Croatian as their second and foreign language has been described by Mikelić Preradović, Beraći, Boras (2015).

Monitor corpus is a corpus that monitors changes in a language (Hunston, 2002). This corpus is upgraded on a daily, monthly or annual basis, which means its size increases rapidly. However, the ratio of the types of texts in the corpus is a constant, so it can be directly compared to other corpora on a daily, monthly or annual basis. Its main advantage is that it allows lexicographers to monitor new words entering the language or the changes in meaning of existing words (Miangah, 2012) in the process of building a dictionary. Sinclair (1991) calls it "monitor corpus" because it has "the ability to monitor the state of a language", which means that it monitors changes and novelties that appear in a language. In other words, it provides the user with "efficient evidence of language evolution".

Parallel corpora are composed of two or more corpora in different languages where each of the corpora contains texts translated from one language to the other or the texts have been simultaneously translated to two or more languages (Hunston, 2002). An example is a text translated from English to German or vice versa. They can be used by translators and students to find potential similarities in various terms in each of the languages or to explore the differences between them. Because they contain the same texts which are written in different languages, they provide their users with pedagogically important discoveries of contrastive language data which provides insight into equivalents noticeable in translation, if they exist, and their results can be used to extract useful information for creating bilingual and learner dictionaries (Römer, 2006). O'Keefee, McCarthy and Carter (2007) state that the most popular program applications used for searching parallel corpora in most cases contain instructions that teach and prepare the user for the process of translation, bilingual lexicography and a mechanism (computer software) used for translating. In the process of creating a parallel corpus, it is important to adhere to certain guidelines so that its content can be efficient when it comes to analysing the language it represents. It is therefore important to align the source text and its translation in order to establish a connection between the two texts at the level of words or sentences (McEnery, Xiao, 2007).

In Croatia, in 2000, the project of building a Croatian-English parallel corpus named Croatian-English parallel corpus/Hr-En p-corp was initiated at the Institute of Linguistics of the Faculty of Humanities and Social Sciences, University of Zagreb, under the leadership of Marko Tadić. One of the main goals of building that corpus was to provide the opportunity to analyze text conversion, corpus organization, sentence alignment and corpus decoding

(Tadić, 2000, 2001). The corpus contains newspaper articles from *Hrvatski tjednik* from the period between 1998 and May of 2000 and is composed on average of 1,409,964 million tokens for Croatian and 1,796,744 million tokens for English. It can be found at http://hnk.ffzg.hr/hr-en_p-corp/. That same year began the cooperation with Slovenia concerning the creation of a Slovenian-Croatian corpus under the leadership of Vesna Požgaj Hadži from the Faculty of Arts in Ljubljana and Marko Tadić from the Faculty of Humanities and Social Sciences in Zagreb. The goals and the purpose of creating this bilingual parallel corpus are "to create parallel corpora of Slovenian and Croatian originals and their respective translations, align the corpora on the level of translation equivalents of sentences and provide online access to the corpus via the world wide web (Požgaj, Tadić, 2000).

Apart from the two aforementioned corpora for Croatian, there is also a parallel corpus of English and a group of Balkan languages, which includes Croatian, called SETIMES[8]. In addition to Croatian, it includes Bulgarian, Bosnian, Greek, English, Macedonian, Romanian, Albanian, Serbian and Turkish language. This is a free multilingual parallel corpus composed of articles from the South-East European Times (http://www.setimes.com) website, which publishes news from the southeastern part of Europe. In total, the corpus contains 72 documents, 341,83M of tokens and 11,94M parts of speech (Tyers, Alperen, 2010). In the SETIMES corpus, the process of corpus alignment was undertaken only in the case of English, whereas no alignment was conducted between the Balkan languages (Tyers, Alperen, 2010).

The term online corpora or web-based corpora denotes corpora available on the internet (World Wide Web) which do not require any additional programs to be installed on a computer. They are usually free and offer plenty of options when it comes to searching their content. Croatian computer corpora (HNK, Croatian Language Repository and the website of Miroslav Krleža Institute of Lexicography) are available on the web and can be called online corpora.

Wu (2008) speaks of three types of online corpora and categorizes them as closed, those with paid access and free online corpora. The main feature of closed corpora is that only select groups of people can access them, whereas other users can access them solely in their printed form, as a publication (Wu, 2008). Such corpora include Longman Corpus Network, Cambridge International Corpus and World English Corpus (Wu, 2008). The main feature of corpora with paid access is that users can buy them for a certain fee, while free online corpora are available to everyone who wants to use them via internet. It is this latter type of corpora that is becoming more and more represented on the market. The largest free online English corpus contains more than 400 million tokens and is known as COCA (Corpus of Contemporary American English), followed by BNC (British National Corpus), which has about 100 million tokens (Davies, 2009).

When speaking about corpora available online, it is important to emphasize the difference between three different categories of corpora which can be linked to the internet and the WWW service through one of their characteristics.

The first group is composed of corpora which are available online and can belong to any type of corpora (learner, historical, general, specialized etc.) based on their content and general characteristics. These are online corpora, described in the previous subchapter.

The second group includes corpora that contain texts collected from the web. In other words, they use the web as a source of corpus materials which are then processed by computers in order to meet the linguistic needs for language analysis, research and teaching. Documents, i.e. texts from the web, are collected by using specialized computer programs for web crawling (Pomikálek, 2011) which search websites and store their content. After the language content is collected, the process of filtering texts is undertaken, and this includes "removing all non-textual content, such as HTML tags or JavaScript code, navigation, hyperlinks, headers, footers, advertisements etc. and removing duplicate documents" (Pomikálek, 2011, p. 12) in order to end up with cleansed corpus content.

The third group denotes the web as a corpus, which means that all web content is considered to be a corpus base which can be searched by using search engines such as Google, Yahoo, etc. Kilgarriff and Grefenstette (2003) expand the definition of a corpus and claim that a corpus is "a collection of texts" (Kilgarriff, Grefenstette, 2003, p. 2), meaning that the web can also be considered a corpus. The process of collecting texts does not apply to this type of corpus, and consequently no cleansing of the documents or of the web's content can be done. Google search engine is the most common example of using the web as a corpus. Google search results provide the number of tokens and the context in which the term appears, but because of their size and the amount of uncleansed texts they are considered "dirty" (Kaligarriff, Grefenstette, 2003) content. In the paper *Refining the use of the web (and web search) as a language teaching and learning resource,* a group of authors (Wu, Franken, Witten, 2009) speaks of the disadvantages of using the web as a corpus for language learning and analysis. According to them, the three main flaws are the web's size, the amount of cleansing done on it and its representativeness. The size is not controlled, meaning that the real size of the web's content cannot be precisely determined. The content, apart from including uncleansed and unedited texts, is also very heterogeneous, which can turn out to be a flaw in the teaching process because a professor can never know what kind of results students will get when they start searching the web. The content is not representative of the language being learned. How cleansed the web's content is can also be brought into question because a large number of texts contains grammar and spelling mistakes which represents an obstacle to language learning. On the other hand, the web is used for conducting language studies which confirm the intuition concerning the frequency of individual words, collocations, phrasemes and idioms and is a very valuable source for acquiring information on collocations (Wu, Franken, Witten, 2010).

When it comes to searching the web for the purpose of language learning, a project called GALL (Google Assisted Language Learning) is mentioned because Google search engine offers many other options apart from simple web searches. One of the examples of that is Google Translator which can translate words, texts and even whole websites to multiple languages and also provide a wide array of synonyms and their wider meaning. However, web search engines often do not show enough instances, do not provide wide enough context for every token, often first show the term we searched for in titles and subtitles and do not allow searches according to specific linguistic criteria such as morphosyntactic tags. Kilgarriff and Grefenstette (2003) discuss several shortcomings linguists have to face when using web search engines as a tool for searching the web as a corpus. They claim that web search results do not provide enough language examples and contexts for those same examples, language examples are shown distorted because the engines show the desired term in titles and headers and after that in the documents' paragraphs, search engines do not allow for setting of detailed criteria important for linguistic analyses of the language and the statistical display of the results is unreliable.

That's why web corpora (corpora containing filtered and cleansed texts collected from the web) are extremely popular - they meet all of the aforementioned lexicographic search criteria.

Thanks to web corpora, it is today possible to parse the web and search it according to lemmas and word types, constituents (e.g. a syntagma) and grammatical relations. Dictionaries and lexicons can be developed directly and easily by using the web for different, even very rare languages.

Using the web as a resource was especially popularized by the Wacky initiative (Baroni, Bernardini, Ferraresi, Zanchetta, 2009), which popularized the idea of the web as a corpus and made available tools for creating WaC corpora and created web corpora for a large number of bigger European languages. Such corpora exist today even for smaller languages, such as Hindi, Telugu, Basque, Filipino, Slovenian, Croatian, Bosnian or Serbian.

Croatian web corpus (hrWaC) is currently Croatia's largest computer corpus with more than 1.9 billion tokens and was created as one of WaC web corpora (Ljubešić, Klubička, 2016).

Speech (or spoken) corpora are the corpora that provide the possibility of actively listening to a spoken word or text of a certain language. Native speakers read texts, and this is then recorded and can be listened to in order to gain insight into a language's real use. Thus, the users have the option of hearing certain dialects, correct word accents and the standard version of the language and can note the differences. This a much better option for language learning than students and learners listening to audio materials recorded solely by lecturers or language experts. The representation of speech corpora is low, and there are no publicly available speech corpora for Croatian, which can be considered a flaw because in most cases the curriculum puts a greater emphasis on speech than on writing (Römer, 2006). This type of corpora could be of great help to students in acquiring and improving their language communication competencies. The largest number of speech corpora was created for the English-speaking world, for example the British National Corpus also contains a speech corpus.

General or reference corpus contains different types of texts. It can contain written or spoken language or both, texts collected in one or several different countries (Hunston, 2002). It does not represent a representative whole of a language, but it does have a large amount of texts, about 10 million tokens. A general corpus is much larger than for example a specialized corpus because it is not limited by its content to just one field and contains many different types of texts which can include newspaper articles, blogs, legal acts, conversations, essays etc. It can be used as a source for language learning or for translating and is often used as a basis for comparison with specialized corpora. A feature of general corpora is that they can provide "as complete picture as possible of a language" (Bennett, 2010) that is in use. The most famous corpora of this type include the British National Corpus and the Bank of English, whereas an example for Croatian is the Croatian National Corpus (HNK).

Specialized corpora are composed of a certain type of texts, such as newspaper articles, academic articles from a certain field, lectures, student essays, everyday conversations, geography textbooks etc. (Hunston, 2002). The purpose of this type of corpus is to conduct research and analysis of a certain part of language in order to provide "an answer to a specific question" (Bennett,

2010). This type of corpora has no level of limitation for a specialized field, but there is a limitation when it comes to the type of texts they contain. One of the examples stated by Hunston (2002) is time limitation to, for example, texts created in a certain century or to a social environment which includes conversation on a certain topic. Usually, they are smaller than general corpora and tend to be representative of the language (Bennett, 2010) they refer to. The most famous corpora of this kind are the Cambridge and Nottingham Corpus of Discourse in English (CANCODE) and the Michigan Corpus of Academic Spoken English (MICASE).

A historical or diachronic corpus contains texts created in different time periods. The most common use and purpose of historical corpora is in that they offer their users and researchers a way to analyze a language used in the past and compare it to modern-day language use. In other words, it is used to track changes occurring in a language over time (Hunston, 2002). The first electronic historical corpus of the English language is the Helsinki Corpus which contains texts created between the years 700 and 1710. It is a corpus in which the content is divided by genres, such as law, philosophy, science, fiction, drama, autobiographies, private and official correspondence and the Bible (Kytö, 2011). In Croatian, Croatian Language Repository, which contains literary texts from different phases of the language's development from the 19th century to modern day, can be considered a partially historical corpus.

Comparative corpora are composed of two or more corpora in different languages (e.g. English and French) or their different varieties (e.g. US English and Canadian English) (Hunston, 2002). They contain the same ratio of representation of certain types of texts, such as newspaper articles, novels, essays etc., but not direct translations from one language to another. McEnery (2003) defines this type of corpora as a "corpus that contains components collected by using the same framework and similar balance and pattern representativeness" of a language that has the same ratio of representation of texts of the same genre in the same domain in the span of different languages in the same period of collecting texts. (McEnery, Xiao, 2007)

An example of a comparative corpus is the International Corpus of English (ICE), while this type of corpora is most often used in translations and for contrastive language research.

A pedagogic corpus is composed of all languages a student was exposed to in their educational environment. It is a corpus that contains "language used in the classroom" (Bennett, 2010). For most students, there are no pedagogic corpora in a physical form, but if a teacher or a researcher decides to create a pedagogic corpus, it can contain all textbooks and materials the student has encountered (Hunston, 2002). It can be used to collect all phrases and words a student has encountered in different situations and contexts in order to achieve a certain level of language awareness and knowledge. This corpus can contain various forms of texts, but the only criterion is that they are created in an educational environment, i.e. during the language teaching process. Some of the reasons pedagogic corpora are used for language teaching are "to ensure that the students are learning a useful language, to test the dynamics between a professor and a student or as a tool for evaluation of a professor's development" (Bennett, 2010).

REFERENCES

Baroni, M., Bernardini, S., Ferraresi, A., & Zanchetta, E. (2009). The WaCky wide web: A collection of very large linguistically processed web-crawled corpora. *Language Resources and Evaluation*, *43*(3), 209–226. doi:10.100710579-009-9081-4

Bennett, G. R. (2010). *Using corpora in the language learning classroom: Corpus linguistics for teachers*. University of Michigan Press. doi:10.3998/mpub.371534

Boulton, A. (2017). Corpora in language teaching and learning. *Language Teaching*, *50*(4), 483–506. doi:10.1017/S0261444817000167

Cambridge Dictionary. (n.d.). Available at: https://dictionary.cambridge.org/dictionary/english/

Davies, M. (2009). The 385+ million word Corpus of Contemporary American English (1990–2008+): Design, architecture, and linguistic insights. *International Journal of Corpus Linguistics*, *14*(2), 159–190. doi:10.1075/ijcl.14.2.02dav

Durand, S. (2018). Embracing Computer Corpora in the Language Learning Clasroom and Using It in Your Classroom. In *Applications of CALL Theory in ESL and EFL Environments* (pp. 131–147). IGI Global. doi:10.4018/978-1-5225-2933-0.ch008

Gabrielatos, C. (2005). Corpora and Language Teaching: Just a Fling or Wedding Bells? *Tesl-Ej*, *8*(4), n4.

Girgin, U. (2019). Perceptions of Turkish EFL Student Teachers towards Learning Phrasal-Prepositional Verbs through Corpus Based Materials. *Online (Bergheim)*, *2*(1), 1–19.

Glosar jezičnih tehnologija. (n.d.). Available at: http://www.hnk.ffzg.hr/jthj/glosar.htm

Granger, S., Dagneaux, E., & Meunier, F. (Eds.). (2002). *International Corpus of Learner English. Version 1.1. Université catholique de Louvain*. Centre for English Corpus Linguistics.

Granger, S., Dagneaux, E., Meunier, F., & Paquot, M. (2009). International Corpus of Learner English v2 (Handbook + CD-Rom). Presses universitaires de Louvain.

Huang, L. S. (2018). Taking Stock of Corpus-Based Instruction in Teaching English as an International Language. *RELC Journal*, *49*(3), 381–401. doi:10.1177/0033688217698294

Hunston, S. (2002). *Corpora in applied linguistics*. Ernst Klett Sprachen. doi:10.1017/CBO9781139524773

Hunston, S. (2005). *Corpora in Applied Linguistics*. Cambridge, UK: Cambridge University Press.

Jantunen, J. H. (2016). *Corpora, phraseology and dictionaries: How does corpus research intersect language teaching and learning?* Mémoires de la Société Néophilologique.

Johnes, T. (1991). Should you be persuaded - two samples of data-driven learning materials, Classroom Concordancing. *ELR Journal*, *4*, 1–16.

Kilgarriff, A., & Grefenstette, G. (2003). Introduction to the special issue on the web as corpus. *Computational Linguistics*, *29*(3), 333–347. doi:10.1162/089120103322711569

Kytö, M. (2011). Corpora and historical linguistics. *Revista Brasileira de Lingüística Aplicada*, *11*(2), 417–457. doi:10.1590/S1984-63982011000200007

Leech, G. (1992). Corpora and theories of linguistic performance. *Directions in corpus linguistics, 1992*, 105-122.

Ljubešić, N., & Klubička, F. (2016). *Croatian web corpus hrWaC 2.1.* Academic Press.

McEnery, A. (2003) Corpus linguistics. In U R. Mitkov (Ed.), Oxford handbook of computational linguistics (pp. 448-63). Oxford University Press.

McEnery, A., & Xiao, R. (2007). *Parallel and comparable corpora: What are they up to? Translating Europe*. Multilingual Matters.

McEnery, T., & Wilson, A. (2001). *Corpus Linguistics*. Edinburgh, UK: Edinburgh University Press.

McEnery, T., & Xiao, R. (2011). What corpora can offer in language teaching and learning. Handbook of research in second language teaching and learning, 2, 364-380.

Miangah, T. M. (2012). Different aspects of exploiting corpora in language learning. *Journal of Language Teaching and Research, 3*(5), 1051–1060. doi:10.4304/jltr.3.5.1051-1060

Nesselhauf, N. (2004). Learner corpora and their potential for language teaching. *How to use corpora in language teaching, 12*, 125-156.

Nesselhauf, N. (2005). *Corpus Linguistics: A Practical Introduction*. Available at: http://www.as.uni-heidelberg.de/personen/Nesselhauf/files/Corpus%20 Linguistics%20Practical%20Introduction.pdf Retrieved May, 9, 2019

O'Keeffe, A., McCarthy, M., & Carter, R. (2007). *From corpus to classroom: Language use and language teaching*. Cambridge University Press. doi:10.1017/CBO9780511497650

Pomikálek, J. (2011). *Removing boilerplate and duplicate content from web corpora* (Doctoral dissertation). Masarykova univerzita, Fakulta informatiky.

Požgaj-Hadži, V., & Tadić, M. (2000). Hrvatsko-slovenski paralelni korpus. In *Jezikovne tehnologije / Language Technologies*. Institut Jožef Stefan.

Preradović, N. M., Berać, M., & Boras, D. (2015). Learner corpus of Croatian as a second and foreign language. In *Multidisciplinary Approaches to Multilingualism*. Peter Lang.

Reppen, R. (2011). Using corpora in the language classroom. *Materials development in language teaching*, 35-51.

Rječnik korpusne lingvistike. (n.d.). http://www.hnk.ffzg.hr/bb/definicijekl.doc

Römer, U. (2006). Pedagogical applications of corpora: Some reflections on the current scope and a wish list for future developments. *Zeitschrift für Anglistik und Amerikanistik*, *54*(2), 121–134.

Sinclair, J. (1991). *Corpus, Concordance, Collocation*. Oxford: Oxford University Press.

Sinclair, J. M. (Ed.). (2004). *How to use corpora in language teaching* (Vol. 12). John Benjamins Publishing. doi:10.1075cl.12

Tadić, M. (2000). Building the Croatian-English Parallel Corpus, *LREC2000 Proceedings*, *1*, 523-530.

Tadić, M. (2001). Procedures in Building the Croatian-English Parallel Corpus. *International Journal of Corpus Linguistics*, *6*(special issue), 107–123. doi:10.1075/ijcl.6.si.10tad

Taylor, C. (2008). What is corpus linguistics? What the data says. *ICAME Journal, 32*, 179-200.

Tucker, G. (2009). 12 Exposure, Expectations and Probabilities: Implications for Language Learning. *Advances in Language and Education*, 239.

Tyers, F. M., & Alperen, M. S. (2010). South-east european times: A parallel corpus of balkan languages. In *Proceedings of the LREC Workshop on Exploitation of Multilingual Resources and Tools for Central and (South-) Eastern European Languages* (pp. 49-53). Academic Press.

Utvić, M. V. (2013) *Izgradnja referentnog korpusa savremenog srpskog jezika* (Doctoral dissertation). Filološki fakultet, Univerzitet u Beogradu.

Wallis, S., Cushing, I., & Aarts, B. (2019). Exploiting parsed corpora in grammar teaching. *LiLT (Linguistic Issues in Language Technology), 18.*

Wu, S., Franken, M., & Witten, I. H. (2009). Refining the use of the web (and web search) as a language teaching and learning resource. *Computer Assisted Language Learning*, *22*(3), 249–268. doi:10.1080/09588220902920250

Wu, S., Franken, M., & Witten, I. H. (2010). Supporting collocation learning with a digital library. *Computer Assisted Language Learning*, *23*(1), 87–110. doi:10.1080/09588220903532971

Wu, W. S. (2008). *The marriage between corpus-based linguistics and lexico-grammar instruction: Using advise, recommend, and suggest as an example*. In WorldCALL 2008 Conference. Fukuoka, Japan.

Wynne, M. (Ed.). (2005). *Developing linguistic corpora: A guide to good practice*. Oxbow Books Limited.

ENDNOTES

1 Cambridge dictionary defines cloud asa computer network where files and programs can be stored, especially the internet. Definition is available at: https://dictionary.cambridge.org/dictionary/english/cloud

2 http://www.hnk.ffzg.hr/jthj/glosar.htm

3 Cambridge dictionary defines it as follows: "The process by which an electronic device recognizes printed or written letters or numbers." Definition available at: https://dictionary.cambridge.org/dictionary/english/ocr

4 According to Waynn (2005) transcriptions can be "orthographic, prosodic, or phonetic, or more than one of these." (p. 78)

5 Available at: http://www.hnk.ffzg.hr/bb/definicijekl.doc.

6 http://www.uclouvain.be/en-cecl-icle.html

7 The Tswana language, Setswana, is a language spoken in southern Africa by about five million people. It is a Bantu language belonging to the Niger–Congo language family within the Sotho languages branch of Zone S (S.30), and is closely related to the Northern- and Southern Sotho languages, as well as the Kgalagadi language and the Lozi language. Tswana is an official language and lingua franca of Botswana. Full ddefinition and description is available at: http://dbpedia.org/page/Tswana_language

8 http://opus.lingfil.uu.se/SETIMES.php

Chapter 2
Corpus Tools and Technology

ABSTRACT

This chapter will give insight to available corpus tools that are free for end users and have open language databases with different types of texts. The main corpus tool that will be presented is NoSketch Engine, an online interface for searching, creating, and analyzing corpus data. The chapter will provide information about available corpora in NoSketch Engine and additional corpus tools that are available to users for conducting language analyses, preparing teaching materials, exploring and learning the language.

CORPUS TOOLS AND TECHNOLOGY

To use and search computer corpora, corpus tools which make conducting language analyses a lot easier for lecturers and other language experts are used. To analyze corpus data, lecturers "need software that allows them to search, manipulate and store the data, precisely what corpus tools enable" (Kilgarriff et.al, 2014). Today, most lecturers and linguistics experts use online corpus tools that do not require a special process of installation of the software on a computer, which makes the first step in working with corpora and their tools much simpler and easier. The size of computer corpora is growing by the day, and they contain large databases with several million tokens (Grazib, 2009). In order to speed up and simplify language analysis, corpus tools that make the process of using and searching corpora of millions of tokens a lot simpler and more efficient were created.

DOI: 10.4018/978-1-7998-3680-3.ch002

Each computer corpus needs a certain software, a tool without which it would be impossible to search it. Every corpus uses a different type of software, and the features of those software types differ, but there are certain common characteristics which appear in almost all of them. One such characteristic and the most important function is "the option to search the corpora by request, after which the program most commonly provides information on the number of tokens in the corpus and their examples in the texts in which they appear, called concordances" (Nesselhauf, 2005). In the paper *Corpus Linguistics: A Practical Introduction,* several other common characteristics of corpus tools are enumerated, such as the ability to sort and narrow down search results according to relevance, the option to search for words and phrases which appear at a certain distance, the existence of options to show a larger chunk of context than the one shown in concordances, the option to store search results so that they can be used later on etc. Furthermore, the option to show the frequency of tokens and an overview of all the words the corpus contains together with the display of their frequency is also mentioned as a common characteristic of corpus tools. Apart from the main characteristics of corpus tools, a categorization of those tools which describes them more closely and states their main characteristics also exists.

Kilgarriff and Kosem (2012) give a detailed overview of corpus tools in their paper and categorize them. The first category includes computer-based tools and online tools. As examples of computer-based corpus tools, whose main features are the facts that they have to be installed on a computer and that they operate independently, WordSmith and MonoConcPro are mentioned, while examples of online tools include Sketch Engine developed by Adam Kilgarriff and Pavel Rychlý, the Corpus Retrieval System (CoREST) developed by the Department for Digital Dictionaries and Text Corpora at the Society for Danish Language and Literature, and the tools developed by the linguistics professor Mark Davies, available at http://corpus.byu.edu (Kilgarriff, Kosem, 2012).

The next category includes corpus-dependent and corpus-independent tools. Corpus-dependent tools can only be used for a specific corpus, and this corpus is in most cases created as a part of an institution's project. As examples, Kilgarriff and Kosem (2012) give SARA and BNCWeb user interfaces which were created to search the LPBritish National Corpus and Spanish Corpus de Referencia del Español Actual - CREA. The group of corpus-independent tools includes all the tools that allow the user to load and analyze any corpus.

The examples given in this case are Sketch Engine, Corpus WorkBench, WordSmith Tools, MonoConc Pro and AntConc (Kilgarriff, Kosem, 2012). A special group is formed by the tools that use the same interface to access different previously installed corpora. For example, CoREST is used to access several Danish corpora, while the tools and the software developed by Mark Davies from Brigham Young University are used to access the corpus of Spanish, Portuguese and American English.

The third category describes prepared corpora and the web as a corpus. The corpus tools used with prepared corpora are the most common ones because they are made for linguistic research. Some consider the web to be one giant corpus containing a variety of texts in different languages. That's why Google and other web search engines can be used as corpus tools - they provide results in terms of tokens' frequency and context in which a token appears in the form of concordances. Their function is not to enable linguistic research. They are also called web concordances, the most famous of which is Webcorp (Kehoe, Renouf, 2002).

The fourth category represents simple and advanced corpus tools. Simple corpus tools contain some of the basic functions with which a corpus can be searched, such as concordance, collocations and keywords, with the programs offering that being AntConc and MonoConc Easy. Advanced corpus tools add to that the option of advanced searches and language analysis, such as CQL queries and word sketch, and the programs with installed advanced tools include Sketch Engine, XAIRA and CoREST.

The final, fifth category is based on the type of user or the group of users that are using the corpus. Three main groups that use corpus tools have been defined - lexicographers, researchers and students, and lecturers (language professors) and learners. Considering the defined groups of users, specialized corpus tools have been created for each of them so that they can satisfy their language analysis needs.

Web corpora is developed in certain way and process of creating web corpora consist of few steps which refers to web crawling, removing duplicates, 'cleaning' to remove non-text material, language identification, linguistic processing (tokenisation, possibly also lemmatisation, part-of speech tagging, parsing). (Kilgarriff, Baisa et al., 2014). Web crawlers are used to find new web pages by collecting and following URLs (Uniform Resource Locators). By following an URL and downloading the corresponding web page the links within that web page can be added to the web crawler's URL collection. The web pages are stored for indexing and ranking by internet search engines.

Internet search engines use web page ranking algorithms that relate the links within a web page to the relevance of the web page.

In this chapter several free and open source technologies for creating and searching corpora for any language will be described. It is important to emphasis that these technologies are available for several languages, e.g. English, German, Italian, Croatian, French, etc. These provide free and unpaid access to all interested parties. Users can search and use language database for variety of reasons, e.g. developing personal subcorpora, developing teaching materials for language subjects, using online tools in classroom with students for learning language (first or second language), conducting language and linguistic analyzis, etc.

NOSKETCH ENGINE

NoSketch Engine is an open-source project that is free version of commercial software Sketch Engine which usage must be paid. It is a limited version (with limited options for searching and analysing language) of Sketch Engine which offers users options for creating word sketches, thesauruses, key words, users' own corpora, etc. (Rychlý, 2007). NoSketch Engine has its own interface which enables users to search corpora online without registration process. On home page is a list of all available corpora for use and search.

On the following link users can see NoSketch Engine interface and list of all the corpora:

https://www.clarin.si/noske/index-en.html.

When presenting NoSketch Engine it is crucial to mention from which tool it has been derived, Sketch Engine[1]. This is a tool for creating, managing and searching large languages databases - corpora and refers to the software and the web service where the web service includes, as well as the core software, a large number of corpora pre-loaded and 'ready for use', and tools for creating, installing and managing your own corpora (Kilgarriff, Baisa et al., 2014). Because of its accessibility and various options for searching and analysing language it is one of most commonly used corpus tools worldwide.

It contains 500 corpora in more than 90 languages, each having a size of up to 30 billion words to provide a truly representative sample of language (Kilgarriff, Baisa et al., 2014; Kilgarriff, Rychlý et al., 2004). The biggest corpus in Sketch Engine is TenTen which has from 2 to 15 billion words.

Services which Sketch Engine is offering are used by some of worldwide known companies for developing their dictionaries like Oxford University Press, Cambridge University Press, Dictionnaires Le Robert, Shogakukan etc. (Kaligarriff et.al., 2014).

One of main differences between two software is the number of functionalities and tools that the paid version (Sketch Engine) offers. Main goal and purpose of both software is the same – providing users with large language database for language learning, conducting linguistics researches and language analysis. NoSketch Engine is “combining Manatee and Bonito into a powerful and free corpus management system where Manatee is a corpus management tool including corpus building and indexing, fast querying and providing basic statistical measures and Bonito is a graphical user interface to corpora maintained by Manatee”. It is a web interface written in Python which can be running under any webserver supporting the CGI (Common Gateway Interface)[2] (Rychlý, 2007). Bonito provides many standard functions as many other corpus managers: concordance, word list generating, context statistics and also some advanced features like distributional thesaurus and word sketches (Baisa, Suchomel, 2014). Manatee, Bonito i Finlib are constantly used, developed and upgraded in collaboration with Sketch Engine developed team. NoSketch Engine enables direct access to online corpus and doesn’t require additional software installation on computer so user can access it through any computer with Internet connection. Second characteristic of NoSketch Engine is possibility of uploading and analysing any kind of corpora. User interface of NoSketch Engine is available in English and Slovenian language. Main language analysis which are offered through NoSketch Engine are concordances and lexical sketches. Concordances will display all tokens in corpus which user is searching for and additionally user can see surrounding context of token. Option for creating and working with Word sketches is available in Sketch Engine and this is used for analysing corpus based samples of grammatical and collocational behaviours of certain words in certain language (Kilgarriff et.al., 2014).

It is example of free technology which is used for creating open language database for any language in the world. Main aim of these kind of open technology and its tools is free access for all interested users, mainly teachers, lecturers, students, researches, etc. to have accessible and free entrance to large language materials for educational and research purpose. Corpora within NoSketch Engine have free access for users and do not require registration to access it.

This research was conducted with corpora which are available in NoSketch Engine. For Croatian language were used three corpora, Croatian web corpus (hrWac), Croatian Language Repository (Riznica) and the Croatian National Corpus (HNK) which is available on following link:

http://filip.ffzg.hr/cgi-bin/run.cgi/first_form

For English language was used ukWaC and for German language was used geWaC. In addition were used parallel corpora for German EU DGT-UD: German, for English EU DGT-UD: English and for Croatian EU DGT-UD: Croatian.

The biggest Croatian corpus is Croatian Web Corpus (hrWaC) with more than 1.9 billion tokens and it is built from the .hr top-level domain in 2011 and again in 2014 (Ljubešić, Klubička, 2016). The corpus was near-deduplicated on paragraph level, normalised via diacritic restoration, morphosyntactically annotated and lemmatised (Ljubešić, Klubička, 2016) so it can be used for different types of linguistic researches.

hrWaC was created 2010 at University of Zagreb Faculty of Humanities and Social Sciences, University Zagreb (Ljubešić, Erjavec, 2011) in collaboration with Slovenia.

Because Croatian language has smaller number of speakers then for instance English, French or German language decision was made that for creating hrWaC they use and search entire internet and web sites/places which had .hr top level domain from which texts were crawled (Ljubešić, Erjavec, 2011) .

Ljubešić i Erjavec (2011) state that they collected 15,7 million texts in HTML format which have between 50 and 500 KBand for collecting URL addresses from web they used Yahoo! Search BOSS API.

Because hrWaC has written texts on Croatian language from all .hr top domain there are various types of texts written on different Croatian dialects, slang, comments and posts from social media, posts from forums and blogs, comments on news portals, etc. which are not standard language. It can be claimed that hrWaC corpus has certain amount of incorrect spelling and grammar language constructions which are not part of Croatian standard language but are part of contemporary language. This is the fact which users needs to know, especially teacher who are going to use corpora and corpus tools for teaching in classroom or for preparing teaching materials for their students.

Croatian National Corpus (HNK) is example of balanced corpus that consists of filtered content that is organized into several categories which include Croatian literary work, newspapers, and journals. He is also divided into two main parts regarding the certain time period, content that has been created from year 1990 till now and contend that has been created before year of 1990. Department of Linguistics at Faculty of Humanities and Social Sciences, University Zagreb in 1996. has begun with development of Croatian national Corpus (HNK). From 2015 HNK is installed in NoSketchEngine where users can use same searching methods and corpus tools like in hrWaC. HNK also has free access to it corpus database and everyone can use it. The founder of HNK Marko Tadić (2000) states that they accomplished one of main goals of corpus which is free, remote and unlimited searching of language materials. HNK consists of filtered texts which are organized by categories in 13 subcorpora which include Croatian literary works and news paper editions (Tadić, 2000). Version 3.0 beta which was used during this research has 234,000,000 tokens of which is available through NoSketch Engine 2,559,160 words and 2,130,095 lemmas.

Third corpus that is available online is Croatian Language Corpus which consists of newspaper text and literary work from second half of 19th century till today. It is significantly smaller than hrWaC and HNK but it is interesting because he offers overview of language evaluation through certain period of time. Riznica has 101,782,863 tokens and 85,273,724 words.

Corpus of English language which was used in research is ukWaC (British WaCky Web Corpus) with 2,135 million tokens crawled from 2,525 thousand URLs. The text has been automatically tokenised, part-of-speech tagged and lemmatised with TreeTagger. The TreeTagger is a tool for annotating text with part-of-speech and lemma information. It was developed by Helmut Schmid in the TC project at the Institute for Computational Linguistics of the University of Stuttgart. The TreeTagger has been successfully used to tag German, English, French, Italian, Danish, Dutch, Spanish, Bulgarian, Russian, Portuguese, Galician, Greek, Chinese, Swahili, Slovak, Slovenian, Latin, Estonian, Polish, Romanian, Czech, Coptic and old French texts and is adaptable to other languages if a lexicon and a manually tagged training corpus are available (Schmid, 1994, 1995). The software is freely available for research, education and evaluation and it can be downloaded from following link:

http://www.cis.uni-muenchen.de/~schmid/tools/TreeTagger/.

The same method was used to create German WaCky Web Corpus (geWaC) with 1,627,118,296 tokens and 1,315,999,780 words crawled from 1 750 thousand URLs.

Parallel corpora EU DGT-UD: German, EU DGT-UD: English and EU DGT-UD: Croatian were also used by the teachers which are teaching English and German as second or foreign languages in primary and secondary schools for preparing teaching materials for their classes. EU DGT is abbreviation for Directorate-General for Translation. In year 2007 European Commission's Directorate-General for Translation has made its multilingual Translation Memory for the Acquis Communautaire, DGT-TM, publicly accessible in order to foster the European Commission's general effort to support multilingualism, language diversity and the re-use of Commission information (Steinberger, Andreas et al., 2012).

Extract sentences are aligned and can be used to produce a parallel multilingual corpus of the European Union's legislative documents (Acquis Communautaire) in 24 EU languages and aligned translation units have been provided by the Directorate-General for Translation of the European Commission by extraction from one of its large shared translation memories in EURAMIS (European advanced multilingual information system) (Steinberger, Andreas et al., 2012).

Available corpora through NoSketch Engine interface are:

Gigafida v2.0 (Slovene reference coprus),
Gigafida v2.0 DeDup (Slovene reference coprus without near duplicates),
ssj500k (Slovene manually annotated corpus),
jos1M v1.2 (Slovene partially manually annotated corpus),
slWaC 2.0 (Slovene Web Corpus v2.1),
Gos (Speech reference corpus),
IMP (Corpus of historical texts from 1584 till 1918),
goo300k (corpus of historical texts from 1584 till 1899, word mare manually modernised and lemmatised),
KAS (corpus of theses from the repositories of Slovene universities form 2000 till 2018),
KAS Dipl (corpus of diploma theses from the repositories of Slovene universities form 2000 till 2018),
KAS Mag (corpus of masters theses from the repositories of Slovene universities form 2000 till 2018),
KAS Dr (corpus of doctoral theses from the repositories of Slovene universities form 2000 till 2018),

Janes (corpus of texts from Slovene social media sites),
Janes Blog (corpus of Slovene blogs and comments),
Janes Forum (corpus of Slovene forums),
Janes News (corpus of Slovene news comments),
Janes Wiki (corpus of Slovene Wikipedia page and user talk texts),
Janes Tweet (corpus od Slovene tweets from 2013 till 2017),
Janes TwePo (corpus of tweets by Slovene politicians form 2013 til 2017),
Janes Norm (user generated texts with manually standardized words),
Janes Tag (user generated texts with manually standardized, morphosyntactically tagged and lemmatised words and named entities),
Janes Syn (user generated texts with manual syntactic annotations),
Janes Kratko (tweets with manually annotated shortened words, categorized using the developed typology),
Janes Vejica (tweets with manually annotated correct comma placement, categorized using the developed typology),
Janes Preklop (tweets manually annotated for code switching),
Tweet-sl (old Slovene tweets form 2007 till 2011),
KoRP (corpus with texts from public relations),
Šolar (corpus of school essays from Slovene primary and secondary high schools),
DSI (corpus of informatics),
siParl (corpus of parliamentary debates of the National Assembly of the Republic of Slovenia form 1990 till 2018),
SlovParl (corpus of parliamentary devates of the Republic of Slovenia in the period of secession from Yugoslavia from 1990 till 1992),
ParlaMeter-sl (corpus of parliamentary debates of the Republic of Slovenia: Mandate VII),
GosVL 4.0 (corpus of transcriptions of talks form VideoLectures.Net),
Kapelski (diplomatic transcription),
ZRC16clt (corpus of samples form three XIV century books),
Zaznavanje nasilja nad ućitelji v šolah (Answers of teachers and headmasters to the questionnaire of the Educational Research Institue about cases of student violence against them),
FILMI (corpus of newspaper and magazine film reviews form 2000 till 2009),
Konji (corpus of texts on equestrianism),
VAYNA (corpus of articles verbally assaulting the JNA from 1987 till 1988),
Riznica (Croatian Language Corpus by the institue of Croatian Language and Linguistics),
hrWaC (Croatian Web Corpus),

srWac (Serbian Web Corpus),
bsWaC (Bosnian Web Corpus),
deWaC (German WaCky Web Corpus),
frWaC (French WaCky Web Corpus),
itWaC (Italian WaCky Web Corpus),
ukWaC (British WaCky Web Corpus),
ParlaMeter-hr (corpus of parliamentary debates of the Republic of Croatia: Mandate VI),
Tweet-hr (corpus of Croatian tweets from 2008 till 2014),
hr500k v1.0 (manually annotated Croatian corpus),
ReLDI-hr (corpus of Croatian tweets with manually standardized, morphosyntactically tagged and lemmatized words and named entities),
Tweet-sr (corpus of Serbian tweets from 2008 till 2014),
SETimes.SR (manually annotated Serbian corpus),
jpWaC-L (Japanese Web texts with automatically assigned difficulty levels form 4 (very easy) to 0 (very difficult), crawl and annotation in 2007),
jpWaC-L0 (Japanese Web texts with automatically assigned difficulty level 0 (very difficult)),
jpWaC-L1 (Japanese Web texts with automatically assigned difficulty level 1 (difficult)),
jpWaC-L2 (Japanese Web texts with automatically assigned difficulty level 2 (intermediate)),
jpWaC-L3 (Japanese Web texts with automatically assigned difficulty level 3 (easy)),
jpWaC-L4 (Japanese Web texts with automatically assigned difficulty level 4 (very easy)),
ELIZA (logs of conversations with ELIZA@ijs.si),
TRANS5: angleško (Slovene-English parallel corpus, English part),
TRANS5: slovensko (Slovene-English parallel corpus, Slovene part),
jaSlo (Japanese-Slovene parallel corpus, Japanese part),
jaSlo (Japanese-Slovene parallel corpus, Slovene part),
ISPAC: italiajnsko (Italian-Slovene parallel corpus, Italian part),
ISPAC:slovensko (Italian-Slovene parallel corpus, Slovene part),
LeMonde: francosko (French-Slovene parallel corpus, French part),
LeMonde: slovensko (French-Slovene parallel corpus, Slovene part),
Opus MontenegrinSubs: Montenegrin (Opus Montenegrin subtitles, Montenegrin part),
Opus MontenegrinSubs: English (Opus Montenegrin subtitles, English part),

EU DGT-UD:Bulgarian (Translation Memory (2016) annotated with UD-Pipe: Bulgarian part),

EU DGT-UD:Czech (Translation Memory (2016) annotated with UD-Pipe: Czech part),

EU DGT-UD:Danish (Translation Memory (2016) annotated with UD-Pipe: Danish part),

EU DGT-UD: German (Translation Memory (2016) annotated with UD-Pipe: German part),

EU DGT-UD:Greek (Translation Memory (2016) annotated with UD-Pipe: Greek part),

EU DGT-UD:English (Translation Memory (2016) annotated with UD-Pipe: English part),

EU DGT-UD: Spanish (Translation Memory (2016) annotated with UD-Pipe: Spanish part),

EU DGT-UD:Estonian (Translation Memory (2016) annotated with UD-Pipe: Estonian part),

EU DGT-UD: Finnish (Translation Memory (2016) annotated with UD-Pipe: Finnish part),

EU DGT-UD: French (Translation Memory (2016) annotated with UD-Pipe: French part),

EU DGT-UD:Gaelic (Translation Memory (2016) annotated with UD-Pipe: Gaelic part),

EU DGT-UD: Croatian (Translation Memory (2016) annotated with UD-Pipe: Croatian part),

EU DGT-UD: Hungarian (Translation Memory (2016) annotated with UD-Pipe: Hungarian part),

EU DGT-UD: Italian (Translation Memory (2016) annotated with UD-Pipe: Italian part),

EU DGT-UD: Lithuanian (Translation Memory (2016) annotated with UD-Pipe: Lithuanian part),

EU DGT-UD: Latvian (Translation Memory (2016) annotated with UD-Pipe: Latvian part),

EU DGT-UD: Dutch (Translation Memory (2016) annotated with UD-Pipe: Dutch part),

EU DGT-UD: Polish (Translation Memory (2016) annotated with UD-Pipe: Polish part),

EU DGT-UD: Portuguese (Translation Memory (2016) annotated with UD-Pipe: Portuguese part),

EU DGT-UD: Romanian (Translation Memory (2016) annotated with UD-Pipe: Romanian part),
EU DGT-UD:Slovak (Translation Memory (2016) annotated with UD-Pipe: Slovak part),
EU DGT-UD:Slovenian (Translation Memory (2016) annotated with UD-Pipe: Slovenian part),
EU DGT-UD: Swedish(Translation Memory (2016) annotated with UD-Pipe: Swedish part)._

On Figure 1 we can see home page of NoSketch Engine which is hosted by CLARIN.SI (Common Language Resources and Technology Infrastructure, Slovenia). CLARIN is the European research infrastructure for researchers from fields of humanities and social sciences. Its goal is to enable these research communities access to language resources, technologies and expertise and it is based at the Jožef Stefan Institute in Slovenia. It offers a repository for language resources, many corpora available via two powerful concordancers, and other services for working with Slovene, and other languages. CLARIN aims at providing easy and sustainable access for scholars in the humanities and social sciences to digital language data and advanced tools to discover, explore, exploit, annotate, analyse or combine them, independent of where

Figure 1. Home page of NoSketch Engine

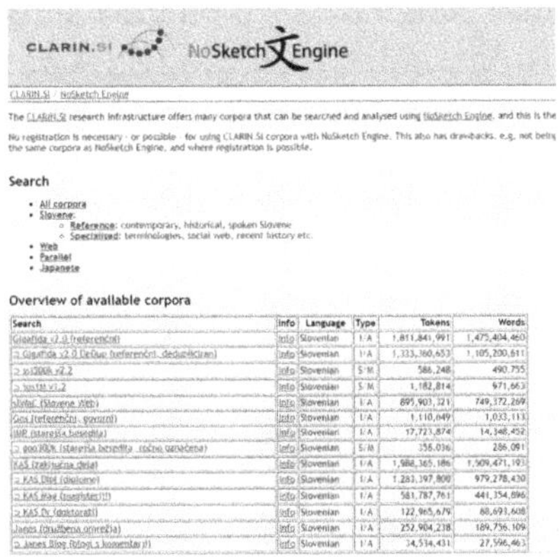

they are located (Krauwer, Hinrichs 2014). CLARIN.SI is Slovenian research infrastructure and it belongs to framework of the European consortium

CLARIN ERIC (European Research Infrastructures Consortium) and it was established in 2013, and became a member of CLARIN ERIC in 2015.

As part of CLARIN through NoSketch Engine are available 94 corpuses in 27 different languages with 17,674,802,304 tokens and 14,285,848,122 words. On the Figure 2 it can be seen representation of corpora in various languages in CLARIN.SI. The most common language is Slovenian (47%) with total number of 44 different corpuses, after Slovenian is Croatian (8%) and Japapnese (8%) with 7 corpuses, then is English (6%) with 5 corpuses, Serbian language (4%) with 4 corpuses, following French (3%) and Italian

Figure 2. Representation of corpora in various languages in CLARIN.SI

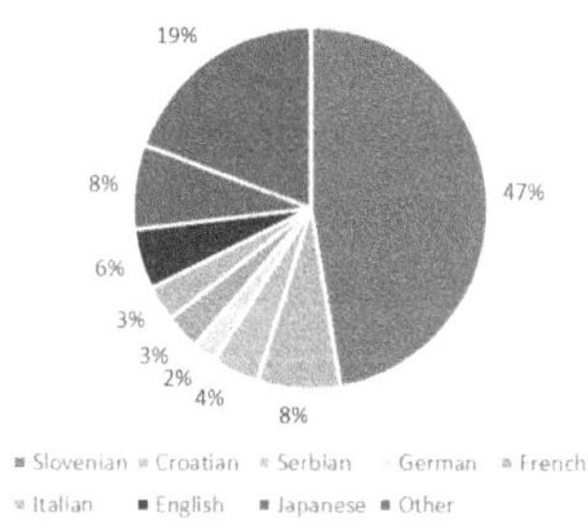

(3%) with 3 corpuses and German (2%) with 2 corpuses. Classification Other with 19% represents languages which have only one corpus available in CLARIN. Bosnian, Bulgarian, Czech, Danish, Greek, Spanish, Estonian, Finnish, Gaelic, Hungarian, Lithuanian, Latvian, Dutch, Polish, Portuguese,

Figure 3. Types of corpora in CLARIN.SI

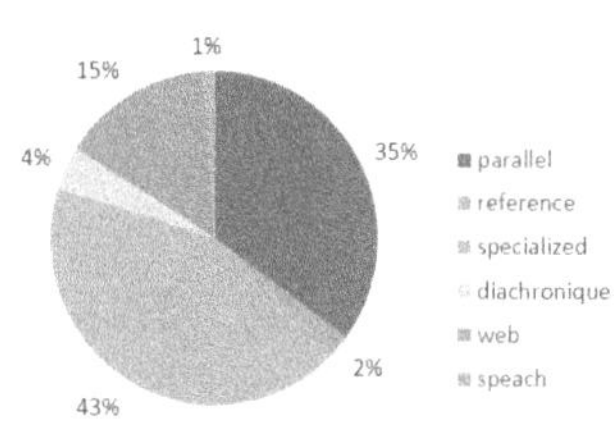

Romanian, Slovak and Swedish languages each have one corpus.

In CLARIN there are different types of corpora represented. At the moment it consists of 6 different corpora: parallel, reference, specialized, diachronique, web and speech corpus. On Figure 3 we can see the number of these corpora represented in CLARIN.SI.

The most numerous corpuses are specialized corpuses with 43%. In this category are included all sort of tweets, posts and comments from social media Tweeter, academic writings, primary and secondary students' essays, political documents, public relation texts, movie reviews, comments from blogs, Wikipedia, forums and new portals. Second main category are parallel multilingual corpora (35%) which are available in 22 different languages. Multilingual corpora include following languages: Slovenian, Croatian, Bulgarian, Czech, Danish, Greek, Spanish, Estonian, Finnish, Gaelic, Hungarian, Lithuanian, Latvian, Dutch, Polish, Portuguese, Romanian, Slovak, Swedish, English, French, Italian, Montenegrin, Japanese and German. Third category are web corpora with 15% which include all texts from certain web domain. There are Slovenia, Croatian, Japanese, British, German, Serbian, Bosnian, French and Italian web corpuses available for use. The biggest web corpus is British with 2,135,658,231 tokens. Forth category are diachronique or historical corpora (4%) which consists of old literary work and texts. There are available three Slovenian and one Croatian diachronique corpus. Reference or general corpora are available in Slovenian language (2%) and there is one spoken or speech reference corpus (1%) also available in Slovenian language. This speech corpus covers 120 hours of spoken communication which occur in different everyday situations. Every concordance in spoken corpus have audio material which pronounce the search results.

Chapter Searching Methods for Corpora in NoSketch Engine will explain all tools and functionalities which NoSketch Engine provides to their users for searching and analysing corpus data. Interface, tools and functionalities of NoSketch Engine is the same for all corpora which is included. Examples for searching available corpora in NoSketch Engine will be presented and explained on English and Croatian language examples.

KONTEXT

Another corpus tool which is available through CLARIN.SI is concordance tool named KonText. KonText was developed for the purposes of the Czech National Corpus, while CLARIN.SI uses the fork developed in the scope of the Czech CLARIN infrastructure. (CLARIN.SI) This is tools for making concordance, but it requires user registration after which the use of the tool is free.

Main functionality of this tools is to provide users with concordance lines based on their search. It offers the same corpora as NoSketch Engine, the only difference is in interface design and this tool require registration for users. Registration is possible with AAI electronical identity3 or with any official institutional account. If user is registered to KonText he or she have possibility to use available additional functionalities for working with search results, e.g. concordance lines. Some of additional functionality is possibility for users to save their search results, the option which isn't available to non-registered users nor in NoSketch Engine interface. Other available options for registered users are functions of enabling setting view options for individual corpora, saving of personal subcorpora, a history of queries, etc. (CLARIN. SI). The interface of KonText is available on following link:

Figure 4. Interface of KonText

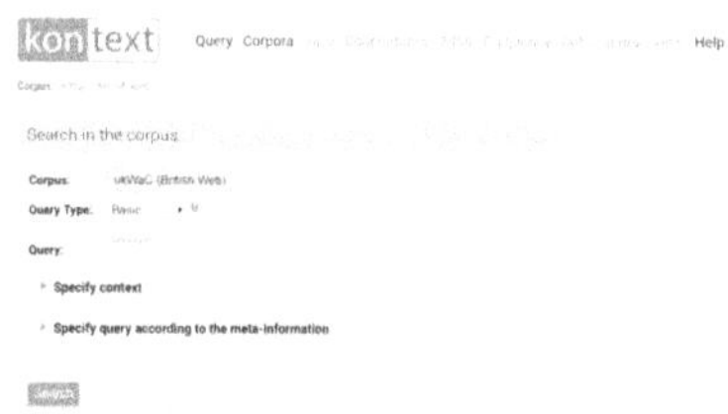

https://www.clarin.si/kontext/corpora/corplist

where user needs to select certain corpus and then search it.

On Figure 4 it can be seen KonText interface for searching ukWaC corpus of English language. The main menu of KonText is located at the top of web page (Figure 4) and provides users with different functions.

Types of searching possibilities (query type) are the same as in NoSketch Engine. CQL language for advanced corpus search is also the same as in NoSketch Engine it offers and supports the same syntaxy. KonText interface is offering possibilities of making queries, save your results, make concordance lists, filter you results, get information about frequency of tokens and words, get information about collocations and changing type of view. The main difference between NoSketch Engine and KonText is mentioned above and refers to saving setting. In KonText registered users have possibility to save their search results, create their own subcorpora, etc. Saving options works as a context selection, meaning that it saves the information currently displayed onscreen and this way it is possible to save a concordance, a list of collocations or for example a frequency distribution (Cvrček, 2017). Available saving formats in drop down menu are CSV, XLSX, XML and Custom format. CSV (comma-separated values) format refers to text files where fields are separated with comma, it contains plain text or number values. XLSX is file extension which refers to Microsoft Excel Spreadsheet or Workbook. It is used for storing data in spreadsheet format where they are arranged in rows, columns and cells. XML (Extensible Markup Language) is markup language like HTML (Hypertext Mark Language) which is used for creating web pages, but it was designed for storing and transporting data. Last type

Figure 5. Options for saving search results in Custom type saving in KonText interface

of listed formats for saving corpus search results is Custom type which offer possibility to save them as text file with txt file extension (Figure 5). TXT extension refers to plain text format which don't include any kind of formats on text. These kind of file formats are often opened with NotePad program or similar application. Additionally, user can choose which will be included or discarded from savings and how much search results they want to save.

Second difference from NoSketch Engine is opportunity for registered users to create their own subcorpora which can include different parts of original corpora. On main interface page users can select option for creating subcorpus. After that they must select corpus from which they want to create subcorpus and specify which part they will use. On Figure 6 it can be seen list of available options for creating subcorpus in ukWaC corpus. First step is to select corpus, after that user must give a name to the subcorpus. Third step is about selecting in which way user would create it, e.g. which kind of content user will use or which text it will be included in subcorpus. There are two options with which user can define what will be in subcorpus, custom ‘within’ condition and attributed list.

Custom ‘within’ condition is option which ensure the search result appears within the structure user want, within the same sentence, paragraph, document or any other structure found in the corpus. Other option is within with exclamation point in front of condition and it refers to negation, e.g. if user want something exclude from search or his subcorpus.

Attributed list is an option which allows users to select from which source they want to use content (texts) in their subcorpora. They can select certain domain[4] or top level domain[5] from menu and after that users will get their corpus which is saved.

Figure 6. Interface for creating subcorpus

When all parameters are selected, user can press Create Subcorpus button and subcorpus is created and saved under the tab Corpora on filed My subcorpora. If user has any subcorpora created, it will show there.

SKELL

Another corpus tool which Sketch Engine offers for free use to its users is SkeLL[6] (Sketch Engine for Language Learning). This is a language learning website in which all the reports are corpus-based, using fully automated methods, and are designed to avoid scaring the students (Baisa, Suchomel, 2014). It is currently available only for English. It offers three reports: word sketch, examples and “similar words” (Kilgarriff, Marcowitz, Smith et.al., 2015). This is corpus tool which has been developed under the Sketch Engine for learning English language but through time its has been developed for learning other languages, Russian[7] (ruSkeLL), German[8] (deSkeLL), Italian[9] (itSkeLL), Czech[10] (csSkeLL), Estonian[11] (etSkeLL). Its main purpose is to help learners to learn specific language. SkeLL language database consists of texts from news, academic papers, Wikipedia articles, open-source (non)-

fiction books, webpages, discussion forums, blogs etc. and there are more than 60 million sentences and more than one billion words in total (Baisa, Suchomel, 2014). Above mentioned reports or corpus search which SkeLL offers to its users refers to searching SkeLL for sentence examples in which

Figure 7. Interface of SkeLL corpus

searched word or a phrase is used (examples search), collocation[12] or word sketch which refers to words which often co-occur together (word sketch) and third option refers to creating a word cloud out of searched word and its similar words. On Figure 7 user can see home page of SkeLL interface where are available all mentioned searching methods/corpus tools.

For example, if user type word *dress* in SkeLL for learning English language first set of results refers to corpus tool Examples. On Figure 8 it can be seen part of the results which are listed in a form of sentence where searched word is showing. At the top of the list is number of tokens of word dress which appears in corpus. Results for word *dress* are in all language forms so user can see where word *dress* is used as noun or verb, singular and plural of word. Second corpus tool refers to Word sketch. On Figure 9 it can be seen results for the same word where the option for context is turned on and is showing results for *dress* as a verb. This tool provides option to see

Figure 8. Search results for word dress created with tool Examples

Figure 9. Search results for word dress created with tool Word sketch

different usage of word in different language form. At the top of results user can switch from verb to noun and can use option to show or hide context in which word *dress* is showing up. On this page user have possibility to see how word is used in sentence, e.g. as subject, object, phrase, which adjectives are commonly used with word etc. If user turns on option to show context,

Figure 10. Search results for word dress created with tool Similar word

page will show extended context which surrounds word. Last tool which is available in SkeLL is called Similar word and it provide user with list of similar word or synonyms. Additionally, it creates word cloud with similar word. On the Figure 10 we can see word cloud for *dress* as verb and list of all similar word which appear with dress in verb form.

All search results have possibility to show complete sentence with the searched word. For example, if user wants to see surrounding content for one or more results, all it takes is to select (click) on it and examples of sentence will be presented. If user on Figure 9 selects *wedding dresses* from the search results where word *dress* is in the function of subject, then results will show sentences in which word appears in this given language form and structure.

All described functionalities and options of SkeLL corpus are available for Russian, German, Italian, Czech and Estonian language. SkeLL options are very simple to use and results are to so it can be useful tool for teaching and learning language. In its simplicity it can be used for primary school teaching especially because of word cloud which is excellent motivation trigger for younger students in primary schools. Visualization helps students to easier learn and remember words therefore word cloud could be used for teaching vocabulary. Another area in which SkeLL would be helpful is learning collocations and synonyms because it provides learners with large amount of words which are similar or in the case of collocation which co-occur one with another. Because of its simple interface and possibility of showing graphic results (word cloud) it can be easily incorporated for learning English and German as second language in primary schools for younger students.

REFERENCES

Baisa, V., & Suchomel, V. (2014, December). *SkELL: Web Interface for English Language Learning*. RASLAN.

Cvrček, V-R. (Ed.). (2017). en:manualy:kontext:index. In *Příručka ČNK*. Retrieved from http://wiki.korpus.cz/doku.php?id=en:manualy:kontext:index&rev=1513343996

Grazib, M. (2009). Electronic Corpora: As Powerful Tools in Computational Linguistic Analyses. CIIA.

Kehoe, A., & Renouf, A. (2002). WebCorp: Applying the Web to linguistics and linguistics to the Web. *World Wide Web (Bussum).*

Kilgarriff, A., Baisa, V., Bušta, J., Jakubíček, M., Kovář, V., Michelfeit, J., ... Suchomel, V. (2014). The sketch engine: Ten years on. *Lexicography*, *1*(1), 7–36. doi:10.100740607-014-0009-9

Kilgarriff, A., & Kosem, I. (2012). *Corpus tools for lexicographers.–S. Granger* (M. Paquot, Ed.). Electronic Lexicography.

Kilgarriff, A., Marcowitz, F., Smith, S., & Thomas, J. (2015). Corpora and language learning with the Sketch Engine and SKELL. *Revue Française de Linguistique Appliquée*, *20*(1), 61–80. doi:10.3917/rfla.201.0061

Kilgarriff, A., Rychly, P., Smrz, P., & Tugwell, D. (2004). Itri-04-08 the sketch engine. *Información Tecnológica*, *105*, 116.

Krauwer, S., & Hinrichs, E. (2014). The CLARIN research infrastructure: resources and tools for e-humanities scholars. In *Proceedings of the Ninth International Conference on Language Resources and Evaluation (LREC-2014)* (pp. 1525-1531). European Language Resources Association (ELRA).

Ljubešić, N., & Erjavec, T. (2011, September). hrWaC and slWaC: Compiling web corpora for Croatian and Slovene. In *International Conference on Text, Speech and Dialogue* (pp. 395-402). Springer. 10.1007/978-3-642-23538-2_50

Ljubešić, N., & Klubička, F. (2016). *Croatian web corpus hrWaC 2.1.* Merriam-Webster.

Nesselhauf, N. (2005). *Corpus Linguistics: A Practical Introduction.* Available at: http://www.as.uni-heidelberg.de/personen/Nesselhauf/files/Corpus%20 Linguistics%20Practical%20Introduction.pdf

Rychlý, P. (2007, December). *Manatee/Bonito-A Modular Corpus Manager.* RASLAN.

Schmid, H. (1994). Probabilistic Part-of-Speech Tagging Using Decision Trees, Intl. In *Conference on New Methods in Language Processing.*

Schmid, H. (1995) Improvements in Part-of-Speech Tagging with an Application to German. *Proceedings of the ACL SIGDAT-Workshop.*

Steinberger, R., Eisele, A., Klocek, S., Pilos, S., & Schlüter, P. (2013). *DGT-TM: A freely available translation memory in 22 languages.* arXiv preprint arXiv:1309.5226

Tadić, M. (2000). Building the Croatian-English Parallel Corpus. *LREC2000 Proceedings, 1*, 523-530.

Tech Terms. (n.d.). Available at: https://techterms.com/definition/cgi

ENDNOTES

1 Available at: https://www.sketchengine.eu/

2 Common Gateway Interface is a set of rules for running scripts and programs on a Web server. It specifies what information is communicated between the Web server and clients' Web browsers and how the information is transmitted. Definition is available on: https://techterms.com/definition/cgi

3 It is the Authentication and Authorisation Infrastructure of science and higher education in Croatia. Source: https://hosting.aaiedu.hr/hfh/?lang=en

4 Definition: a subdivision of the Internet consisting of computers or sites usually with a common purpose (such as providing commercial information) and denoted in Internet addresses by a unique abbreviation (such as com for commercial sites or gov for government sites). Available at: https://www.merriam-webster.com/dictionary/domain

5 Definition: Top-level domain (TLD) refers to the last segment of a domain name, or the part that follows immediately after the "dot" symbol. TLDs are mainly classified into two categories: generic TLDs and country-specific TLDs. Examples of some of the popular TLDs include .com, .org, .net, .gov, .biz and .edu. Available at: https://www.techopedia.com/definition/1348/top-level-domain-tld

6 Available at: https://skell.sketchengine.co.uk/run.cgi/skell

7 Available at: https://ruskell.sketchengine.co.uk/run.cgi/skell

8 Available at: https://deskell.sketchengine.co.uk/run.cgi/skell

9 Available at: https://itskell.sketchengine.co.uk/run.cgi/skell

10 Available at: https://csskell.sketchengine.co.uk//run.cgi/skell

11 Available at: https://etskell.sketchengine.co.uk/run.cgi/

12 Collocates of a word are words which occur frequently together with the word—they "co-locate" with the word (Baisa, Suchomel, 2014).

Chapter 3
Searching Methods for Corpora in NoSketch Engine

ABSTRACT

In this chapter, readers will get insight into a free online system for creating and searching corpora, NoSketch Engine, and its abilities. The chapter will provide valuable information about all corpus tools and functionality that users can use for conducting linguistic research, preparing teaching materials, exams, or exercise for their students. The basic syntax for querying corpus, a corpus query language (CQL), will be explored. Along with that, the chapter will provide examples of CQL syntax so that users can easier comprehend the basics for searching and exploring large language databases in different languages.

INTRODUCTION

Searching Methods for Corpora in NoSketch Engine

With NoSketch Engine, users can search corpora based on different kind of query. There are six types of query: simple, lemma, phrase, word, character and CQL. Additional options which corpus offers to its users is view of context which provides additional analysis of lemmas and words. Also, there is an option of analysis text type in which searched tag is shown. In this chapter author will show all query types and additional possibilities of query analysis which are available in NoSketch Engine. In category query

DOI: 10.4018/978-1-7998-3680-3.ch003

type user can select which type of search he or she wants to conduct. Query type simple refers to most simple searching method of selected corpora. In this search user can type word or a phrase and based on it user can get all language forms.

Query type lemma[1] refers to searching lemmas in corpus. For example, if user wants to find all tags of the headword[2] *žena* (eng. woman) result of this search would be exclusively for nominative of singular in all other forms in singular and plural like *žene, ženama*, resume and so on.

With query type word user can search exact word in her exact morphosyntactic form without lemmatization[3]. For example, if user wants to search corpus for word the *dog* he will get results only for genitive singular but he will not get all the rest forms. This query type offers to the user additional possibility where user can specify which form or word he or she wants to find. In drop down menu PoS (Part of Speech) user can choose from different available language forms. Tadić (2009) states that PoS tagging is associating language categories to each headword in text, this is also called morphosyntactic tagging. This process enables user to select which type of word he or she wants to find in corpus, e.g. noun, verb, adverb, preposition, etc. For example, if user wants to search for word *pila* (eng. chainsaw) as noun than in field Word Form he or she will type *pila* and from drop down menu at PoS will select *noun common.* Search result will show just headword in this searched form.

Query type character is used for searching certain string of characters, e.g. if user wants to find string of characters (letters) which occur together in certain word. Figure 1 shows search results for string *potr* in Croatian hrWaC corpus. This search doesn't have any restrictions and it will find all word in corpus which contains string of mentioned characters no matter on which position in word they appear (beginning, middle or end of the word). On the Figure 1 is example for string of characters *hyper* in English ukWaC corpus.

Last query type which is available in NoSketch Enigine is CQL (Corpus Query Language) a query language which is used for creating advance search queries with morphosyntactic tags. This is advanced query method for searching corpora with which user can narrow down his/hers results. Possibilities of CQL query which are available for users will be in more detailed explained in following subchapter.

Figure 1. Example of corpus search for sting "potr" in hrWaC corpus

Figure 2. Example of corpus search for sting hyper in ukWaC corpus

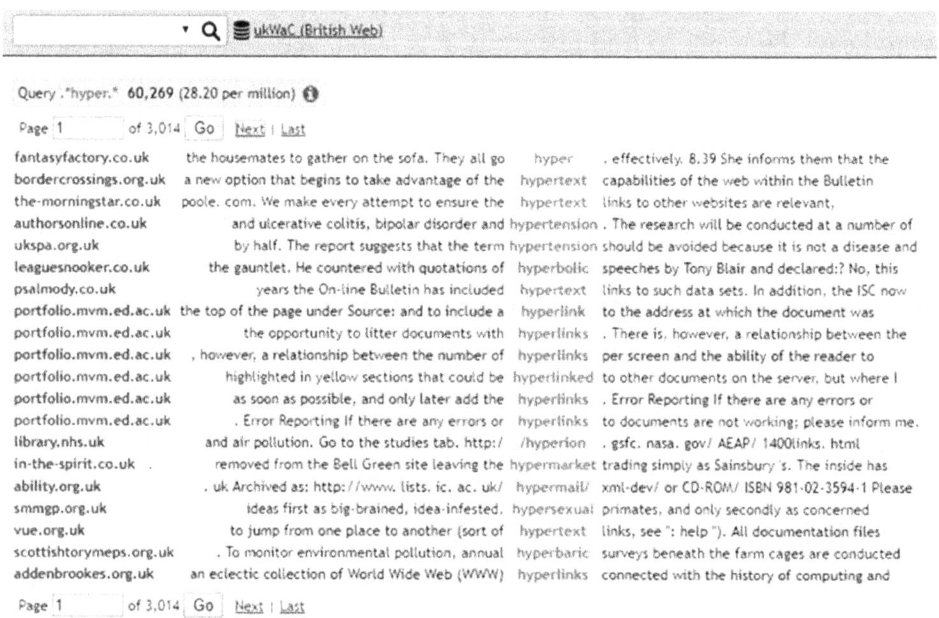

CQL QUERY

In CQL search we can choose what we want to find based on attribute we choose. Attribute can be word, lemma, tag, lc, lema_lc and lempos. Each attribute has its own meaning and depending on the attribute the search results will be different. Attribute word is uscd when user wants to find certain word in her exact form. Searching by lemma is explained above an it is one of the basic searches types in corpus. Attribute tag is used when user wants to search corpus by morphosyntactic tags or specifications. When user wants to find headwords, which are written in lower or upper case letters or if they start with capital letter then user will use attribute lc. Second attribute, lemma_lc is used for searching lemmas which are written with lower or upper case letters or if they starts with capital letter. For example, if word *što* (eng. what) appears in corpus written in following forms *što*, *Što* or *ŠTO* search results will show all forms. If we want to narrow down the search results only to show word written in upper case than the CQL query will be [lc="ŠTO"]. The same principle applies for attribute lemma_lc except it is used for searching lemmas. Example for use of lemma_lc attribute can be seen if user wants to search corpus for lemma *Višnja* (eng. cherry, in Croatian language word Višnja can be type of fruit and the name of a person) where user wants to

Figure 3. Search results for CQL in ukWaC: [lemma_lc="Butterfly" & tag="Np."]*

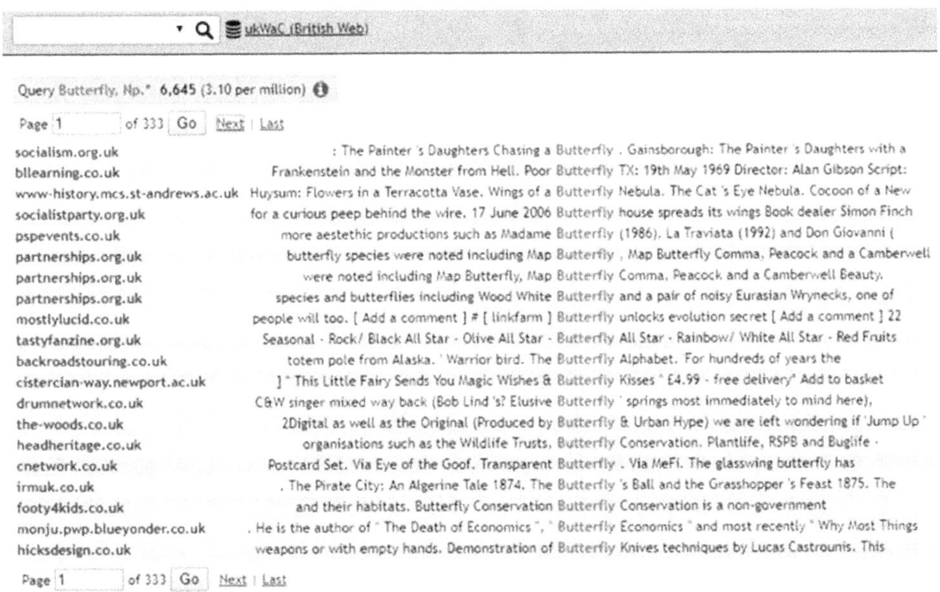

get results only for common noun in all grammatical case in singular and plural. CQL query will be: [lemma_lc="Višnja" & tag="Np.*"]. Example of this for English language can be seen on Figure 3 where are showed search result for word *butterfly* which is used as proper noun and refers to the name (e.g. name of a person, book, etc.) not the type of insect. CQL query is the same as for Croatian language, we just need to replace lemma or a word, i.e. [lemma_lc="Butterfly" & tag="Np.*"] (Figure 3).

Figure 4. Search results for CQL query with attribute lc

Left context	KWIC	Right context
.00 h organizira 1. biciklističko natjecanje	osnovnih škola	grada Zaprešića u vožnji biciklom kroz pre
... i namjenjena je prije svega curama po	osnovnim školama	. Probajte zainteresirat neke nove cure z
je namijenjena djeci od 1. do 4. razreda	osnovne škole	. U igraonici djeca provode vrijeme pišući
e na poziv Ureda donirao i već je stigla u	Osnovnu školu	podjednaka količina vode. ¢ Zagrebački h
e već iste, 1845. godine bila je to Ženska	osnovna škola	. Veliki interes za školovanje kod sestara
ljima u suradnji sa Zdravim gradom Poreč	Osnovna škola	Poreč provodi program Afirmacija uspješn
od navršene 4. godine života do polaska u	osnovnu školu	. Igraonicu vodi Vanja Blažek, odgojiteljica
od navršene 4. godine života do polaska u	osnovnu školu	. Igraonica upoznaje djecu s elementima
od navršene 4. godine života do polaska u	osnovnu školu	. Igraonicu vodi Dalia Jurenec, odgojitelji
djeca od navršene 3. godine do polaska u	osnovnu školu	. ¢ Program se temelji na suvremenim sp
djeca od navršene 3. godine do polaska u	osnovnu školu	. ¢ Program se temelji na suvremenim sp
a su pravila ovogodišnjih natjecanja ekipa	osnovnih škola	naše županije. Učenice će prvi krug natje
miranju za minice, učenike nižih razreda	osnovnih škola	potpuna su zagrebačka i hrvatska posebn
adnom dijelu pohoda biskup je boravio u	osnovnoj školi	, gdje se susreo s učenicima i djelatnicim
jerak... ¢ U sklopu proslave Dana škole u	Osnovnoj školi	Mato Lovrak predstavljena je knjiga Naših
da. ¢ Zato je važno da djeca od, ne samo	osnovne škole	, nego i od vrtića, dobivaju ta osnovna zn
u Lekenik. Radovi su to djece koja polaze	osnovnu školu	, grafički su riješeni bez prevelike interve
a kuna. ¢ U sportskoj dvorani lepoglavske	osnovne škole	, u srijedu, 29. svibnja održana je svečan
a Lokrumu. Bilo je prelijepo vidjeti djecu	osnovnih škola	kao i djecu sa posebnim potrebama koji s
rešimirom Roginom. Od listopada 1990., u	osnovnoj školi	u Dugavama počinje školski vjeronauk za
2013. ¢ Unikom već godinama surađuje s	osnovnim školama	između ostaloga i tako što organizira eduk
nji s Udrugom ' ' Ozana ' '. ¢ Godine 2001.	Osnovna škola	Voltino uključila se u projekt Eko škola te
prašinu i u protueksplozivnoj izvedbi ¢ U	osnovnoj školi	Novigrad, od 4. do 6. studenog 2011., održ
s Turističkom zajednicom, Komunalcem i	Osnovnom školom	Vela Luka. Djeluje edukativno preko lokal
ri. Na upražnjeno mjesto tiflopedagoga u	osnovnoj školi	Plokite primljena je gđa Marija Španjić, u
a gimnazija s pravom javnosti iz Zagreba,	Osnovna škola	Vijenac iz Osijeka te Srednja škola Zlatar
obratio učenicima 7. i 8. razreda porečkih	osnovnih škola	te roditeljima i stručnjacima u prostorima
te za što uspješniji polazak u prvi razred	osnovne škole	. ¢ Program predškole i ove godine bit će
manifestacija Cvjetni korzo. Dok su djeca	osnovnih škola	na svoj način oslikavala uskrsne pisanice,
ža volontera u SMŽ ". Učenici i nastavnici	osnovnih škola	Dragutin Tadijanović iz Petrinje, Katarine
ici Zadarske privatne gimnazije i Privatne	osnovne škole	Nova poklonili su gradu Zadru nešto zaist
sam učenika od drugog do šestog razreda	osnovne škole	, podijeljenih u dvije starosne grupe; mla
ni rezultati naših članova ¢ 26.03.2010. ¢	Osnovne škole	- LOGO Evo prijevremenih neslužbenih re
. Teoretska nastava održavana je u zgradi	Osnovne škole	. ¢ Industrijska kamenoklesarska škola ¢ S
-a Petar Zrinski, male gimnastičarke iz II.	Osnovne škole	Vrbovec te djeca vrbovečkih dječjih vrtić
organizaciju tribine o katalogu znanja za	osnovnu školu	, koji je od strane Ministarstva tada aktua

Additional example of attribute lc can be seen on adjective *osnovni* (eng. basic) which in Croatian language can be written with capital or small first letter. If adjective *osnovni* is written with capital letter than he refers to the name of primary school (in Croatian language primary school is called *osnovna škola* and adjective *osnovna* is written always with capital letter because it is the name of the school). CQL query will be: [lc="osnovn.*" & tag="A.*"] [lc="škol.*"]. Figure 4 presents part of search results according to attribute lc where it can be seen, by the surrounding content in which case we will write this adjective with capital letter and in which situation we will leave it in small letter.

Last attribute which we can use for creating CQL query is lempos and it refers to query type where corpus is searched by morphosyntactic descriptors of lemmas. This means that with lemma user will see her morphosyntactic tag so user can get insight into grammatical annotations of lemma her or she is searching. CQL query is using programming language which is developed for conducting advanced search and analyzing language which is placed in corpus. For that reason, CQL use certain rules and phrases which must be properly used for conducting this type of search.

Burnard (1996) describes CQL as typical Boolean style retrieval language, with a number of additional features particularly useful for corpus work. Like many other such languages, its syntax is designed for convenience of machine processing, rather than elegance or perspicuousness. To use CQL queries user must know language specification for language corpus he will use. These specifications are called morphosyntactic specifications and every language has its own description of it. CQL syntax and rules for searching are the same for every corpus and language. In following text, author will explain these rules on hrWaC corpus for Croatian language. Search methods are applicable in all available corpora in NoSketch Engine. List of morphosyntactic specifications can be found on home page of corpus under the general info, in field Tagset and the document is called Description. In Tagset every word form has its own specification which is used for conducting CQL query. Figure 5 shows table of specifications for verbs in Croatian language.

Table is divided into three columns. First column refers to attribute for category in Croatian language (table shows type of verbs, verb forms, person, number, gender and negative). Second column refers to value of attribute and third column refers to the code which is used for conducting CQL search in corpus. Code for searching verbs in NoSketch Engine is upper case V. Codes for verb tenses are as following: infinitive (n), participle (p), present (r), future (f), imperative (m), aorist (a), imperfect (e). Codes for persons

Figure 5. Specifications for verbs in Croatian language

P	Attribute (en)	Value (en)	Code (en)
0	CATEGORY	Verb	V
1	Type	main	m
		auxiliary	a
		copula	c
2	VForm	infinitive	n
		participle	p
		present	r
		future	f
		imperative	m
		aorist	a
		imperfect	e
3	Person	first	1
		second	2
		third	3
4	Number	singular	s
		plural	p
5	Gender	masculine	m
		feminine	f
		neuter	n
6	Negative	no	n
		yes	y

are: first person (1), second person (2) third person (3). Marks for number is singular (s) and plural (p). Codes for gender are: masculine (m), feminine (f) and neuter (n). Codes for negative is no (n) and yes (y). Below the table with specifications for Croatian language is table with morphosyntactic descriptions (MSD) with code for creating CQL query. Figure 6 shows MSD table for verbs in Croatian language.

Figure 6. Table with MSD for Croatian verbs

MSD	Features	Lexical entries	Examples of usage
Vmn	Verb Type=main VForm=infinitive	2017	imati, pomoći, nastaviti, ostati, pronaći, vidjeti, raditi, postati
Vmp-sm	Verb Type=main VForm=participle Number=singular Gender=masculine	1806	izjavio/izjaviti, kazao/kazati, rekao/reći, dodao/dodati, sastao/sastati
Vmp-sf	Verb Type=main VForm=participle Number=singular Gender=feminine	1772	mogla/moći, izjavila/izjaviti, trebala/trebati, priopćila/priopćiti
Vmp-sn	Verb Type=main VForm=participle Number=singular Gender=neuter	1597	moglo/moći, došlo/doći, trebalo/trebati, pokazalo/pokazati, priopćilo/priopćiti
Vmp-pm	Verb Type=main VForm=participle Number=plural Gender=masculine	1742	potpisali/potpisati, trebali/trebati, mogli/moći, imali/imati
Vmp-pf	Verb Type=main VForm=participle Number=plural Gender=feminine	1607	mogle/moći, trebale/trebati, potpisale/potpisati, složile/složiti
Vmp-pn	Verb Type=main VForm=participle Number=plural Gender=neuter	1491	ostala/ostati, dosegnula/dosegnuti, završila/završiti, zapošljavala/zapošljavati
Vmr1s	Verb Type=main VForm=present Person=first Number=singular	1514	mislim/misliti, nadam/nadati, vjerujem/vjerovati, smatram/smatrati

First column is containing MSD code or index which must be typed in field for creating CQL query. Second column provides explanation of MSD code while last column gives lexical examples. For example, if user wants to find all verb forms of present tense in singular, he or she will use MSD code Vmr1s.

The same situation is for all other word forms. Figure 7 shows table of specifications for nouns in Croatian language.

It is the same principle as for verbs. Table is divided into three columns. First column shows attributes for category: type, gender, number, case and animate. Second column contains value of the attribute. MSD code for nouns is N, upper case. For nouns there are common (c) and proper (p) nouns. Code for gender are: masculine (m), feminine (f), neutral (n). Code for case are: nominative (n), genitive (g), dative (d), accusative (a), vocative (v), locative (l), instrumental (i). Code for animate are yes (y) and no (n).

Below the table with specifications for Croatian language is table with morphosyntactic descriptions (MSD) with code for creating CQL query. Figure 8 shows MSD table for nouns in Croatian language.

Figure 7. Specifications for noun in Croatian language

P	Attribute (en)	Value (en)	Code (en)
0	CATEGORY	Noun	N
1	Type	common	c
		proper	p
2	Gender	masculine	m
		feminine	f
		neuter	n
3	Number	singular	s
		plural	p
4	Case	nominative	n
		genitive	g
		dative	d
		accusative	a
		vocative	v
		locative	l
		instrumental	i
5	Animate	no	n
		yes	y

First column is containing MSD code or index which must be typed in field for creating CQL query. Second column provides explanation of MSD code while last column gives lexical examples. For example, if user wants to find all common noun masculine in singular of genitive case, user will use MSD code Ncmsg.

For conducting CQL query it is essential to be familiar with MSD code and its syntax. CQL query language has been developed at Institute for Natural

Figure 8. Table of MSD code for nouns in Croatian language

MSD	Features	Lexical entries	Examples of usage
Ncmsn	Noun Type=common Gender=masculine Number=singular Case=nominative	1869	predsjednik, ministar, premijer, dio, broj, cilj, ured, šef, sporazum
Ncmsg	Noun Type=common Gender=masculine Number=singular Case=genitive	1787	posto, tjedna/tjedan, lipnja/lipanj, studenog/studeni, sporazuma/sporazum
Ncmsd	Noun Type=common Gender=masculine Number=singular Case=dative	1425	premijeru/premijer, razvitku/razvitak, parlamentu/parlament, dnevniku/dnevnik
Ncmsan	Noun Type=common Gender=masculine Number=singular Case=accusative Animate=no	1367	ponedjeljak, utorak, petak, četvrtak, sporazum, proces, napredak
Ncmsay	Noun Type=common Gender=masculine Number=singular Case=accusative Animate=yes	376	predsjednika/predsjednik, premijera/premijer, kandidata/kandidat
Ncmsv	Noun Type=common Gender=masculine Number=singular Case=vocative	1336	prosječe/prosjek, predsjedniče/predsjednik, župniče/župnik, živote/život
Ncmsl	Noun Type=common Gender=masculine Number=singular Case=locative	1579	putu/put, sjeveru/sjever, svijetu/svijet, sklopu/sklop, procesu/proces
Ncmsi	Noun Type=common Gender=masculine Number=singular Case=instrumental	1502	tijekom/tijek, obzirom/obzir, predsjednikom/predsjednik, početkom/početak
Ncmpn	Noun Type=common Gender=masculine Number=plural Case=nominative	1606	dužnosnici/dužnosnik, izvori/izvor, građani/građanin, čelnici/čelnik
Ncmpg	Noun Type=common Gender=masculine Number=plural Case=genitive	1722	eura/euro, poslova/posao, milijuna/milijun, ljudi/čovjek, dana/dan
Ncmpd	Noun Type=common Gender=masculine Number=plural Case=dative	1396	novinarima/novinar, naporima/napor, građanima/građanin, dužnosnicima/dužnosnik
Ncmpa	Noun Type=common Gender=masculine Number=plural Case=accusative	1557	izbore/izbor, napore/napor, zločine/zločin, napade/napad, odnose/odnos
Ncmpv	Noun Type=common Gender=masculine Number=plural Case=vocative	1332	mediji/medij, župnici/župnik, životi/život, živci/živac, žiriji/žiri

Figure 9. Table of MSD categories in ukWaC

kategorija (en)	vrednost (en)	koda (en)	kategorija (sl)	vrednost (sl)	koda (sl)	Atributi
CATEGORY	Noun	N	besedna_vrsta	samostalnik	S	2
CATEGORY	Verb	V	besedna_vrsta	glagol	G	5
CATEGORY	Adjective	A	besedna_vrsta	pridevnik	P	2
CATEGORY	Pronoun	P	besedna_vrsta	zaimek	Z	2
CATEGORY	Determiner	D	besedna_vrsta	določilnik	I	1
CATEGORY	Adverb	R	besedna_vrsta	prislov	R	2
CATEGORY	Adposition	S	besedna_vrsta	predlog	D	1
CATEGORY	Conjunction	C	besedna_vrsta	veznik	V	1
CATEGORY	Numeral	M	besedna_vrsta	števnik	K	1
CATEGORY	Particle	Q	besedna_vrsta	členek	L	0
CATEGORY	Interjection	I	besedna_vrsta	medmet	M	0
CATEGORY	Abbreviation	Y	besedna_vrsta	okrajšava	O	0
CATEGORY	Residual	X	besedna_vrsta	neuvrščeno	N	1

Language Processing, University of Stuttgart in the early 90's. It consists of regular expressions which are used with attribute expressions and structures. The main condition for conducting CQL search is that corpus is annotated (part of speech or MSD codes).

For English language MSD codes are available at link:

http://nl.ijs.si/spook/msd/html-sl/msd-en.html

In following section there will be explained MSD codes for ukWaC British corpus which is available in NoSketch Engine. The structure of MSD codes is similar to MSD codes for Croatian language which is explained aforementioned. Figure 9 shows all categories which are available in ukWaC corpus for English language. The codes are the same as for Croatian language, verbs have code V, nouns have code N, adjectives have code A, etc.

Figure 10 shows table of verbs in ukWaC corpus and Figure 11 shows MSD codes for searching different types of verbs for English language. Tables have English and Slovenian translation of descriptions. Figure 11 shows MSD codes which user can use if he or she wants to search for base form of verb *be* in ukWaC corpus than CQL query will be [word="be" & tag=V-b].

Figure 10. Attributes for verbs in English language in ukWaC

P	Atribut (en)	Vrednost (en)	Koda (en)	Atribut (sl)	Vrednost (sl)	Koda (sl)
0	CATEGORY	Verb	V	besedna_vrsta	glagol	G
1	Type	modal	o	vrsta	naklonski	n
2	VForm	base	b	oblika	osnovna_oblika	o
		indicative	i		povednik	i
		participle	p		deležnik	d
3	Tense	present	p	čas	sedanjik	s
		past	s		preteklik	r
4	Person	third	3	oseba	tretja	t
5	Number	singular	s	število	ednina	e

Figure 11. Table of MSD codes for verbs in ukWaC

MSD (sl)	Lastnosti (sl)	MSD (en)	Lastnosti (en)	TreeTagger	Opis	Primeri
G-o	glagol oblika=osnovna_oblika	V-b	Verb VForm=base	VB	Verb, base form	be, have, see, do, go, get, know, tell, take
G-is	glagol oblika=povednik čas=sedanjik	V-ip	Verb VForm=indicative Tense=present	VBP	Verb, non-3rd person singular present	do, are be, have, 're be, 'm be, know, 've have, think, am be
G-iste	glagol oblika=povednik čas=sedanjik oseba=tretja število=ednina	V-ip3s	Verb VForm=indicative Tense=present Person=third Number=singular	VBZ	Verb, 3rd person singular present	is be, 's be, has have, does do, says say, 's have, knows know, seems seem, comes come
G-ir	glagol oblika=povednik čas=preteklik	V-is	Verb VForm=indicative Tense=past	VBD	Verb, past tense	was be, had have, said say, were be, did do, looked look, came come, thought think, seemed seem
G-ds	glagol oblika=deležnik čas=sedanjik	V-pp	Verb VForm=participle Tense=present	VBG	Verb, gerund or persent participle	going go, looking look, being be, trying try, doing do, coming come, taking take, sitting sit, saying say
G-dr	glagol oblika=deležnik čas=preteklik	V-ps	Verb VForm=participle Tense=past	VBN	Verb, past participle	been be, got get, seen see, come, done do, gone go, made make, left leave, taken take
Gn	glagol vrsta=naklonski	Vo	Verb Type=modal	MD	Modal verb	could, would, will, can, 'll will, must, should, might, 'd will

Figure 12 shows attributes for searching nouns in ukWaC corpus. User can search just nouns with code N or common and proper nouns with code c for common nouns and p for proper nouns. Also, user can specify plurality or singularity of the noun with code s for singular noun and p for plural noun. CQL query for plural proper nouns in ukWaC corpus would be: [tag="Np-p"]

Figure 12. Attributes for nouns in English language in ukWaC

P	Atribut (en)	Vrednost (en)	Koda (en)	Atribut (sl)	Vrednost (sl)	Koda (sl)
0	CATEGORY	Noun	N	besedna_vrsta	samostalnik	S
1	Type	common	c	vrsta	občno_ime	o
		proper	p		lastno_ime	l
3	Number	singular	s	število	ednina	e
		plural	p		množina	m

. This syntax will list plural proper nouns in corpus, e.g. States, Americans, Croatians, et. The example of MSD codes for searching nouns can be seen on Figure 13 with following examples of words (nouns) which user can search and get results from corpus.

Figure 13. Table of MSD codes for nouns in ukWaC

MSD (sl)	Lastnosti (sl)	MSD (en)	Lastnosti (en)	TreeTagger	Opis	Primeri
So-e	samostalnik vrsta=občno_ime število=ednina	Nc-s	Noun Type=common Number=singular	NN	Noun common singular	time, man, way, head, something, hand, room, door, nothing
So-m	samostalnik vrsta=občno_ime število=množina	Nc-p	Noun Type=common Number=plural	NNS	Noun common plural	eyes eye, people, things thing, 's, years year, men man, feet foot, hands hand, words word
Sl-e	samostalnik vrsta=lastno_ime število=ednina	Np-s	Noun Type=proper Number=singular	NP	Proper noun singular	Harry, Langdon, Ron, Dumbledore, Sophie, Hermione, Samad, Archie, Stefan
Sl-m	samostalnik vrsta=lastno_ime število=množina	Np-p	Noun Type=proper Number=plural	NPS	Proper noun plural	Dursleys Dursley, Harrys Harry, Fords, Brothers, States, Jews, Muslims, Catholics, Americans

Syntax for CQL Query

Using CQL query for corpus search gives the user the ability of diversify and comprehensive search of available text in corpora. Thus, this type of search is the most demanding to users and presents one of the obstacles for using the corpus and corpus tools. CQL query allows corpus search for words, morphosyntactic tags or individual parts of a word, tags, or expressions.

There are certain rules and guidelines for how to use CQL query. The search type is similar to the database search and it is based on similar rules and syntagma. It requires for user to have advanced level of computer literacy and also requires time for the user to master rules for conducting this type of the search. Table 1 contains some of the basic parameters used in the CQL query. Each of them has a certain meaning that the user needs to know in order to use this type of search. In CQL queries, the search term/word must always be entered within the quotation (“ “) characters. The quotation must be English therefore the words should be positioned above on both sides. The CQL query is not case-sensitive, as well as for spaces, except for a term that is entered within the quotation marks - then no spaces are used because the search cannot be performed. The general form used to search a certain attribute value is [attribute = “value”]. For example, if user wants to find a certain word (e.g. *žena*, eng. *women*) CQL query will looks like this: [word=”žena”]. In this syntax attribute is word and his value is *žena.* If user

Table 1. Table of signs and characters for CQL query

SIGN	DESCRIPTION
[]	Replaces any element or one word. It is used for Boolean expression.
‘’ ‘’	Sign for defining value
.	Replaces one character
*	Replaces all letters or characters between 0 and 100
|	Searches two or more different values (words)
!	It is used for negation
{}	Sign for searching defined range of values which appears inside default search
&	Sign for bond between to attribute values
\	Sign for excluding element from search
=	Sign for defining attribute value
?	Sign for searching one or none previous character
tag	Attribute for searching word forms
word	Attribute for word search
<s/>	Sign for structure - sentence
within	Command for searing inside sentence structure
containing	Command for searching by content
meet	Command for searching context
union	Command for expanding parameters of meet command

wants to find certain value/code (e.g. Vmr1s - main verbs in the first person singular) attribute is tag and her value is “Vmr1s”. CQL query will look like this: [tag=”Vmr1s”].

It is not always necessary to enter the attribute word. If a user wants to search corpus without this attribute, then the requested term/word is entered into the quotation characters. For example, if user wants to find words *''preispitati''* (eng. to question a decision) and *''ispitati''* (eng. to question) CQL query will be: ''(pre)?ispitati''. In this example is used the question mark (?) which is used for finding zero or one occurrence of a particular expression in front of a given word. Figure 14 shows search results for mentioned CQL query for words ''preispitati'' and ''ispitati''. Situation in ukWac corpora can be

Figure 14. Results for CQL query: ''(pre)?ispitati''

seen on Figure 15 which shows the example of this type of search for English language with words *possible* and *impossible*: ''(im)?possible''

Figure 15. Results for CQL query: ''(im)?possible'' in ukWaC

The equality sign (=) is used is to define the value of the attribute that user wants to search for. For example, if user wants to find the usage of the word in context, CQL the query would be: word=''vrt'' (eng. garden). In this example, one can see how the attribute value is always inside the quotation. If user wants to expand the query to find more values, the user will use square brackets [] and within add the required attributes.

In addition to defining limits for corpus search, square braces can also be used to replace any sign or word. If user wants to leave an arbitrary place where any word can appear, then empty square brackets will be used ([]). For example, if user wants to find all the words that appear between the word "*kroz*" (eng. through) and all the words "*prozor*" (engl. window) then the CQL query will be: "kroz" [] "prozor.* " . Since empty square brackets are used between the two default words, the query results will only show one word

Figure 16. CQL query for: "kroz" [] "prozor.".*

ovog puta sunce već dobrano prodire	kroz otvoreni prozor	. Još jedan topao i sunčani dan
ći od slabog svijetla koje je prodiralo	kroz malene prozore	. Ušli smo u sobu u kojoj je bilo
klo, pa se činilo kao da mi se ukazala	kroz zamagljen prozor	. Na koji je opet zakucala jesen
emena hladan zrak se uvlačio u sobu	kroz otvoreni prozor	... Vani u vrtu vukao se jež ispo
enicama ili s namještaja, s balkona ili	kroz otvoren prozor	. Zato je potrebno unaprijed ra:
oz zatvoren prozor) i ventilacijski (oni	kroz otvoren prozor	). Kada se zbroje jedni i drugi, I
i se događaju kako kroz staklo, tako i	kroz okvir prozora	. Okvir može biti PVC, ali s čelič
zloženo moguće je promatrati s ulice	kroz veliki prozor	galerije. Međunarodni program
krio taj pogled, morao sam pogledati	kroz drukčiji prozor	. ¢ Lindsay Brown u Zagrebu ¢ l
ija Fino si kaza maloj ' ', dobaci netko	kroz otvoren prozor	u susjedstvu. ¢ Nova se pokunji
gađaja i zapažamo da gusti dim izlazi	kroz podrumski prozor	. ¢ Voditelj intervencije vrši izv
storije, zidovi se hlade, a topliji zrak	kroz otvorene prozore	izlazi vani. ¢ Sobnim programat
željni nerijetko, istražujući, ulijeću i	kroz otvorene prozore	naših domova. Ne zna se, zapra
ena soba, u koju se može tek provući	kroz omaleni prozorčić	, a u njoj najviše vole boraviti d
bici kroz prozore su transmisijski (oni	kroz zatvoren prozor	) i ventilacijski (oni kroz otvorer
avati kad je prozor otvoren. I kad mi	kroz otvoren prozor	jutro uđe u sobu i pozdravi me.
čekali. Kratko vremena nakon što je	kroz otvoreni prozor	dopro podnevni pucanj topa s L
iti razinu buke za 33 dB. Na taj način	kroz zatvoren prozor	nećete čuti buku s ulice. Ukolik
konska vrata ¢ Prirodna je ventilacija	kroz otvorene prozore	i balkonska vrata najintenzivniji
na toplijima. ¢ Prirodna je ventilacija	kroz otvorene prozore	i balkonska vrata najintenzivniji
ugu kosu svoje Sanjinke. Naginjem se	kroz otvoren prozor	, želim joj doviknuti, objaviti joj
su se osloboditi u nadi da će pobjeći	kroz otvoreni prozor	. Tu borbu za život i smrt između
govih biografa, Bog je provirio glavom	kroz njegov prozor	i on je počeo kričati. Možete li t
li ne navučemo tamne zastore, često	kroz zatvoreni prozor	ulaze sunčeve zrake koje imaju
parkinga u rikverc, jer loša vidljivost	kroz bočne prozore	otežava i povećava rizik izlaska
Ona se odvija putem infiltracije zraka	kroz zazore prozora	i vrata, te zidova, otvaranjem p
na prste noge zavirujemo i ne znamo	kroz koji prozor	ući. ¢ â žMislim da su ipak rekl
avajuće svjetlo, istu može prodirati i	kroz otvorene prozore	ili vrata. ¢ Pružaju li metaliziran
lašenu djevojku i oboje se zagledaju	kroz veliki prozor	sa kojeg je pucao vidik na mnog
lašenu djevojku i oboje se zagledaju	kroz veliki prozor	sa kojeg je pucao vidik na mnog
je sunce užarenom pesnicom udaralo	kroz otvoren prozor	i vrijeđalo oči, usprkos napola s
jnim medijima) kao tmuran i oblačan,	kroz ogroman prozor	u mom uredu zasjalo sunce. Go
ćete uvijek biti u mogućnosti gledati	kroz kuhinjski prozor	. Katastrofa može nastati u trep
otkrovlju, u koju se može tek provući	kroz mali prozor	, a u njoj najviše vole biti djeca

between them. Figure 26 shows the hrWaC corpus results for the specified CQL query. Part of results shows different words in between, for example:

kroz otvoreni prozor, (eng. through open window),
kroz maleni prozor (eng. through tiny window),
kroz veliki prozor (eng. through big window),
kroz okvir prozora (eng. through frame of window),
kroz zamagljen prozor (eng. through blurred window),

kroz podrumski prozor (eng. through basement window),
kroz drugačiji prozor (eng. through different window),
kroz zatvoren prozor (eng. through closed window),
kroz ogroman prozor (eng. through huge window),
kroz kuhinjski prozor (eng. through kitchen window).

Figure 17 shows CQL query for English version of this search: "through" [] "window.*" The results shows all the word that appears between word *through* and *window.* Figure 17 shows just part of the search results, for example: *through a window, through the window, through stained-glass windows, through opaque window, through your window, through our window, through her window, through this window, through glass window, through their window.* This example shows which type of the words, articles or pronouns can be used between these two words.

Figure 17. CQL query for: "through" [] "window."*

The attribute tag is used to search the tagged/annotated words, it is used when a user wants to find a certain type of word, such as a verb, noun, adjective, etc. An example of this type of search is following if user wants to find all the verbs in the corpus - then the CQL query will be: tag = ''V.*''

. If user only wants to find the main verbs in the first person singular, he or she will use a specific tag (Vmr1s), i.e. tag = "Vmr1s".

When tagged words are searched within the corpus, often is used syntax . * because it includes any string of characters after a particular character. For example, tag = '' V. * '' will find all verbs (main, auxiliary or copulas, any verbal time, any single or plural face), in other words, the syntax .* (the full stop and the star) replaces any string of characters in tag attribute.

Sign & denotes a bond between the two values of the attribute which are could be searched in corpus. For example, a query can be set up to find all the verb forms which appear in the corpus and begin with "razgovara" (eng. talk). In this example, the CQL query would be: [word=''razgovara.*'' & tag=''V.*''] So the value & is used as a link between the string of " razgovara " and the type of word - the verb can be in any verbal time, any single or plural face, so the search results will include the following forms:

razgovarati, razgovaram, razgovaraš, razgovara, razgovaramo, razgovarate, razgovaraju, razgovarat, razgovarah, razgovaraše, razgovarasmo, razgovaraste, razgovarahu, razgovarao, razgovarala, razgovaralo, razgovarali, razgovaraj, razgovarajmo, razgovarajte te razgovarajući.

If CQL query would be: [word=''razgovara.*'' & tag='' Vmr3s''], result would be: *razgovara.*

If CQL is: [word=''razgovara.*'' & tag='' Vmr.*'], result would include just verbs in present tense of verb: *razgovaram, razgovaraš, razgovara, razgovaramo, razgovarate, razgovaraju.*

Curly brackets ({}) are used when searching the word range within a default search, or when user wants to see which words appear between 2 or more terms that he or she want to find. For example, if user wants to find the words that appear between all the verb forms *projuriti* (eng. run) and adverb *kroz* (eng. through), inside the curly brackets he or she will enter a number that refers to the number of words user wants to see between these two words. The CQL query for this example would be: ''projur.*''[]{2}''kroz''. This means that the results will show zero to the maximum of two words which may appear between those two terms. In Figure 18 it is possible to see hrWaC results for the given example. Figure 19 shows example of CQL query for English language with words *run* and *through.* Results show which two deferent words can appear between these words. CQL query is: "run"[]

Figure 18.

Figure 19. CQL query for: "run"[]{2}"through"

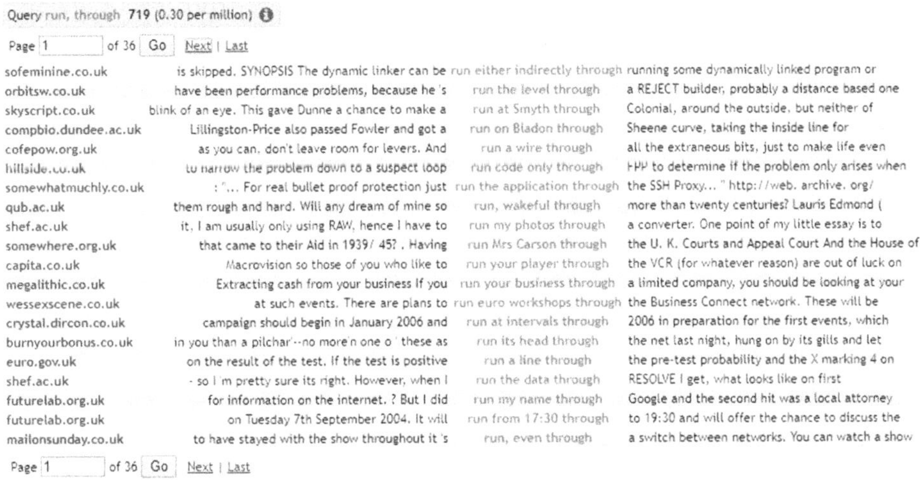

Query run, through 719 (0.30 per million)

Page 1 of 36 Go Next | Last

sofeminine.co.uk	is skipped. SYNOPSIS The dynamic linker can be	run either indirectly through	running some dynamically linked program or
orbitsw.co.uk	have been performance problems, because he 's	run the level through	a REJECT builder, probably a distance based one
skyscript.co.uk	blink of an eye. This gave Dunne a chance to make a	run at Smyth through	Colonial, around the outside, but neither of
compbio.dundee.ac.uk	Lillingston-Price also passed Fowler and got a	run on Bladon through	Sheene curve, taking the inside line for
cofepow.org.uk	as you can, don't leave room for levers. And	run a wire through	all the extraneous bits, just to make life even
hillside.co.uk	to narrow the problem down to a suspect loop	run code only through	FPP to determine if the problem only arises when
somewhatmuchly.co.uk	: "... For real bullet proof protection just	run the application through	the SSH Proxy... " http://web. archive. org/
qub.ac.uk	them rough and hard. Will any dream of mine so	run, wakeful through	more than twenty centuries? Lauris Edmond (
shef.ac.uk	it, I am usually only using RAW, hence I have to	run my photos through	a converter. One point of my little essay is to
somewhere.org.uk	that came to their Aid in 1939/ 45? . Having	run Mrs Carson through	the U. K. Courts and Appeal Court And the House of
capita.co.uk	Macrovision so those of you who like to	run your player through	the VCR (for whatever reason) are out of luck on
megalithic.co.uk	Extracting cash from your business If you	run your business through	a limited company, you should be looking at your
wessexscene.co.uk	at such events. There are plans to	run euro workshops through	the Business Connect network. These will be
crystal.dircon.co.uk	campaign should begin in January 2006 and	run at intervals through	2006 in preparation for the first events, which
burnyourbonus.co.uk	in you than a pilchar'--no more'n one o ' these as	run its head through	the net last night, hung on by its gills and let
euro.gov.uk	on the result of the test. If the test is positive	run a line through	the pre-test probability and the X marking 4 on
shef.ac.uk	- so I 'm pretty sure its right. However, when I	run the data through	RESOLVE I get, what looks like on first
futurelab.org.uk	for information on the internet. ? But I did	run my name through	Google and the second hit was a local attorney
futurelab.org.uk	on Tuesday 7th September 2004. It will	run from 17:30 through	to 19:30 and will offer the chance to discuss the
mailonsunday.co.uk	to have stayed with the show throughout it 's	run, even through	a switch between networks. You can watch a show

Page 1 of 36 Go Next | Last

{2}"through". It is used without full stop at verb *run* because the difference in language. If the full stop is added then the results would include all forms of verb *run*, e.g. *running*, *runs*, etc., because sign full stop and asterisk replaces all the characters/letters which can appear after them at given word or a string of characters.

The exclamation point (!) is used as a negation in corpus search, or it can be used when something wants to be excluded from the search. For example, if user wants to find all the words *žena* (eng. women) in the corpus, but he or she do not want to get the results where an adjective appears in front of the search term, the CQL query for this example would be: [tag!="A.*"] [word ="žena"]. It can be noticed that the exclamation point is always placed behind the attribute (which is in this case a tag), or in front of the equality sign. It is never used within the attribute value. If the exclamation point is used in front of the parentheses, then attributes and their associated values will be excluded from the search.

The backslash sign (\) is used when user wants to exclude all tokens that contain only one character from the search. For example, if user wants to exclude punctuation signs that appear inside paragraphs such as a full stop, a comma, an exclamation point, a question mark, a colon, a dot, etc.

Vertical Line (|) is used in search where user wants to see two or more terms simultaneously, i.e. two or more attribute values are defined in query. In the program language, this sign is called OR (Boolean operator) and it includes members of both defined search set in search results. For example, if user wants to find words starting with a string of *trub* which can be nouns and verbs, the CQL query for this type of search would be: [word = ʻʼ trub. * ʻʼ & (Tag = ʻʼ N. * ʻʼ I tag = ʻʼ V. * ʻʼ)]. The results will include following verb forms: *trubiti* (eng. honk), *trubi, trube*, and also nouns *truba* (eng. klaxon),, *trubač* (eng. trumpeter),, *trubadur* (eng. troubadour), and all forms of these nouns. In this query there are also plain brackets because in the search are defined two values i.e. two types of words, nouns and verbs beginning with "*trub*". Figure 20 shows an overview of the concordance sequence for a CQL query.

Figure 20. Concordance list for CQL query: [word=''trub.'' & (tag=''N.*'' | tag=''V.*'')]*

utno najbolji klub na ovim prostorima, ali u Evropi su	truba	. ¢ Ovaj vas Mamic koliko god da je budala, covek zna po
om ritualu zavođenja koje uključuje trčanje, pjesmu,	trublje	, bičevanje i krv. Sve završava njegovim konačnim izboror
zdanju Alfe objavljuje i svoj prvi roman za djecu Plavi	trubač	. ¢ Godinu dana kasnije tiskan mu je još jedan roman za
alo problema zna svirati još dva glazbena instrumenta	trubu	i klavir. ¢ Nebahat Cehre (sultanova majka) jedva dočeka
i ključnih figura francuske šansone, jedan od najvećih	trubadura	francuskog jezika. Rođen 8. travnja 1929. u Bruxellesu, n
lnih čudovišta. Vlada negira da on postoji, iako mediji	trube	o njemu na sve strane. Jest da si čovjek brusi rogove, ali i
će mjesto. ¢ U finalu su svi navijači uzbuđeno gledali,	trubili	i skakali od uzbuđenja. Snage su odmjerili Zagreb i Senj.
e će tako bilježiti brzinu, potrošnju, kočenje, pa čak i	trubljenje	, a svi podaci biti će pohranjeni u datoteci. Premda mnog
ne zaletim. ¢ Kad ono na prvoj ravnoj i glatkoj dionici	trubi	mi par koje sam ostavio u prošloj grupi. To the left. Ko da
žio im se Ivan Bralić. Na programu su se našla djela za	trubu	i orgulje čuvenih majstora glazbenoga baroka, J. Pachelb
treću godinu su poznati glazbeni umjetnici i pedagozi	trubač	prof. Stanko Arnold iz Slovenije te orguljašica prof. Ljerka
ranije za bariton i orgulje. U orkestar dodaje rogove,	trube	i trombone, i, naravno, bariton solo. Takva verzija Requie
ske sredine svog doba. S devet godina počeo je svirati	trubu	zaslugom oca, nekadašnjega svirača u kapeli, da bi poslij
enu isprogramiranosti se radi. Svi premijeri i državnici	trube	u istu tikvu kao da ih je ista majka rodila. Zašto nema rev
gled te sam morala naslijepo izaći. Vozač mi je počeo	trubiti	, i ja sam krenula za njim jer me iživcirao. Počela sam ga
sa, mokra. Pada kiša kao iz kabla. Automobili prolaze,	trube	, ona ne zna gdje je. Samo hoda, pa trči, pa hoda sve dol
ađen je 1942. godine. ¢ Prva odijela, kao i vatrogasnu	trubu	, vatrogasnu časničku sablju, te raznu sitniju opremu Dru
ovjeri ministar. ¢ Srednjovjekovni biografski tekstovi o	trubadurima	vrlo su staro svjedočanstvo o zanimanju koje izazivaju živ
io da se dočekuju neki sportski junaci. Dočekali su nas	trubači	, kolege su bili u narodnim nošnjama a u rukama im bila
hovim inozemnim gazdama, trn su u oku. Paralelno sa	trubadurima	iz prodanih udarnih medija, gejevi vrlo perfidno igraju ul
ča koji prebire po strunama gitare. Prepoznah uličnog	trubadura	iz naše mladosti i stavih želju u šešir koji je ležao na astr
ča koji prebire po strunama gitare. Prepoznah uličnog	trubadura	iz naše mladosti i stavih želju u šešir koji je ležao na astr
ča koji prebire po strunama gitare. Prepoznah uličnog	trubadura	iz naše mladosti i stavih želju u šešir koji je ležao na astr
Bernarda na čelo komisije, da je do njega Dragačevski	trubači	bi imali ljetnu tezgu u Areni. ¢ 12 Srijeda, 14 Travanj 201
eti nikakvu korist, to jest neće donijeti, kako se stalno	trubi	, bolju kvalitetu usluga i razvoj konkurentskog tržišta. On
već uobičajna praksa dijeljenja razne racing opreme,	truba	i boja za automobile. Svoje umijeće opet možete pokaza
ju poezije, pripovjedne proze i esejistike. ¢ Tršćanski	trubač	i skladatelj Marco Fragiacomo glazbenu je naobrazbu stel
povijesnog značaja ovog kompleksa, motive poštanske	trube	koja predstavlja poštansku postaju i preslika netom spom
ke ili romaničke katedrale ¢ feudalni dvorci, vitezovi,	trubaduri	¢ samostani s knjižnicama i prepisivačima knjiga ¢ kršćan
vijet dobiti upozorenje od Boga Ondak neću ja morati	trubiti	što je ispravno a što ne ¢ nije lose i glavno da je to sve p
ler i basist Mario Torbica te gosti, gitarist Elvis Penava,	trubač	Antonio Geček i tenor saksofonist Mario Bočić. ¢ LEKAP Q
ački orkestar. Božićnim melodijama tube, horna (rog),	trube	, klarineta, flauta, blok flauta, picolo flauta, krilnica i sa
¢ Poznat kao jedan od najsvestranijih jazz glazbenika,	trubač	, skladatelj, voditelj big banda i glazbeni pedagog, Wynt
ičnih nema previše zar ne? ¢ Bio Massa super vozač, ili	truba	u jedno možeš bit siguran; teško da bi ijedan drugi vozač
a za učenjem. Osim toga slobodno možemo reći da su	truba	i orgulje na neki način prepoznati kao izvanredan spoj gl
Zvonimir organizirali su Treći međunarodni seminar za	trubu	i orgulje, održan u razdoblju od 26. do 29. kolovoza. Pre
asvjetnog generatora, startera, reflektorskih svjetala i	trube	koje su se uskoro počele primjenjivati u konstruiranju aut
nastupio s vlastitim skladbama u Studiju Bajsić, švedski	trubač	, skladatelj, aranžer i bandleader Lasse Lindgren vraća se

This sign can also be used when user wants to find two or more words at once. For example, if user wants to find the word "*malen*" (eng. small) or "*sićušan*" (eng. tiny) the CQL query will be: [word = "malen | sićušan"]. It is important to emphasize that the attribute can contain as many values as the user wants to search within the query, it is not limited to just two values as in this example.

Example of this sign for English language can be seen on Figure 21 with words *small* and *tiny*. It can be seen which term is more often use in English language and in what contexts certain word will be used. The structure of CQL query is the same as for the Croatian language but it is important just to type words in English: [word = "small | tiny"]. From the corpus results it can be seen that word *small* is frequently used in regards to *tiny*. Later in this chapter author will present how user can get information about frequency of vocabulary or phrase, words, etc. through analysis of corpus results.

Figure 21. CQL query in ukWaC: [word = "small | tiny"].

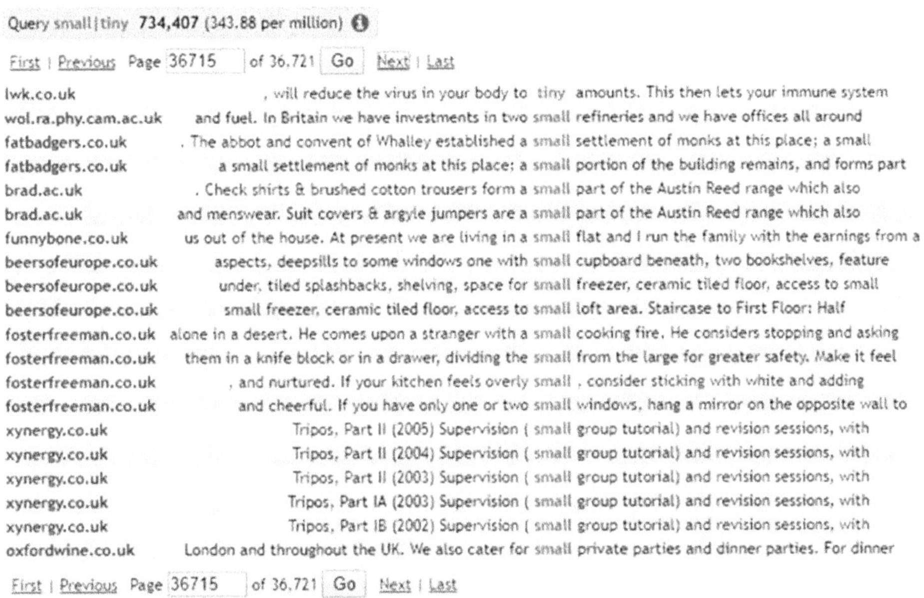
Query small|tiny 734,407 (343.88 per million)

First | Previous Page 36715 of 36,721 Go Next | Last

lwk.co.uk	, will reduce the virus in your body to	tiny	amounts. This then lets your immune system
wol.ra.phy.cam.ac.uk	and fuel. In Britain we have investments in two	small	refineries and we have offices all around
fatbadgers.co.uk	. The abbot and convent of Whalley established a	small	settlement of monks at this place; a small
fatbadgers.co.uk	a small settlement of monks at this place; a	small	portion of the building remains, and forms part
brad.ac.uk	. Check shirts & brushed cotton trousers form a	small	part of the Austin Reed range which also
brad.ac.uk	and menswear. Suit covers & argyle jumpers are a	small	part of the Austin Reed range which also
funnybone.co.uk	us out of the house. At present we are living in a	small	flat and I run the family with the earnings from a
beersofeurope.co.uk	aspects, deepsills to some windows one with	small	cupboard beneath, two bookshelves, feature
beersofeurope.co.uk	under. tiled splashbacks, shelving, space for	small	freezer, ceramic tiled floor, access to small
beersofeurope.co.uk	small freezer, ceramic tiled floor, access to	small	loft area. Staircase to First Floor: Half
fosterfreeman.co.uk	alone in a desert. He comes upon a stranger with a	small	cooking fire. He considers stopping and asking
fosterfreeman.co.uk	them in a knife block or in a drawer, dividing the	small	from the large for greater safety. Make it feel
fosterfreeman.co.uk	, and nurtured. If your kitchen feels overly	small	, consider sticking with white and adding
fosterfreeman.co.uk	and cheerful. If you have only one or two	small	windows, hang a mirror on the opposite wall to
xynergy.co.uk	Tripos, Part II (2005) Supervision (	small	group tutorial) and revision sessions, with
xynergy.co.uk	Tripos, Part II (2004) Supervision (	small	group tutorial) and revision sessions, with
xynergy.co.uk	Tripos, Part II (2003) Supervision (	small	group tutorial) and revision sessions, with
xynergy.co.uk	Tripos, Part IA (2003) Supervision (	small	group tutorial) and revision sessions, with
xynergy.co.uk	Tripos, Part IB (2002) Supervision (	small	group tutorial) and revision sessions, with
oxfordwine.co.uk	London and throughout the UK. We also cater for	small	private parties and dinner parties. For dinner

First | Previous Page 36715 of 36,721 Go Next | Last

The command *meet* refers to the contextual query type which enables the user to see the context of the searched term, or to see how a certain term or word behaves in a given language environment. For example, if user wants to

Figure 22. Concordance list for CQL query: (meet [tag="V."] [tag="R.*"] -2 2) in Croatian language*

see how the verbs and surrounding adverbs are behaving in authentic language (language in use) then user will use the meet command. The CQL query which will enable user to see all the verbs which are surrounded with adverbs within range from a maximum of two words before or after the verb would be: (meet [tag = "V. *"] [tag = "R. *"] -2 2). The last two query parameters that are numeric are related to the range of words that user wants to establish in the search results (specifically, -2 refers to the position of the adverb that can be up to a maximum of two places to the left of the verb, while 2 refers to the position of the adverb that can be up to a maximum of two places on

Figure 23. Concordance list for CQL query: (meet [tag="V."] [tag="R.*"] -2 2) in English language*

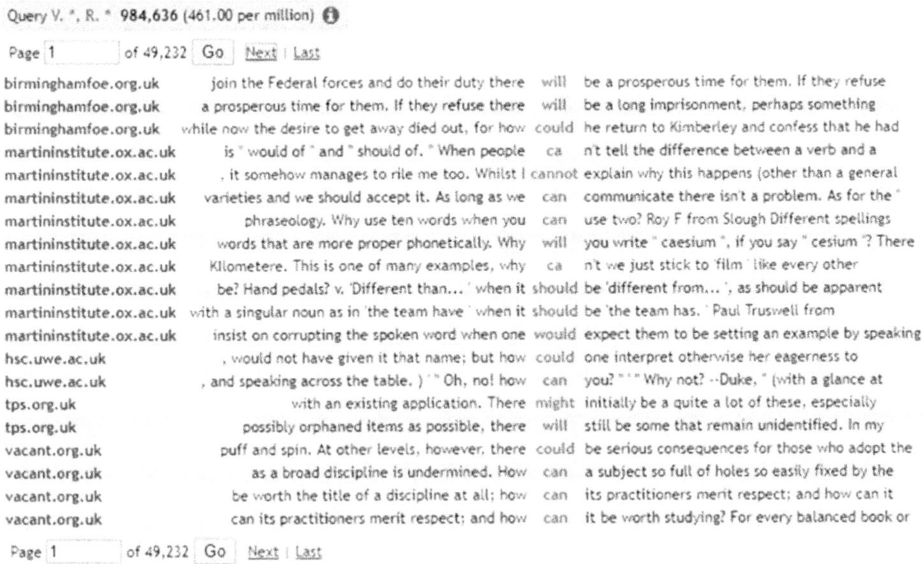

the right of the verb) (Figure 22). The same CQL query is used for English language and results can be seen on Figure 23.

It is also possible to use the union command to expand search and get detailed results. The union command is always used for expanding CQL search with meet command. For example, if user wants to find all common nouns in female gender which are located before common noun (up to 2 places left) and in addition all common nouns in female gender which are located before an adjective (up to 2 places left) then a CQL query is formed like this: (union

Figure 24. Concordance list for CQL query: (union (meet [tag="Ncf."] [tag="Nc.*"] -2 0) (meet 7[tag="Ncf.*"] [tag="A.*"] -2 0))*

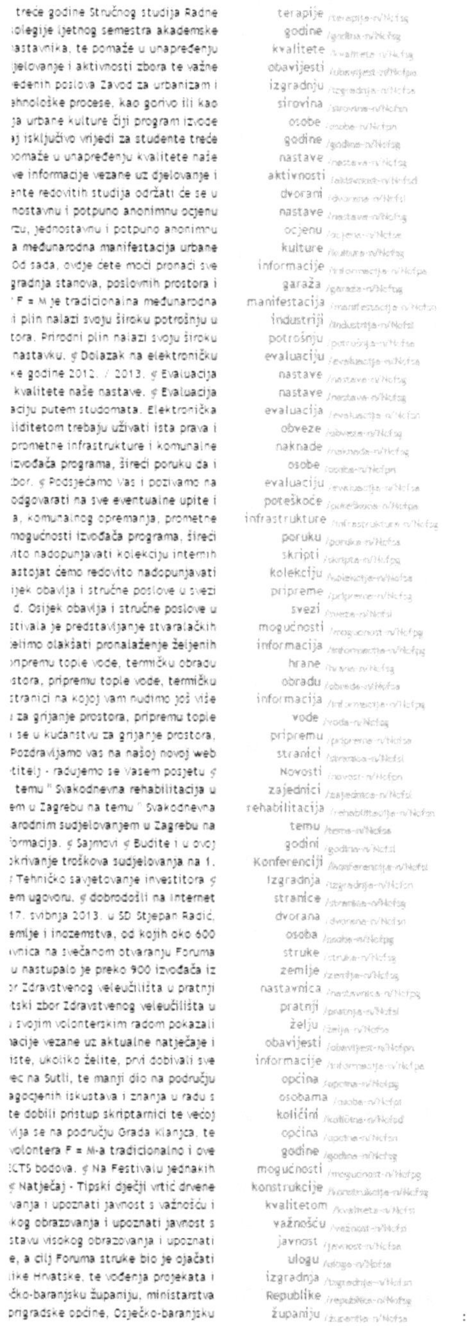

(meet [tag="Ncf.*"] [tag="Nc.*"] -2 0) (meet [tag="Ncf.*"] [tag="A.*"] -2 0)) (Figure 24). This example in ukWaC corpus gives empty results so author alter it to find all common nouns which are located before common noun (up to 2 places left) and in addition all common nouns which are located before an adjective (up to 2 places left). CQL query for his type of search is: (union (meet [tag="Nc.*"] [tag="Nc.*"] -2 0) (meet [tag-"Nc.*"] [tag="A.*"] 2 0)) . Results of the search are visible on Figure 25.

Figure 25. CQL query for union command in ukWaC (union (meet [tag="Nc."] [tag="Nc.*"] -2 0) (meet [tag="Nc.*"] [tag="A.*"] -2 0))*

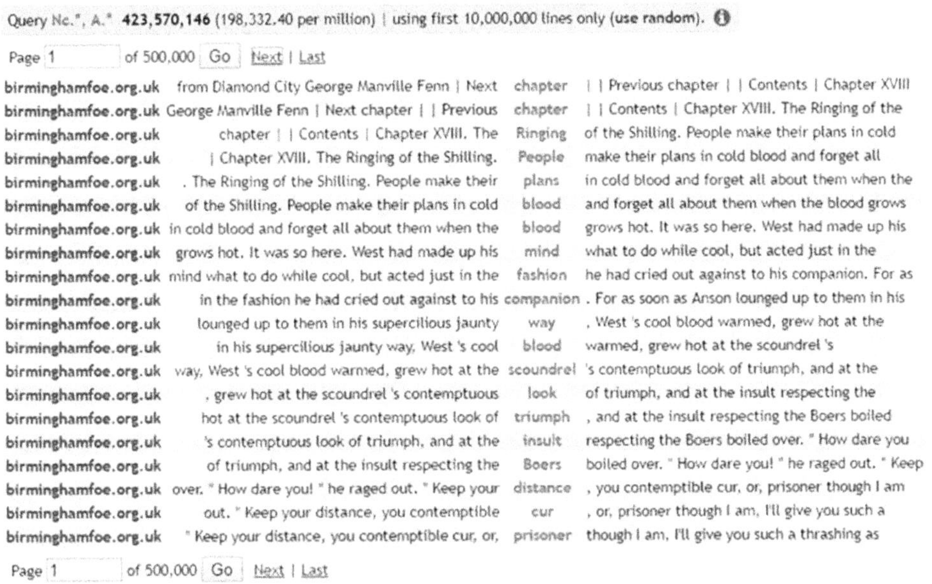

Query Nc.", A.* **423,570,146** (198,332.40 per million) | using first 10,000,000 lines only (**use random**).

Page 1 of 500,000 Go Next | Last

birminghamfoe.org.uk from Diamond City George Manville Fenn | Next chapter | | Previous chapter | | Contents | Chapter XVIII
birminghamfoe.org.uk George Manville Fenn | Next chapter | | Previous chapter | | Contents | Chapter XVIII. The Ringing of the
birminghamfoe.org.uk chapter | | Contents | Chapter XVIII. The Ringing of the Shilling. People make their plans in cold
birminghamfoe.org.uk | Chapter XVIII. The Ringing of the Shilling. People make their plans in cold blood and forget all
birminghamfoe.org.uk . The Ringing of the Shilling. People make their plans in cold blood and forget all about them when the
birminghamfoe.org.uk of the Shilling. People make their plans in cold blood and forget all about them when the blood grows
birminghamfoe.org.uk in cold blood and forget all about them when the blood grows hot. It was so here. West had made up his
birminghamfoe.org.uk grows hot. It was so here. West had made up his mind what to do while cool, but acted just in the
birminghamfoe.org.uk mind what to do while cool, but acted just in the fashion he had cried out against to his companion. For as
birminghamfoe.org.uk in the fashion he had cried out against to his companion . For as soon as Anson lounged up to them in his
birminghamfoe.org.uk lounged up to them in his supercilious jaunty way , West 's cool blood warmed, grew hot at the
birminghamfoe.org.uk in his supercilious jaunty way, West 's cool blood warmed, grew hot at the scoundrel 's
birminghamfoe.org.uk way, West 's cool blood warmed, grew hot at the scoundrel 's contemptuous look of triumph, and at the
birminghamfoe.org.uk , grew hot at the scoundrel 's contemptuous look of triumph, and at the insult respecting the
birminghamfoe.org.uk hot at the scoundrel 's contemptuous look of triumph , and at the insult respecting the Boers boiled
birminghamfoe.org.uk 's contemptuous look of triumph, and at the insult respecting the Boers boiled over. " How dare you
birminghamfoe.org.uk of triumph, and at the insult respecting the Boers boiled over. " How dare you! " he raged out. " Keep
birminghamfoe.org.uk over. " How dare you! " he raged out. " Keep your distance , you contemptible cur, or, prisoner though I am
birminghamfoe.org.uk out. " Keep your distance, you contemptible cur , or, prisoner though I am, I'll give you such a
birminghamfoe.org.uk " Keep your distance, you contemptible cur, or, prisoner though I am, I'll give you such a thrashing as

Page 1 of 500,000 Go Next | Last

The <s /> tag refers to the annotated text within the corpus. More precisely, this sign represents a sentence within the corpus. If the corpus is annotated, then this sign can be used when the search is restricted to the sentence. In order to search corpus in this way, we will use the command within and containing. The command within is used when the search is conducted within the structure which represents sentence. For example, if user wants to analyze the verb "*otkriti*" (engl to revel) and its object supplements in the form of a noun "*tajna*" (eng. secret), then the CQL query will be: "otkri.*" []{0,5} "tajn.*" within <s/>. Figure 26 shows the hrWaC results for the specified CQL query.

Figure 26. Search results for CQL query with command within

The command containing is used when user wants to see what the specified structure contains. For example, if user wants to see all sentences containing more than one noun it will be: <s /> containing [tag = “N. *”] [] {0,5} [tag = ‘’ N. *’’] In Figure 27, it is possible to see the CQL query results for this example using the command containing in the hrWaC corpus. Figure 28 shows the same use of containing command just in ukWaC for English language.

ADDITIONAL ANALYSIS OPTIONS IN THE TEXT TYPE CATEGORY

The last search category in the NoSketch Engine corpus tool is **text type**. This category provides the option of conducting an additional analysis of

Figure 27. Search results for CQL query with command containing in hrWaC

Izgradnja stanova, poslovnih prostora i garaža
Cijena povratne karte je 50 kn.
Iz današnje perspektive nezamislivo je življenje bez električne energije.
Ne propustite ništa - prijavite se na naš besplatni servis noviteta
Tehničko savjetovanje investitora
Budite i u ovoj godini ponovno nas posjetitelj - radujemo se Vasem posjetu
Elektromaterijal pokreće svijet
Polazak ispred crkve u 09,00 sati, a povratak oko 17,00 sati.
Uštedite korištenjem plina...
Novosti - Newsletter
U nedjelju 19.05. 2013. je tradicionalno isusovačko hodočašće u Mariju Bistricu.
Ukupan razvoj i napredak našeg planeta stoljećima se bazira na tehnološkim dostignućima praktičnosti korištenja električne energije.
Toplinu Vašeg doma u tehničkom smislu stvara energija ljudi koji u njemu žive.
U uredu Hrvatske pošte otvorena je filatelistička izložba Europske integracije i Republika Hrvatska autora Stjepana Zdenka Brezarića.
ične poslove u svezi pripreme građevinskog zemljišta, komunalnog opremanja, prometne infrastrukture i komunalne naknade za Grad Osijek po god
nitelja, policije i vojne policije iz Domovinskog rata predvođeni Antom Jurićem održali su radni sastanak s predsjednikom Republike Hrvatske dr. s
Pored navedenih poslova Zavod za urbanizam i izgradnju d. d.
Ovim načinom želimo Vam približiti profil naše tvrtke i asortiman ponude u interesu stvaranja partnerskih odnosa s Vama.
Prirodni plin nalazi svoju široku potrošnju u industriji za tehnološke procese, kao gorivo ili kao sirovina, te za grijanje i hlađenje prostora.
Osnovne škole Vrbovec te djeca vrbovečkih dječjih vrtića.
dobrodošli na Internet stranice studentskog zbora Zdravstvenog veleučilišta u Zagrebu.
ako možete upoznati dio naše poslovne tradicije koja govori o trajnim vrijednostima koje se stvaraju ustrajnim promicanjem odnosa korektnosti.
le su mlađe skupine vrbovečkih mažoretkinja, baletna skupina POU Vrbovec, najmlađa folklorna skupina HKUD-a Petar Zrinski, male gimnastičarke i
Izložbu je otvorio gradonačelnik Vladimir Bregović, a o izložbi je govorio autor Stjepan Zdenko Brezarić.
za pokrivanje troškova sudjelovanja na 1. Konferenciji radnih terapeuta s međunarodnim sudjelovanjem u Zagrebu na temu " Svakodnevna rehabilit
ićnu ispovijed za starije i nemoćne osobe naše župe biti će od 10. do 15. prosinca, a u narednom tjednu od 17. do 21. prosinca svećenici će prijavl
Pučko otvoreno učilište Vrbovec priredilo je na Trgu Petra Zrinskog glazbeno-scenski program pod nazivom Poleti, pjesmo, prema Europi.
e rezultate izbora za gradonačelnika Grada Vrbovca, Odluku o održavanju drugog kruga glasovanja u izboru za gradonačelnika Grada Vrbovca te Rezul
tronička evaluacija jamči nam brzu, jednostavnu i potpuno anonimnu ocjenu nastave i nastavnika, te pomaže u unapređenju kvalitete naše nastave.
Članak 2. Dijete ima pravo da ga se jednako poštuje i cijeni, bez razlike na rasu, nacionalnost, spol, jezik, vjeru, podrijetlo i imovinsko stanje.
Zavod za urbanizam i izgradnju Osijek
ZELENJAK PLIN d. o. o. ovlašten je od HRVATSKE STRUČNE UDRUGE ZA PLIN za ispitivanje plinskih instalacija.
odni plin upotrebljava se u kućanstvu za grijanje prostora, pripremu tople vode, termičku obradu hrane, a koristi se i sve više za hlađenje prostora
Od ponedjeljka, 3. prosinca u našoj crkvi započinjemo sa misama zornicama u 6.00 sati.
U četvrtak, 9. svibnja 2013., u Vrbovcu je obilježen Dan Europe.
Podsjećamo Vas i pozivamo na evaluaciju putem studomata.

Figure 28. Search results for CQL query with command containing in ukWaC

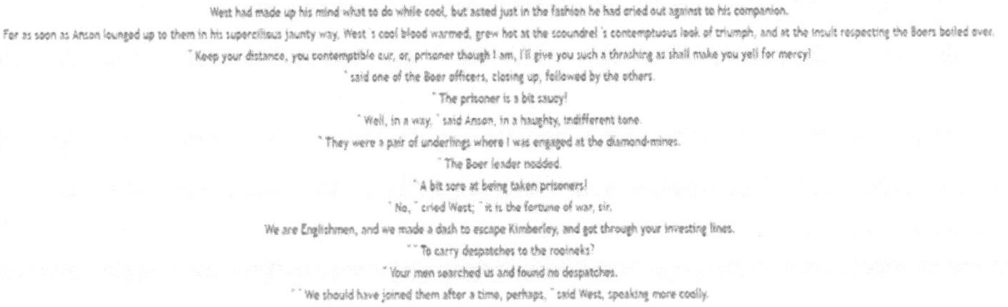

A Dash from Diamond City George Manville Fenn | Next chapter | | Previous chapter | | Contents | Chapter XVIII.
The Ringing of the Shilling.
People make their plans in cold blood and forget all about them when the blood grows hot.
West had made up his mind what to do while cool, but acted just in the fashion he had cried out against to his companion.
For as soon as Anson lounged up to them in his supercilious jaunty way, West 's cool blood warmed, grew hot at the scoundrel 's contemptuous look of triumph, and at the insult respecting the Boers boiled over.
" Keep your distance, you contemptible cur, or, prisoner though I am, I'll give you such a thrashing as shall make you yell for mercy!
" said one of the Boer officers, closing up, followed by the others.
" The prisoner is a bit saucy!
" Well, in a way, " said Anson, in a haughty, indifferent tone.
" They were a pair of underlings where I was engaged at the diamond-mines.
" The Boer leader nodded.
" A bit sore at being taken prisoners!
" No, " cried West; " it is the fortune of war, sir.
We are Englishmen, and we made a dash to escape Kimberley, and got through your investing lines.
" " To carry despatches to the rooineks?
" Your men searched us and found no despatches.
" " We should have joined them after a time, perhaps, " said West, speaking more coolly.

the tokens that are searched by **query type** or **context**. It has options that help us search for tokens in accordance with the type of text in which they appear. Depending on the corpus, the search options will also vary. Some of the options offered by hrWaC are searches according to the text's year of publication, its URL, the number of words in the text etc. In order to use it, a desired query has to be created in the **query type** or the **context** category after which the **text type** category also has to be selected. Additional options will appear, as seen in Figure 29, where user can input or choose the desired option.

Figure 29. Interface for searching by category text type in hrWaC

Figure 30 shows the same interface just for ukWaC corpus for English language.

CONCORDANCE

One of the most basic and most common corpus tools used for language analysis is the concordance tool, i.e. the tool used to create concordances. According to Bekavac (2001), the concordance tool is "at the very heart of corpus linguistics and is a fundamental tool for any corpus linguist". Moreover, "the main goal of a concordance tool is to provide insight into numerous

Figure 30. Interface for searching by category text type in ukWaC

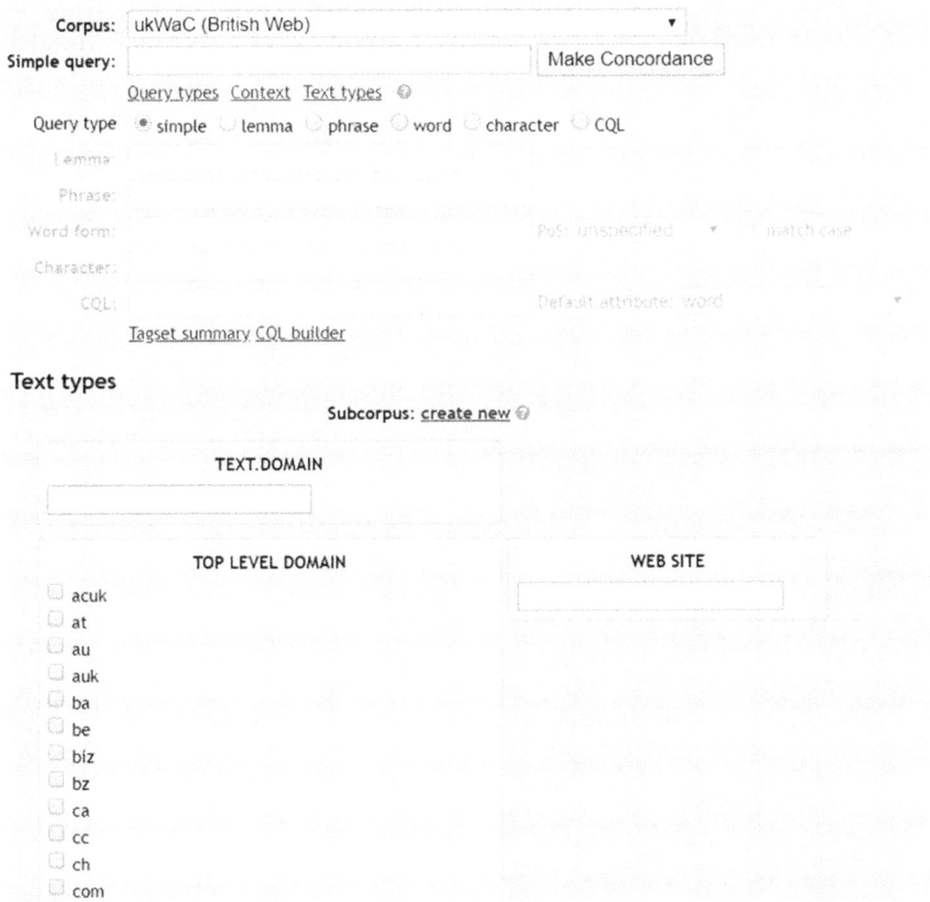

examples of a certain token or a phrase in the environment in which they appear. This insight often allows us to find a meaning or a use of the word which is not described in dictionaries or to notice a previously unknown regularity" (Bekavac, 2001, p. 73). The glossary in the NoSketch Engine tool defines concordances as all tokens from a corpus found on the basis of a given query and represents the main tool for using a corpus. John Sinclair (1991) defines concordances as a collection of tokens of a single word where each appears in its own textual environment. One of the programs which enables the use of concordances is Sketch Engine, a program which "creates lists of words that can be sorted alphabetically or according to their frequency" (Reppen, 2010). The main feature of all concordance tools is displaying the searched token in its textual environment along with its total frequency, i.e. the number of times it appears in a corpus. Concordance tools show concordances of a given token in a corpus. By using this corpus tool, it is possible to quickly see how a given word or a phrase behaves in the context of a sentence. In other words, we can see how it is used in a text. Figure 31 provides an example of a KWIC display for the tokens of the lemma "*pitanje*" (eng. question).

Figure 31. KWIC view of search results for noun question

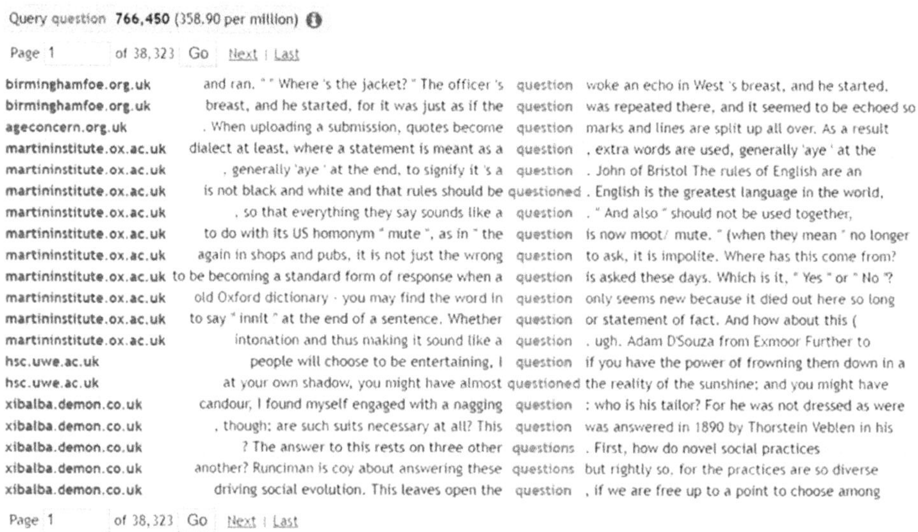

KWIC display is composed of several parts. At the centre of the interface, the searched word is displayed in bold red letters.

Dictionary of corpus linguistics[4] calls that word a headword. "Headword, in the concordance context, is a token that is being searched for. It is usually found in the middle of a concordance line."

On its left and right side is the text that surrounds the given word in order to provide insight into the context in which the word is being used. To display additional information about the text in which the given word appears, we only need to choose one of the results and a dialog box with the complete text in it will appear in the lower part of the interface. The left side of the KWIC interface is reserved for the source, i.e. the place where the text was published. These sources are also in bold letter, only in blue colour. Should we need more information about the source, we need to select any of the sources and another dialog box will appear in the lower part of the interface with additional information such as the year and place of publication, author, total word count etc. The third feature of the KWIC display is providing information about the total number of tokens in the corpus, something that can be found at the very top of the interface. For our lemma "*pitanje*", the total number is 1,283.295 tokens in hrWac and 766,450 tokens in ukWac corpus. Apart from the KWIC display, concordances offer several other options to their user for further analysis and displaying search results. These options can be found on the left side of the concordances. One of the options is to choose that the results are displayed in the form of complete sentences, not just parts of a text as is the case with the KWIC display. The concordance tool also has the option of sorting the results according to several criteria, including right and left side (meaning the tokens will be sorted according to the left and right context), as well as sorting according to the desired concordance and data (meaning they will be sorted alphabetically according to the sources in which the token appears).

The next option the concordance tool offers is the creation of patterns of a word in which we can choose the size of the random sample whose display we want to get. Figure 32 shows the results of creating a random pattern for 20 examples of different forms of the verb "rasti" (eng. to grow).

Apart from creating patterns, it is also possible to filter search results with a negative and a positive filter. If user wants to see the results for a certain phrase alone, we can use the positive filter which will only show results for the given phrase, whereas the negative filter will be used if user wants to exclude a certain term/context that can appear next to the token

Figure 32. Search results for random sample for concordance for context of verb "rasti"

user is searching for. The way search results are filtered will be explained in the following example. In order to be able to use the filtering option, user first have to create a CQL query. In this example, the corpus was searched according to the following CQL query: [tag="A.*"] [word="voda"]. This means that we wanted to see which adjectives appear in front of the word "*voda*" (eng. water). After further analysis, we wanted to exclude the results for the adjective "*hladna*" (eng. cold). In that case, a negative filter will be used, and we will get the results for all other adjectives appearing in front

Figure 33. Search results of positive filter for term "hladna voda"

je rashlađena voda. Osim temperaturnog šoka za tijelo,	hladna voda	loše djeluje na probavu usporavajući je, iako će tijel
le vode je učinilo svoje. Đank fud, svježe voće i povrće,	hladna voda	, sladoled. Kao dijete u trgovini igračaka. ¢ Vraćam s
o ukus snijega. Istopljen i ne izgleda toliko loše, štaviše,	hladna voda	nas je okrijepila i ulila dodatnu snagu da istrajemo i
mi se lijeva ruka počela užasno tresti. Nije pomagala ni	hladna voda	ni smirivanje, dok nisam uzela tabletu za smirenje. M
odjeću zaprljanu od voćnog soka pod hladnom vodom.	Hladna voda	će oslabiti mrlje od soka. Namačite odjeću u smjesi v
ivna kamena litica iz čijeg dna na površinu izvire bistra i	hladna voda	. To je mjesto rođenja rijeke Grab. Kažu da se u toj r
oji je dokazano povezan s upalama i pojavom prištića. ¢	Hladna voda	sužava pore Većinu pora naslijedili ste od svojih rodit
svojih roditelja i tu ne možete promijeniti mnogo toga.	Hladna voda	sužava krvne žile tako da imate osjećaj da vam je ko
io da sinoć ništa nije bilo u tavici. Može opet. Obrije se,	hladna voda	ispod pazuha i odmah negdje napolje. Nećeš njega n
su bili u stanju reći gdje se šta zatvara, gdje topla, gdje	hladna voda	, (ali zato silom hoće da mi nekakvi njihovi majstori p
n. Neki fitness stručnjaci smatraju da je to pametno jer	hladna voda	ubrzava rad metabolizma, a to znači da tijelo sagorij
gluposti (i baš me zanima hoćete li ga prepoznati?) ¢ …	hladna voda	je klizila… Da, jučer navečer, prije spavanja, uhvati
ne a nenudiju ništa posebno barem meni, meni je tamo	hladna voda	, pa kad idem sa dragim on okolo pikira komade a ja
om zavarivanju, zbog uvjeta u kojima boravi zavarivač (	hladna voda	od koje prijeti pothlađivanje tijela i ograničenje s ob
Hop mala bosonoga, kako živiš bez onoga. Sladak šećer,	hladna voda	, hajde mala dok je zgoda. ¢ Povjerenstva za upravlj
olijevao ga je vodom. Ne sjećam se je li to bila vruća ili	hladna voda	. Opačić mu je dao šamar, a sjećam se i da ga je dok
uristi pokušavaju se na različite načine rashladiti: šeširi,	hladna voda	, što deblji hlad… No, sunce je bilo neumoljivo. Foto
evljeni puno komaraca (ili nekih drugih letećih gamadi),	hladna voda	u bazenu, a i vani je bilo hladno… tako da mi je dra
e hladne vode nakon obroka = rak ¢ Možete li vjerovati?	Hladna voda	će očvrsnuti masne tvari koje ste upravo konzumirali,
im, a zatim mlazom hladne vode uklone ostaci iz ćelija.	Hladna voda	neće ukloniti vosak, ali će ukloniti sve ostatke. Takovi
na znači da ćete tijekom dana unositi manje kalorija. ¢	Hladna voda	Vjerojatno ste čuli da vodu treba piti kada ogladnite
idinamike, toplija voda će strujati prema gore dok će se	hladna voda	kretati prema dolje. Kada ne možemo osigurati uvije
i kroz gotovo pola stoljeća. Princip rada je jednostavan:	hladna voda	upumpava se na vruće granitne stijene koje se nalaze
de nalaze se slojevi vode različite temperature od dna (	hladna voda	) prema vrhu (topla voda) pa su stoga dobri rezervoai
a jutros nas je zateklo veoma neugodno iznenađenje tj.	hladna voda	u jezeru. Ali šta je tu je i kako svima tako i Karli sam
agu pridonose kolonizaciji. Zbog toga u sustavima vode,	hladna voda	treba biti doista hladna, a temperatura vode na slavi
osvijeste boli u nosu, u obrazima, u ušima i u rukama…	Hladna voda	kano da je raskvasila brazgotine i otekline, pa hrabro
e sam Heleni dala krčag da ga drži pod slavinom. Dok je	hladna voda	tekla u krčag, ja sam Heleni u slobodnu ruku opet sni
hranjivati. ¢ Ljeti se travnjak zalijeva ujutro ili navečer.	Hladna voda	izaziva termički šok kod biljaka, a kapljice vode koje
alja zalijevati sredinom dana, ljeti ujutro ili navečer jer	hladna voda	izaziva termički šok kod biljaka, a kapljice ostale na l
noga, kako zivis bez onoga lole > garavoga. Sladak secer,	hladna voda	, hajde mala dok je zgoda, ajde mala dok > je zgoda
slite da se previše znojite, pokušajte s hladnim tušem. ¢	Hladna voda	stimulira plavu točku u mozgu i potiče proizvodnju nc
kalorija, a onda je shvatio da je u pitanju voda. Naime,	hladna voda	prisiljava Phelpsovo tijelo da se stalno bori kako bi oc
on obroka može zbilja naštetiti vašem zdravlju. Naime,	hladna voda	će očvrsnuti masne tvari koje ste upravo konzumirali
ci: ¢ 1 kg sušenog slanutka ¢ 2 žlice morske soli ¢ obična	hladna voda	¢ vezica svježeg peršina ¢ 1 - 2 žlice maslinovog ulja,
e bilo mnogo manje no kad se išlo spavat na vrijeme, no	hladna voda	i umivanje brzo rasane čovjeka. Dorčak i put u školu
ko biste potaknuli cirkulaciju krvi na području oko očiju,	hladna voda	nije dovoljna. Nanesite obloge, primjerice vrećice oc
u iskovani u nove jesenske boje, a iz fontana je sukljala	hladna voda	, koja je prije tri sedmice bila topla od sunčeve vatre
o kako postići ljepši pogled u ogledalo svakog jutra: ¢ 1.	Hladna voda	¢ Izvrstan način za razbuđivanje je brzinsko umivanje
z zelenih cijevi vode koji se spajaju na spremnik. Topla,	hladna voda	i recirkulacija. Kad to kupim mogu sve stegnuti i da, p

of the word "*voda*", without the adjective "*hladna*" (Figure 34). If we want to find solely examples for the phrase "*hladna voda*" (eng. *cold water*), we will use the positive filter into which we will input the term "*hladna*" (Figure 33). Figure 33 shows the results of applying the positive filter for the phrase "*hladna voda*", while Figure 34 shows the results of applying the negative filter that excluded the word "*hladna*" from the search. Exact same situation can be made for English language in ukWaC corpus for term *cold water.*

Figures and examples used to explain concordance tools were taken from NoSketch Engine's interface, but it is important to emphasize that the general functionality does not differ from other concordance tools and programs – the only differences (if there are any) can be found in interface and menu design. Naturally, some discrepancies in options and functions these tools

Figure 34. Search results of negative filter for word "hladna"

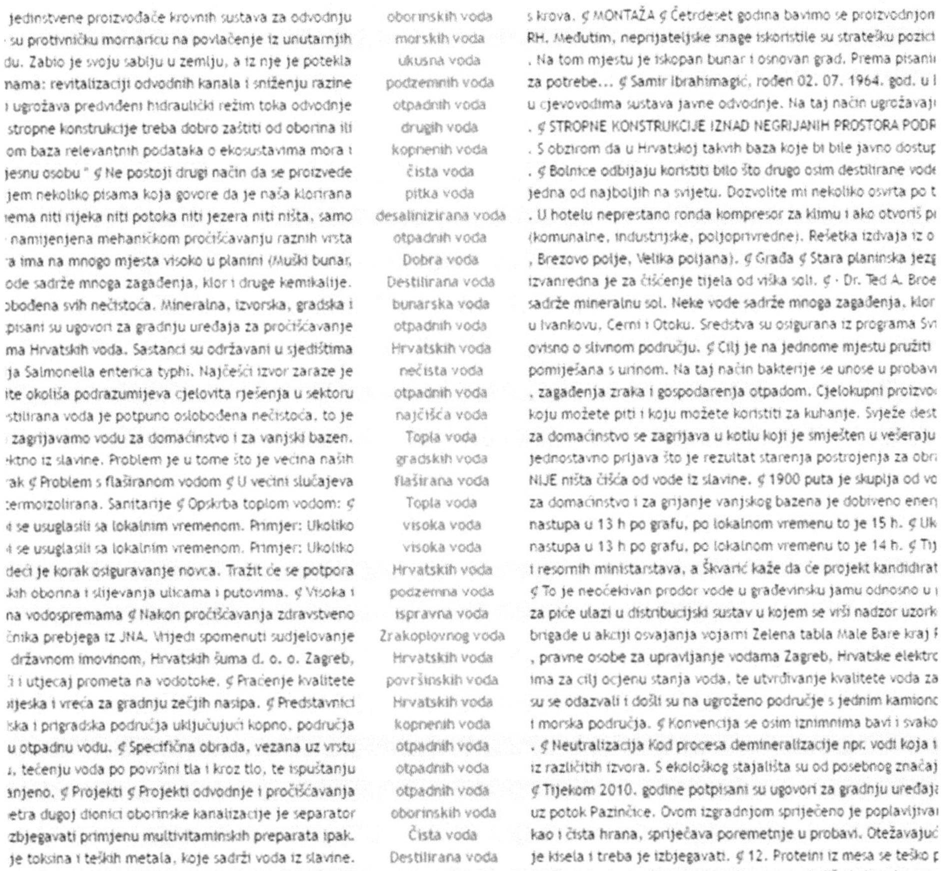

jedinstvene proizvođače krovnih sustava za odvodnju	oborinskih voda	s krova. ¢ MONTAŽA ¢ Četrdeset godina bavimo se proizvodnjom
su protivničku mornaricu na povlačenje iz unutarnjih	morskih voda	RH. Međutim, neprijateljske snage iskoristile su stratešku pozici
du. Zabio je svoju sablju u zemlju, a iz nje je potekla	ukusna voda	. Na tom mjestu je iskopan bunar i osnovan grad. Prema pisani
nama: revitalizaciji odvodnih kanala i sniženju razine	podzemnih voda	za potrebe... ¢ Samir Ibrahimagić, rođen 02. 07. 1964. god. u I
i ugrožava predviđeni hidraulički režim toka odvodnje	otpadnih voda	u cjevovodima sustava javne odvodnje. Na taj način ugrožavaju
stropne konstrukcije treba dobro zaštiti od oborina ili	drugih voda	. ¢ STROPNE KONSTRUKCIJE IZNAD NEGRIJANIH PROSTORA PODF
om baza relevantnih podataka o ekosustavima mora i	kopnenih voda	. S obzirom da u Hrvatskoj takvih baza koje bi bile javno dostup
jesnu osobu " ¢ Ne postoji drugi način da se proizvede	čista voda	. ¢ Bolnice odbijaju koristiti bilo što drugo osim destilirane vode
jem nekoliko pisama koja govore da je naša klorirana	pitka voda	jedna od najboljih na svijetu. Dozvolite mi nekoliko osvrta po t
iema niti rijeka niti potoka niti jezera niti ništa, samo	desalinizirana voda	. U hotelu neprestano ronda kompresor za klimu i ako otvoriš p
namijenjena mehaničkom pročišćavanju raznih vrsta	otpadnih voda	(komunalne, industrijske, poljoprivredne). Rešetka izdvaja iz o
a ima na mnogo mjesta visoko u planini (Muški bunar,	Dobra voda	, Brezovo polje, Velika poljana). ¢ Građa ¢ Stara planinska jezg
ode sadrže mnoga zagađenja, klor i druge kemikalije.	Destilirana voda	izvanredna je za čišćenje tijela od viška soli. ¢ · Dr. Ted A. Broe
bođena svih nečistoća. Mineralna, izvorska, gradska i	bunarska voda	sadrže mineralnu sol. Neke vode sadrže mnoga zagađenja. Klor
pisani su ugovori za gradnju uređaja za pročišćavanje	otpadnih voda	u Ivankovu, Cerni i Otoku. Sredstva su osigurana iz programa Sv
ma Hrvatskih voda. Sastanci su održavani u sjedištima	Hrvatskih voda	ovisno o slivnom području. ¢ Cilj je na jednome mjestu pružiti
ja Salmonella enterica typhi. Najčešći izvor zaraze je	nečista voda	pomiješana s urinom. Na taj način bakterije se unose u probavi
ite okoliša podrazumijeva cjelovita rješenja u sektoru	otpadnih voda	, zagađenja zraka i gospodarenja otpadom. Cjelokupni proizvo
stilirana voda je potpuno oslobođena nečistoća, to je	najčišća voda	koju možete piti i koju možete koristiti za kuhanje. Svježe dest
zagrijavamo vodu za domaćinstvo i za vanjski bazen.	Topla voda	za domaćinstvo se zagrijava u kotlu koji je smješten u večeraju
ktno iz slavine. Problem je u tome što je većina naših	gradskih voda	jednostavno prljava što je rezultat starenja postrojenja za obr
ak ¢ Problem s flaširanom vodom ¢ U većini slučajeva	flaširana voda	NIJE ništa čišća od vode iz slavine. ¢ 1900 puta je skuplja od vo
ermoizolirana. Sanitarije ¢ Opskrba toplom vodom: ¢	Topla voda	za domaćinstvo i za grijanje vanjskog bazena je dobiveno ener
i se usuglasili sa lokalnim vremenom. Primjer: Ukoliko	visoka voda	nastupa u 13 h po grafu, po lokalnom vremenu to je 15 h. ¢ Uk
i se usuglasili sa lokalnim vremenom. Primjer: Ukoliko	visoka voda	nastupa u 13 h po grafu, po lokalnom vremenu to je 14 h. ¢ Tij
deći je korak osiguravanje novca. Tražit će se potpora	Hrvatskih voda	i resornih ministarstava, a Škvarić kaže da će projekt kandidirat
ih oborina i slijevanja ulicama i putovima. ¢ Visoka i	podzemna voda	¢ To je neočekivan prodor vode u građevinsku jamu odnosno u
na vodospremama ¢ Nakon pročišćavanja zdravstveno	ispravna voda	za piće ulazi u distribucijski sustav u kojem se vrši nadzor uzork
čnika prebjega iz JNA. Vrijedi spomenuti sudjelovanje	Zrakoplovnog voda	brigade u akciji osvajanja vojarni Zelena tabla Male Bare kraj F
državnom imovinom, Hrvatskih šuma d. o. o. Zagreb,	Hrvatskih voda	, pravne osobe za upravljanje vodama Zagreb, Hrvatske elektro
i i utjecaj prometa na vodotoke. ¢ Praćenje kvalitete	površinskih voda	ima za cilj ocjenu stanja voda, te utvrđivanje kvalitete voda za
rijeska i vreća za gradnju zečjih nasipa. ¢ Predstavnici	Hrvatskih voda	su se odazvali i došli su na ugroženo područje s jednim kamionc
ska i prigradska područja uključujući kopno, područja	kopnenih voda	i morska područja. ¢ Konvencija se osim iznimnima bavi i svako
u otpadnu vodu. ¢ Specifična obrada, vezana uz vrstu	otpadnih voda	. ¢ Neutralizacija Kod procesa demineralizacije npr. vodi koja i
, tečenju voda po površini tla i kroz tlo, te ispuštanju	otpadnih voda	iz različitih izvora. S ekološkog stajališta su od posebnog značaj
njeno. ¢ Projekti ¢ Projekti odvodnje i pročišćavanja	otpadnih voda	¢ Tijekom 2010. godine potpisani su ugovori za gradnju uređaja
etra dugoj dionici oborinske kanalizacije je separator	oborinskih voda	uz potok Pazinčice. Ovom izgradnjom spriječeno je poplavljivai
zbjegavati primjenu multivitaminskih preparata ipak.	Čista voda	kao i čista hrana, sprječava poremetnje u probavi. Otežavajuć
je toksina i teških metala, koje sadrži voda iz slavine.	Destilirana voda	je kisela i treba je izbjegavati. ¢ 12. Proteini iz mesa se teško p
atskih akreditiranih laboratorija za analizu otpadnih i	prirodnih voda	. ¢ Za potrebe izrade studija utjecaja na okoliš (Jadransko mor

offer are also possible. But given that the subject of this paper are Croatian and English computer corpora, it was logical to choose the NoSketch Engine tool because this tool is also used by the hrWaC and ukWaC corpus.

Corpus Tools for Concordance Analyses

Concordances can be subject to additional text analyses which are very important for linguists, lecturers, professors and students themselves. Apart from the ability to manage how the results of concordances are displayed, it is also possible to conduct additional linguistic analyses such as displays of frequencies and lexical phrases (more precisely, collocations). Both types of analyses are important for linguistic analysis, and their functionality can ease and improve the preparation of materials needed for teaching Croatian as a first language and English as second or foreign language. In the rest of this text each of these analyses will be elaborated on more thoroughly in order to provide a deeper insight into their functionality and show how they are used.

Frequency

One of the most important and most useful corpus analyses concordance tools allow us to conduct is frequency, i.e. the ability to create frequency lists. A token's frequency shows words that appear in the corpus along with the number of their appearances (Bennett, 2010). Frequency analysis is very useful for linguistic analysis because lecturers and linguists can get

Figure 35. Main menu for creating frequency lists

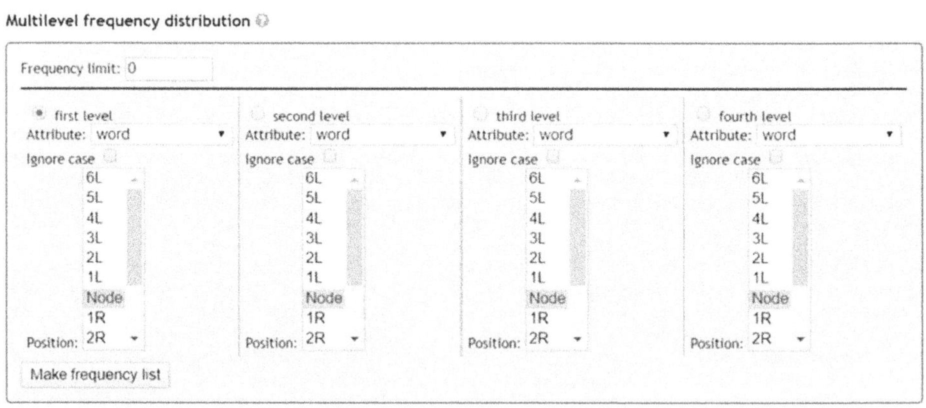

exact numbers concerning tokens' frequency and the frequency of certain collocations in a corpus.

The interface for creating frequency lists is shown in Figure 35. It is possible to create a frequency list containing up to four levels, which means that we can get results for four words or terms that appear on the left or right of the term (token, lemma) we searched for.

Figure 36. Frequency list for verb that starts with letter u- in hrWaC

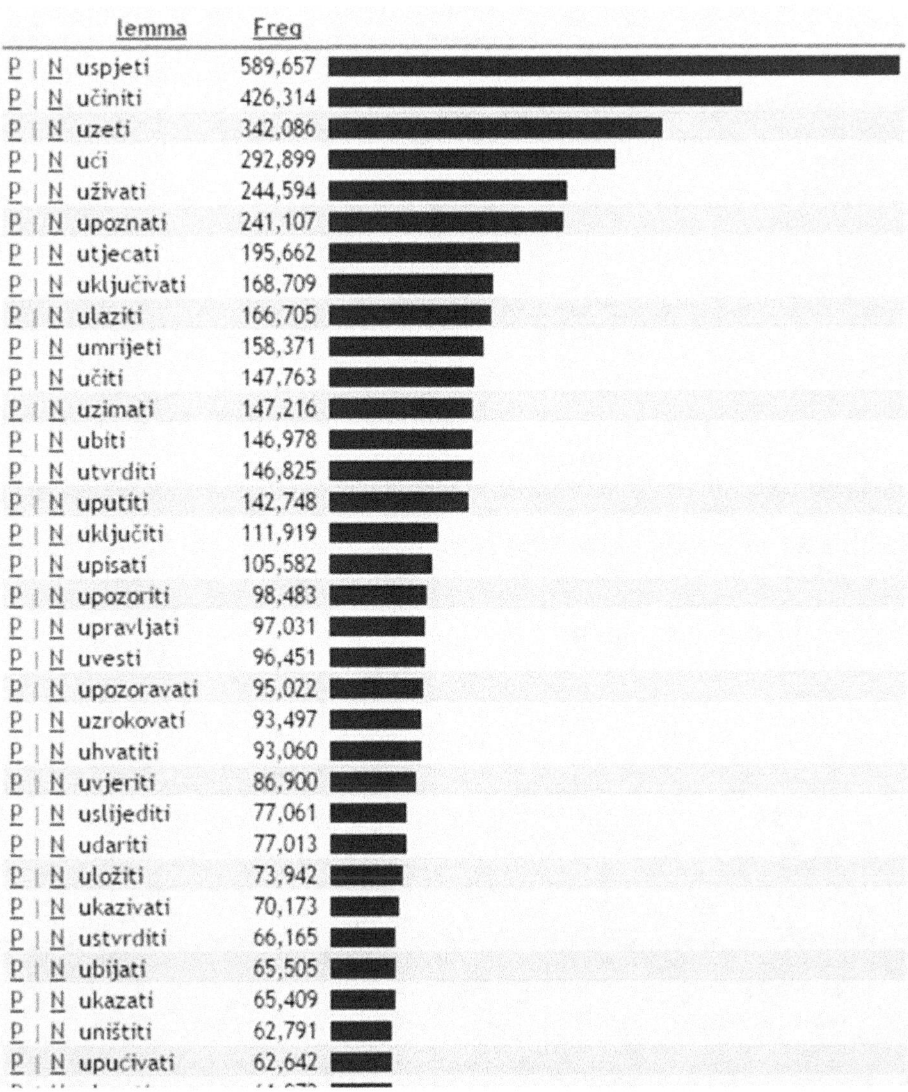

If we need, for example, to get results for the most common nouns that start with a certain letter or a sequence of symbols, we will use the first level with default settings. On the other hand, if we want to check the frequency of collocations (the words that most often appear next to the term that interests us, be that a noun, a verb, an adjective, etc.), we are going to use the other levels. Each level allows us to choose the position in which the word appears

Figure 37. Frequency list for verb that starts with letter u- in ukWaC

	lemma	Frequency	Items: 5,414 || Total frequency: 4,746,539
P | N	use	3,251,803	
P | N	understand	389,299	
P | N	undertake	216,974	
P | N	update	183,678	
P | N	urge	60,057	
P | N	underlie	53,649	
P | N	undergo	45,071	
P | N	upgrade	41,178	
P | N	unite	38,703	
P | N	utilise	37,339	
P | N	undermine	29,944	
P | N	underpin	29,370	
P | N	underline	29,145	
P | N	upset	21,059	
P | N	uphold	18,805	
P | N	uncover	18,540	
P | N	unveil	18,226	
P | N	unfold	15,081	
P | N	unlock	14,752	
P | N	utilize	12,200	
P | N	underestimate	10,326	
P | N	unload	7,543	
P | N	utter	7,358	
P | N	unleash	7,324	
P | N	uplift	6,599	
P | N	undo	6,528	
P | N	uploaded	6,304	
P | N	upload	6,296	
P | N	unravel	5,784	
P | N	unwind	4,871	
P | N	unearth	4,867	
P | N	unpack	4,531	
P | N	understate	4,240	
P | N	undulate	3,822	
P | N	usher	3,622	
P | N	unify	3,615	

and where it's positioned (to the right or to the left of the term that is the subject of our search). The designations spanning from 1L to 15L denote up to 15 places on the left side of the given token, while the designations from 1D to 15D denote places on the right. An example of frequency analysis can be seen in Figure 36, which shows the results for the most common verb starting with the letter "u". In this case, the frequency list has been created by using only the first level of the given concordance. The results show that the most common verb that starts with a "*u*" in the hrWaC corpus is the verb "*uspjeti*" (eng. to succeed). Its frequency is 589,657. In English language the most common verb that starts with a "*u*" letter (in the ukWaC corpus) is the verb *use*. Its frequency is 3,251,803 (Figure 37).

The bigger the corpus user is searching, the more transparent the results will be. The frequency of the searched terms will vary from corpus to corpus due to their construction, type and the number of tokens they contain. Frequency lists can also offer information on the frequency of lexical phrases. Figure 38 shows which adjectives most commonly appear on the left side of the noun "*žena*" (eng. woman).

The result with the highest frequency is "*mlada žena*" (eng. young woman), with the frequency of 2.425. Next in line is "*prva žena*" (eng. "first woman",

Figure 38. Most frequently used adjectives on the left side of noun "žena"

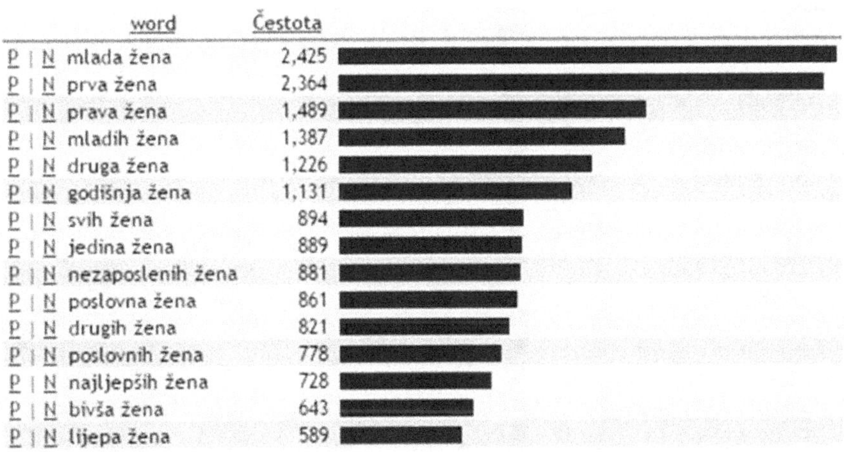

but also "first wife") with 2.364, etc.

In English language situation is different which can be seen on Figure 39. Adjective which most commonly appear on the left side of the noun *woman* is *young woman,* with the frequency of 6,280. The rest of adjectives with high frequency are: *old*, *first*, *pregnant*, *beautiful*, *married*, *elderly*, *only*, *black*, *poor*, etc. Frequency of adjectives was possible with certain CQL query which for this type of search is: [tag=”A.*”][word=”woman”] . Based on that CQL query corpus gave frequency analyses of most common adjectives which

Figure 39. Most frequently used adjectives on the left side of noun "woman"

	word	Frequency	Items: 3,381 || Total frequency: 42,820
P | N	young woman	6,280	
P | N	old woman	3,622	
P | N	first woman	1,956	
P | N	pregnant woman	1,413	
P | N	beautiful woman	892	
P | N	married woman	775	
P | N	elderly woman	634	
P | N	only woman	523	
P | N	black woman	517	
P | N	poor woman	489	
P | N	other woman	462	
P | N	older woman	452	
P | N	single woman	383	
P | N	American woman	358	
P | N	white woman	349	
P | N	Muslim woman	349	
P | N	good woman	329	
P | N	British woman	318	
P | N	local woman	279	
P | N	remarkable woman	247	
P | N	middle-aged woman	238	
P | N	younger woman	217	
P | N	little woman	212	
P | N	same woman	205	
P | N	Samaritan woman	203	
P | N	French woman	202	
P | N	dead woman	201	
P | N	wise woman	189	
P | N	English woman	188	
P | N	new woman	184	
P | N	attractive woman	183	
P | N	modern woman	177	
P | N	Jewish woman	154	
P | N	naked woman	140	
P | N	disabled woman	140	
P | N	average woman	140	
P | N	African woman	139	

appears on the left side of the noun *woman*, if CQL query was vice versa, [word=”woman”][tag=”A.*”] that the results will show the most common adjectives which can be found on the right side of the noun *woman*.

As a part of frequency analyses, it is possible to create an automatic comparison between two or more terms in order to find out which one is more frequent in language use. The option **Concordance forms** in the frequency menu gives us a way to compare frequencies when the query has multiple values. If user wants to conduct an analysis of the frequency of use of the words “*velik*” (eng. “big”) and “*ogroman*” (eng. “huge”), the Concordance forms option will show how represented these two words are in a corpus.

Figure 40. Parallel view of frequency for adjective “velik” and “ogroman”

Figure 40 shows the results of a corpus search for the aforementioned example. Apart from comparing how the words are represented, through frequency analysis it is also possible to see which forms of the terms are the most common in a corpus. For this type of analysis user needs to select the option **Concordance tags**. The result is shown in the form of morphosyntactic tags and can be seen in Figure 41.

Figure 41. Results for frequency of adjectives just in the form of morphosyntactic tags in hrWAc

We can see from the results that the most common form of the words “velik” and “ogroman” in language use is a positive (p) of a descriptive (g) adjective (A) of masculine gender (m) in nominative (n) singular (s), i.e. Agpmsn, whereas the second highest frequency belongs to a positive (p) of an indefinite (n) descriptive (g) adjective (A) of masculine gender (m) in accusative (a) singular (s), i.e. Agpmsan.

The last type of analysis user can connect to frequency is the analysis of content. This means that user can analyse documents in which the given terms most often appear. This type of display can be accessed if user selects the **Documents** tab in the menu. The results can be seen in Figure 42, which shows a list of websites containing the highest frequency of the words "*velik*" and "*ogroman*". Since hrWaC is a web corpus, the sources are only websites whose domain is .hr. The most frequent use of the terms is on the forum.hr, then on blog.hr, while the third place takes the website belonging to newspaper Slobodna Dalmacija at www.slobodnadalmacija.hr.

Figure 42. List of websites containing the highest frequency of the words "velik" and "ogroman"

	text.urldomain	Freq
P | N	forum.hr	18,033
P | N	blog.hr	8,673
P | N	slobodnadalmacija.hr	6,710
P | N	index.hr	6,378
P | N	vecernji.hr	5,147
P | N	tportal.hr	4,944
P | N	nacional.hr	4,690
P | N	zadarskilist.hr	2,867
P | N	monitor.hr	2,455
P | N	poslovni.hr	2,296
P | N	ezadar.hr	2,151
P | N	24sata.hr	1,756
P | N	glas-koncila.hr	1,464
P | N	net.hr	1,446
P | N	gorila.hr	1,361
P | N	jutarnji.hr	1,331
P | N	pollitika.com	1,288
P | N	bug.hr	1,256
P | N	business.hr	1,209
P | N	dnevnik.hr	1,200

Examples for English language in ukWaC corpus have the same principal as in hrWaC corpus for Croatian language the only difference is that user will type words in English. For example, analysis of synonyms for *big* and *huge* can be conducted using CQL query [word="big|huge"]. Based on this syntax user can see which of these two words are commonly used in English corpus.

Results for frequency of these words can be seen on Figure 43. The word *big* is more frequently used than the word *huge*. Figure 44 shows results for tag option which shows that *big* in language use is a positive (p) Adjective (A) and *huge* in language use is a positive (p) general (g) Adverb (R).

Figure 43. Parallel view of frequency for "big" and "huge"

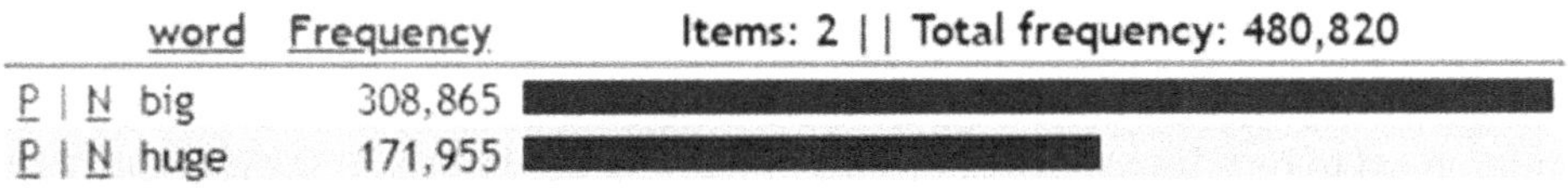

Figure 44. Results for frequency of adjectives just in the form of morphosyntactic tags in ukWAc

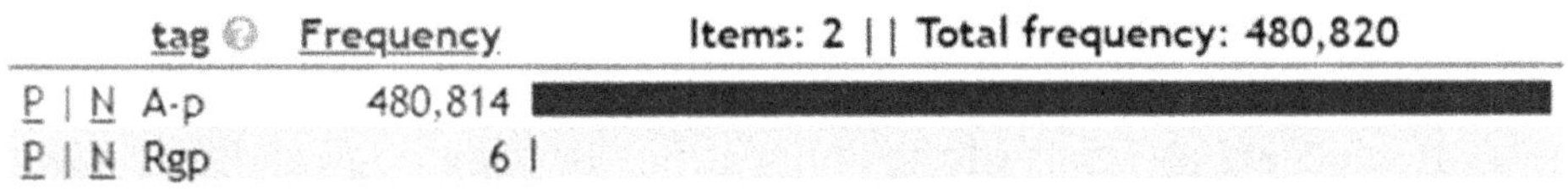

Collocations

One of the most basic and most important linguistic analyses we can conduct through corpus tools are collocations. There is a wide array of definitions and explanations of collocations and their meaning and role in corpus linguistics.

According to Hrvatski jezični portal, a collocation is an obligatory or a common link between words not prescribed by grammar ["*podnijeti molbu*" (eng."submit an application"), but "*uložiti žalbu*" (eng. "submit an appeal")].

Dictionary of corpus linguistics[5] states that collocations are characteristic co-occurrences of tokens' patterns. They are combinations of a headword and those tokens that appear in its immediate surrounding. Furthermore, a headword is, in the context of concordances, the token that is being searched for. It is most commonly found in the middle of a concordance line.

On the other hand, NoSketch Engine's glossary states that these are sequences or combinations of words that occur together more often than would be expected by chance.

Collocations are one of the most prevalent methods of analysing and researching language phraseology because "when one word is used, there is a high statistical probability that a certain word or several words will appear next to it" (Bennett, 2010).

The term collocations comes from the Latin word *com*, which means "together", and the word *locare*, which means "placement". Based on that, Ivir (1992-1993) defines collocations as "co-placed, i.e. contrasting or combining words in a syntagmatic sequence."

Authors Stojić and Murica (2010) state that collocations can be viewed in a broader and in a narrower sense and that in a narrower sense, a collocation is understood to be a linguistic phenomenon connected to typical, conventional and recurring way of combining lexemes, whereas in a broader sense every syntactically and semantically compatible phrase is considered a collocation.

The book "From Corpus to Classroom" (O'Keeffe, McCarthy, Carter, 2007) states that collocations are not absolute and determined language expressions but probable events that result in recurring combinations of word use and expressions created in the spoken process. As an example of that, the authors provide the word "barking" which is explicitly connected to the word "dog", most often occurs as a part of the collocation "barking dog" and will never occur next to the word "cat".

Computer corpora contain a built-in function which automatically and in a simple way shows collocations based on the basic search. Computer programs compare presumed similarity between two words which will appear together in the same environment to their real appearances in that same environment (O'Keefee, McCarthy, Carter, 2007) when displaying collocations.

In his book "Corpus, Concordance, Collocation", Sinclair (1991) defines collocations as prevalence of two or more words located close to each other in a text. The same author also provides insight into two main types of collocations. Sinclair (1991) writes: "collocations can be dramatic and interesting because they are unexpected, or they can be important in the lexical structure of a language due to their frequency. This second type of collocations, often associated with the concept of statistical significance, is the type usually discussed in linguistic discussions" (p. 170).

This second type of collocations Sinclair (1991) mentions are those collocations whose prevalence frequency is significant, something that can be checked in a corpus by using frequency lists. Unexpected collocations, on the other hand, do not appear often in a corpus, i.e. their frequency index is very low.

Another possible division of collocations is provided by Ewa Donesch-Jezo (2013) in her paper "Using Language Corpus in Teaching Foreign Language Vocabulary" where she states that collocations can be grammatical and lexical. She gives an example of grammatical collocations in which she emphasizes that some nouns co-occur with particular prepositions, for example *in the end, to hell with something* etc., whereas with lexical collocations word combinations have a certain semantic context, for example ''cruise ship'', ''merchant ship'', ''blonde hair'' etc.

Furthermore, as stated by Bartolec (2012, p. 56): "In scientific literature, binary approach is the dominant approach to parsing collocational relations into their constituent parts, according to which the main constituent is distinguishable. Its semantic potential adapts to the semantic potential of changeable constituents with which it forms a phrase. Usual and most frequent term for a changeable constituent is a collocate". Furthermore, Bartolec (2012, p. 56): "The main, i.e. the unchanging constituent of every collocational relation has several names. In lexicologically-lexicographical discussions Hausmann's term base is applied. In domestic scientific literature, apart from the term base (Borić 2002), basis (Petrović, 2007) and keyword (Pritchard, 1998) also appear. In the same context, in discussions concerning corpus linguistics, the term node is used".

Figure 45 shows the results of collocation candidates for the node/basis "*letjeti*"[6] (eng. to fly), where the range for defining the position of the word that co-occurs with the node (the so-called collocate) is from 0 to 5, meaning that the collocate can appear up to five places away on the right (5) of the node, i.e. of the term "*letjeti*".

The result for the collocation candidates (collocates) is a list of words (which appear next to the node "*letjeti*" in the range of 0 to 5 words after that word) and a series of numbers showing different statistics. For example, **Freq (frequency)** shows us how often the word "avionom" (eng. by plane) appears next to the verb "letjeti" inside the given range (the frequency is 181). Apart from frequency, the figure also shows us some other measures: T-score, *Mutual information* and logDice's coefficient.

The results in Figure 47 have been sorted according to logDice's statistical coefficient, the most relevant coefficient when it comes to collocational relations (so, "*avionom*" is statistically the most significant collocation candidate for the node "letjeti" in the corpus, not the word that most often follows "*letjeti*" in the given range. As can be seen in Figure 47, "*treće*" (eng. "third") is a much more frequent collocate than "*avionom*", but it's not as statistically significant).

Figure 45. Collocation candidates for the node "letjeti" sorted by the descending logDice coefficient

Kolokacijski kandidati

Stranica 1 Idi Sljedeća >

	Freq	T-score	MI	logDice
P | N avionom	181	13.448	11.262	7.878
P | N zrakom	109	10.433	10.557	7.156
P | N terenom	61	7.808	11.566	6.773
P | N Starijim	53	7.280	14.407	6.764
P | N avionima	64	7.996	11.050	6.743
P | N perje	59	7.678	11.099	6.658
P | N zrakoplovom	66	8.118	10.373	6.612
P | N helikopterom	55	7.412	10.678	6.493
P | N zrakoplovima	52	7.207	10.713	6.436
P | N treće	308	17.505	8.598	6.411
P | N krilima	70	8.355	9.514	6.353

There are many statistical measures of connection which identify good collocations. Most of them provide a formula for the degree of connection which shows the amount of statistical connection of two words. The result is then calculated for all possible word pairs, with the pairs with the highest degree of connection being presented as collocations.

Almost all formulas for calculating the measure of connection use frequency features mentioned by Rychlý (2008) in his article (Table 2), which measure the relationship between two words (W_1 and W_2). f_x represents the number of tokens of the word X, f_y represents the number of tokens of the word Y, f_{xy} represents the number of co-occurrences of the words X and Y, R_x is the relative frequency of the word X, and R_y is the relative frequency of the word Y. The relative frequency R_x can be calculated using the formula f_{xy} / f_x, while the relative frequency R_y is calculated by using the formula f_{xy}/f_y.

Among the most famous measures for calculating the connection of words in a collocation are the T-score, Mutual information and Dice's coefficient.

Equation 1.

$$\log_2 \frac{f_{xy} N}{f_x f_y} \tag{1}$$

Mutual information points to the collocation's strength (Evert, 2004). It represents the ratio of log-likelihood of occurrence of the collocate and the node (basis) together and the product of them appearing individually. The measure compares real co-occurrences of the collocate and the node with their expected co-occurrences in a corpus. For example, the collocation "*trudna žena*" (eng. "pregnant woman") will have a very high MI because it is expected in the corpus that "*trudna*" will be followed by "*žena*". On the other hand, the collocation "*crna zemlja*" (eng. "black soil") will have a significantly lower MI because after the adjective "*crna*" we expect many other nodes (apart from "*zemlja*") in the corpus, such as panther, crow etc. So, the MI calculates the amount of non-randomness present in the collocate's and the node's co-occurrence. The measure's results range from zero to 18, with the higher number denoting a stronger connection between the node and the collocate. According to Hunston (2002), the MI score of 3 or more is often considered as significant for a collocation.

MI's flaw is that it can't be applied to collocations whose constituents have large discrepancies in their frequency, but it is important for discovering interesting collocations because it does not depend on the frequency of the words in a corpus as much as other measures do.

Equation 2.

$$\frac{f_{xy} - \frac{f_y f_B}{2}}{\sqrt{f_{xy}}} \tag{2}$$

T-score is a measure very similar to frequency. It is a version of Student's t-test (T-score is the test's statistics), which makes sure that the non-randomness of two words' co-occurrence is substantiated by a large amount of evidence in the corpus (Evert, 2004).

Equation 3.

$$D = \frac{2f_{xy}}{f_x + f_y} \tag{3}$$

Dice's coefficient (Dice, 1945) divides the intersection of sets f_x and f_y (in other words, f_{xy} - the number of co-occurrences of words X and Y) by the sum of sets f_x and f_y and normalizes the result by multiplying the numerator by 2.

Equation 4. Marking frequency of words X and Y[7]

	$W_1 = X$	$W_1 \neq X$	
$W_2 = Y$	f_{xy}	$f_y - f_{xy}$	f_y
$W_2 \neq Y$	$f_x - f_{xy}$	$N - f_{xy}$	$N - f_y$
	f_x	$N - f_x$	N

(4)

Dice's coefficient gives very good results for collocation candidates. The only problem is that its values are usually very small numbers. That's why logDice coefficient was defined (Richly, 2008).

$$\log Dice = 14 + \log_2 D = 14 + \log_2 \frac{2f_{xy}}{f_x + f_y} \tag{5}$$

The theoretical maximum is 14, in the case when all tokens of the word X co-occur with all tokens of the word Y and vice versa. Usually, the value is lower than 10. If the value is 0, this means there is less than one co-occurrence of the words X and Y per 16000 tokens of X or 16000 tokens of Y. A negative value means there is no statistically relevant connection between X and Y which would allow us to consider them a collocation. This measure does not depend on the corpus' total size and combines relative frequencies XY compared to X and Y.

For search results for collocations in NoSketchEngine in Figure 28, logDice's coefficient gives a list of words from the corpus which have the

Figure 46. Collocation candidate for node "letjeti" sorted by descending frequency

Kolokacijski kandidati

Stranica 1 Idi Sljedeća >

		Freq	T-score	MI	logDice
P | N	,	4,703	56.390	2.492	0.509
P | N	.	3,362	49.688	2.805	0.822
P | N	i	2,649	42.135	2.463	0.480
P | N	u	1,999	36.580	2.459	0.476
P | N	na	1,795	37.556	3.139	1.155
P | N	je	1,505	27.501	1.780	-0.203
P | N	su	1,222	31.259	3.241	1.257
P | N	se	942	22.912	1.980	-0.003
P | N	a	699	22.979	2.934	0.949
P | N	iz	679	24.265	3.861	1.875
P | N	za	652	19.942	2.191	0.207
P | N	od	639	21.535	2.755	0.771
P | N	s	576	20.893	2.949	0.964
P | N	?	566	22.181	3.886	1.899
P | N	ili	558	21.752	3.659	1.672
P | N	da	548	14.732	1.432	-0.552
P | N	po	507	21.320	4.234	2.245
P | N	do	506	20.931	3.847	1.859
P | N	će	441	18.218	2.916	0.931
P | N	ne	424	16.543	2.347	0.362
P | N	sve	416	18.824	3.698	1.710
P | N	"	404	15.191	2.034	0.049
P | N	iznad	386	19.563	7.878	5.793
P | N	prema	376	18.729	4.872	2.876
P | N	bi	365	16.450	2.847	0.861
P | N	kao	357	16.556	3.014	1.028
P | N	-	351	14.717	2.221	0.236
P | N	nešto	338	17.849	5.101	3.101
P | N	sam	332	15.721	2.865	0.879
P | N	to	320	14.049	2.220	0.235
P | N	Više	311	17.571	8.110	5.980
P | N	treće	310	17.562	8.607	6.420
P | N	samo	290	15.267	3.272	1.284
P | N	sa	288	14.844	2.996	1.009
P | N	strane	286	16.587	5.704	3.690
P | N	preko	275	16.231	5.559	3.547
P | N	(	257	11.368	1.781	-0.204
P | N	ali	255	13.692	2.810	0.823
P | N	...	245	13.371	2.778	0.791
P | N	smo	239	14.132	3.541	1.550
P | N	što	228	11.284	1.985	-0.001
P | N	jer	221	13.001	2.995	1.006
P | N	pa	189	11.915	2.907	0.918
P | N	puta	184	13.006	4.600	2.595
P | N	avionom	184	13.559	11.285	7.902

statistically most significant connection with the given word, i.e. the node. Therefore, in the hrWaC corpus, statistically, the most significant relation is "*letjeti avionom*" (eng. "fly by plane"). In other words, the statistically most significant candidate-collocate for the word "*letjeti*" is the token "*avionom*".

If we display the search results from Figure 47 according to descending frequency of the candidates instead of descending logDice's coefficient, we will get what is shown on Figure 38. What can be seen there is that, within the given framework, after the verb "letjeti" (eng. "to fly") in most cases (apart from punctuation marks) appear function words: conjunctions *i, u*, prepositions *na, iz, za, od* or auxiliary forms of the verb *biti* (eng. *to be*). Such relations are called colligations in scientific literature. As stated by Bartolec and Ivanković (2013), compared to collocations as relations based on the semantic relationship between individual constituents, colligations can be defined as formal relationships between words which are a reflection of a language's systematicness. So, the words at the top of the list in Figure 38 are colligation, not collocation candidates.

The importance of the aforementioned statistical measures for linguistic research when it comes to collocations and colligations can be seen in Figures 45, 46, 47 and 48. Figure 45 shows candidates-collocates for the node/basis "*soba*" (eng. room), according to descending logDice coefficient (range from -3 to 0). The list of words from the corpus with statistically most significant connection contains: "*spavaća* soba" (eng. bedroom), "*dnevna* soba" (eng. living room), "*hotelska* soba" (eng. hotel room), etc.

On the other hand, Figure 47 shows candidates-colligations for the node/basis "*soba*", shown according to descending frequency (range from -3 to 0). Some very interesting colligations can be found there, such as: "*u sobu*" (eng. in the room) "*iz sobe*" (eng. out the room), *od sobe*" (eng. from the room), "*po sobi*" (eng. around the room) etc.

Furthermore, Figure 47 shows candidates-collocates for the node/basis "soba" according to descending MI (range -3 to 0). Here we find collocations that are rare in the hrWaC corpus, although they are still linguistically relevant, such as "*jednokrevetna soba*" (eng. single room), "*trokrevetna soba*" (eng. triple room), "*dvoposteljna soba*" (eng. double room), "*dnevno-spavaća soba*" (eng. bedroom-living room), "*preluksuzna soba*" (eng. too luxurious room), "*motelska soba*" (eng. motel room), which do not appear in the top 100 results according to the descending list based on logDice's coefficient.

Finally, Figure 48 shows candidates-collocates for the node/basis "soba" according to descending T-score (range -3 to 0). These results are very similar to the descending frequency list, but they are not identical. For example, the

Figure 47. Collocation candidate for node "soba" sorted by descending logDice coefficient

Collocation candidates

Page 1 Go Next >

		Freq	T-score	MI	logDice
P | N	spavaće	7,586	87.086	12.820	10.231
P | N	spavaćoj	4,124	64.212	13.249	9.397
P | N	spavaću	3,145	56.074	13.217	9.013
P | N	spavaća	2,933	54.151	13.154	8.913
P | N	dnevnoj	2,643	51.393	11.579	8.723
P | N	hotelskoj	1,711	41.358	12.672	8.140
P | N	dnevnu	1,563	39.513	10.837	7.966
P | N	svojoj	3,426	57.921	6.583	7.632
P | N	hotelske	1,075	32.772	11.058	7.452
P | N	spavaćih	993	31.509	13.190	7.367
P | N	dvije	4,855	68.577	5.984	7.329
P | N	mojoj	1,161	33.885	7.502	7.180
P | N	dnevna	919	30.278	9.670	7.180
P | N	dvokrevetne	860	29.321	12.538	7.157
P | N	dnevne	868	29.386	8.605	7.021
P | N	hotelsku	781	27.942	12.493	7.018
P | N	svoju	3,544	58.273	5.564	6.901
P | N	sobe	880	29.472	7.265	6.820
P | N	Spomen	694	26.317	9.939	6.805
P | N	dječju	700	26.421	9.507	6.799
P | N	vrata	1,621	39.587	5.899	6.798
P | N	istoj	905	29.853	7.032	6.792
P | N	dvokrevetnoj	652	25.532	13.235	6.763
P | N	moju	916	30.002	6.845	6.752
P | N	dvokrevetnim	613	24.756	13.113	6.674
P | N	hotelskih	613	24.740	10.385	6.645
P | N	apartmana	619	24.809	8.457	6.565
P | N	dvokrevetnih	566	23.788	12.856	6.558
P | N	soba	655	25.441	7.395	6.505
P | N	drugu	1,024	31.464	5.901	6.490
P | N	branitelja	950	30.336	5.987	6.471
P | N	prozor	624	24.827	7.354	6.440
P | N	Ženska	536	23.123	9.655	6.436
P | N	jednoj	1,105	32.595	5.683	6.435
P | N	drugoj	936	30.088	5.918	6.428
P | N	dječjoj	528	22.953	9.846	6.421
P | N	kutu	533	23.032	8.731	6.385
P | N	radnoj	515	22.651	9.061	6.356
P | N	ulazi	655	25.340	6.658	6.350
P | N	susjednoj	514	22.626	8.954	6.348
P | N	Spavaća	475	21.792	13.241	6.308
P | N	Ženske	479	21.868	10.281	6.294
P | N	radnu	517	22.640	7.859	6.273
P | N	njegovoj	692	25.947	6.196	6.271
P | N	spavace	462	21.492	13.123	6.267
P | N	dječje	537	23.026	7.302	6.250
P | N	spavaćim	434	20.830	12.865	6.177
P | N	jednu	1,328	35.239	4.921	6.065
P | N	kat	457	21.252	7.407	6.064
P | N	m2	542	22.985	6.297	6.054
P | N	ušao	559	23.313	6.161	6.048
P | N	ušla	460	21.292	7.110	6.031

Figure 48. Collocation candidate for node "soba" sorted by descending frequency

Collocation candidates

Page 1 Go Next >

		Freq	T-score	MI	logDice
P | N	u	74,488	256.264	4.034	5.690
P | N	,	22,530	80.435	1.107	2.767
P | N	i	13,205	62.616	1.136	2.794
P | N	.	13,174	62.355	1.131	2.789
P | N	je	11,088	53.249	1.017	2.674
P | N	iz	8,447	85.548	3.853	5.470
P | N	spavaće	7,586	87.086	12.820	10.231
P | N	se	7,127	49.040	1.255	2.908
P | N	od	5,311	56.632	2.165	3.805
P | N	dvije	4,855	68.577	5.984	7.329
P | N	U	4,659	62.427	3.550	5.145
P | N	po	4,518	62.202	3.745	5.328
P | N	spavaćoj	4,124	64.212	13.249	9.397
P | N	na	3,880	21.353	0.606	2.257
P | N	su	3,662	33.791	1.179	2.825
P | N	svoju	3,544	58.273	5.564	6.901
P | N	svojoj	3,426	57.921	6.583	7.632
P | N	za	3,390	27.544	0.924	2.572
P | N	da	3,292	13.087	0.373	2.025
P | N	(	3,256	40.670	1.800	3.433
P | N	spavaću	3,145	56.074	13.217	9.013
P | N	sam	3,017	44.551	2.404	4.020
P | N	spavaća	2,933	54.151	13.154	8.913
P | N	dnevnoj	2,643	51.393	11.579	8.723
P | N	ima	2,290	42.747	3.228	4.783
P | N	s	2,247	27.721	1.268	2.902
P | N	sa	2,127	36.330	2.236	3.839
P | N	do	2,013	35.060	2.194	3.796
P | N	ili	1,969	31.917	1.833	3.447
P | N	a	1,941	18.083	0.762	2.401
P | N	svoje	1,933	40.684	3.744	5.228
P | N	1	1,856	41.264	4.567	5.917
P | N	:	1,854	26.907	1.415	3.038
P | N	tri	1,810	40.139	4.145	5.562
P | N	)	1,722	17.764	0.806	2.441
P | N	hotelskoj	1,711	41.358	12.672	8.140
P | N	vrata	1,621	39.587	5.899	6.798
P | N	dnevnu	1,563	39.513	10.837	7.966
P | N	2	1,540	36.744	3.973	5.381
P | N	"	1,530	7.559	0.310	1.950
P | N	-	1,516	14.752	0.687	2.321
P | N	te	1,388	21.851	1.274	2.890
P | N	jednu	1,328	35.239	4.921	6.065
P | N	3	1,176	31.829	3.799	5.170
P | N	smo	1,162	26.555	2.178	3.738
P | N	mojoj	1,161	33.885	7.502	7.180
P | N	jednoj	1,105	32.595	5.683	6.435
P | N	hotelske	1,075	32.772	11.058	7.452
P | N	jedna	1,043	30.315	4.027	5.316
P | N	drugu	1,024	31.464	5.901	6.490
P | N	mi	1,018	20.765	1.518	3.106
P | N	spavaćih	993	31.509	13.190	7.367

Figure 49. Collocation candidate for node "soba" sorted by descending MI mesurment

Collocation candidates

Page 1 Go Next >

		Freq	T-score	MI	logDice
P | N	Jednokrevetna	51	7.141	13.366	3.092
P | N	Spavace	6	2.449	13.338	0.004
P | N	Sadr¾i	5	2.236	13.338	-0.259
P | N	žova	6	2.449	13.338	0.004
P | N	SPAVACA	10	3.162	13.338	0.741
P | N	spavaæe	11	3.316	13.338	0.879
P | N	Preluksuzna	5	2.236	13.338	-0.259
P | N	porotnu	10	3.162	13.338	0.741
P | N	DVOKREVETNOJ	8	2.828	13.338	0.420
P | N	Minibarovi	5	2.236	13.338	-0.259
P | N	družinskoj	10	3.162	13.338	0.741
P | N	spvaće	9	3.000	13.338	0.589
P | N	Spavaćih	8	2.828	13.338	0.420
P | N	Rugovčevu	5	2.236	13.338	-0.259
P | N	dvoposteljnu	6	2.449	13.338	0.004
P | N	spavaæu	5	2.236	13.338	-0.259
P | N	dnevno-spavaća	96	9.797	13.338	4.004
P | N	spavačih	11	3.316	13.338	0.879
P | N	POTOPLJENO	13	3.605	13.338	1.120
P | N	redekoracijom	5	2.236	13.338	-0.259
P | N	dvo-krevetnim	5	2.236	13.338	-0.259
P | N	http://acp.carnet.hr/maturahr/	184	13.563	13.330	4.942
P | N	motelske	17	4.123	13.255	1.507
P | N	motelsku	17	4.123	13.255	1.507
P | N	spavaćoj	4,124	64.212	13.249	9.397
P | N	Andrea-Beata	15	3.873	13.244	1.326
P | N	Spavaća	475	21.792	13.241	6.308
P | N	SPAVAĆA	56	7.483	13.238	3.226
P | N	Trokrevetna	14	3.741	13.238	1.227
P | N	dvokrevetnoj	652	25.532	13.235	6.763
P | N	spavaću	3,145	56.074	13.217	9.013
P | N	Dvokrevetna	85	9.219	13.208	3.828
P | N	SPAVAĆOJ	10	3.162	13.200	0.741
P | N	spavaćih	993	31.509	13.190	7.367
P | N	polutamnoj	27	5.196	13.186	2.174
P | N	okrečenoj	27	5.196	13.186	2.174
P | N	dnevno-spavaca	8	2.828	13.168	0.419
P | N	trokrevetnim	164	12.805	13.164	4.776
P | N	spavaća	2,933	54.151	13.154	8.913
P | N	jednokrevetnoj	170	13.037	13.147	4.828
P | N	Bhaironovu	7	2.645	13.145	0.227
P | N	trokrevetnoj	63	7.936	13.145	3.396
P | N	motelskih	7	2.645	13.145	0.227
P | N	spavace	462	21.492	13.123	6.267
P | N	motelskoj	55	7.415	13.119	3.200
P | N	primaćih	6	2.449	13.115	0.004
P | N	dvoposteljnih	6	2.449	13.115	0.004
P | N	višekrevetnoj	12	3.464	13.115	1.004
P | N	dvokrevetnim	613	24.756	13.113	6.674
P | N	spavačoj	57	7.549	13.104	3.252
P | N	Vandinoj	11	3.316	13.097	0.879
P | N	jednokrevetnu	357	18.892	13.096	5.896

Figure 50. Collocation candidate for node "soba" sorted by descending T-mesurment

Collocation candidates

Page 1 Go Next >

		Freq	T-score	MI	logDice
P | N	u	74,488	256.264	4.034	5.690
P | N	spavaće	7,586	87.086	12.820	10.231
P | N	iz	8,447	85.548	3.853	5.470
P | N	,	22,530	80.435	1.107	2.767
P | N	dvije	4,855	68.577	5.984	7.329
P | N	spavaćoj	4,124	64.212	13.249	9.397
P | N	i	13,205	62.616	1.136	2.794
P | N	U	4,659	62.427	3.550	5.145
P | N	.	13,174	62.355	1.131	2.789
P | N	po	4,518	62.202	3.745	5.328
P | N	svoju	3,544	58.273	5.564	6.901
P | N	svojoj	3,426	57.921	6.583	7.632
P | N	od	5,311	56.632	2.165	3.805
P | N	spavaću	3,145	56.074	13.217	9.013
P | N	spavaća	2,933	54.151	13.154	8.913
P | N	je	11,088	53.249	1.017	2.674
P | N	dnevnoj	2,643	51.393	11.579	8.723
P | N	se	7,127	49.040	1.255	2.908
P | N	sam	3,017	44.551	2.404	4.020
P | N	ima	2,290	42.747	3.228	4.783
P | N	hotelskoj	1,711	41.358	12.672	8.140
P | N	1	1,856	41.264	4.567	5.917
P | N	svoje	1,933	40.684	3.744	5.228
P | N	(	3,256	40.670	1.800	3.433
P | N	tri	1,810	40.139	4.145	5.562
P | N	vrata	1,621	39.587	5.899	6.798
P | N	dnevnu	1,563	39.513	10.837	7.966
P | N	2	1,540	36.744	3.973	5.381
P | N	sa	2,127	36.330	2.236	3.839
P | N	jednu	1,328	35.239	4.921	6.065
P | N	do	2,013	35.060	2.194	3.796
P | N	mojoj	1,161	33.885	7.502	7.180
P | N	su	3,662	33.791	1.179	2.825
P | N	hotelske	1,075	32.772	11.058	7.452
P | N	jednoj	1,105	32.595	5.683	6.435
P | N	ili	1,969	31.917	1.833	3.447
P | N	3	1,176	31.829	3.799	5.170
P | N	spavaćih	993	31.509	13.190	7.367
P | N	drugu	1,024	31.464	5.901	6.490
P | N	branitelja	950	30.336	5.987	6.471
P | N	jedna	1,043	30.315	4.027	5.316
P | N	dnevna	919	30.278	9.670	7.180
P | N	drugoj	936	30.088	5.918	6.428
P | N	moju	916	30.002	6.845	6.752
P | N	istoj	905	29.853	7.032	6.792
P | N	sobe	880	29.472	7.265	6.820

second item on this list is the very strong collocation "*spavaća soba*", whereas that same collocation ranks only seventh on the frequency list.

The initial screen for creating collocation lists offers several search results display options. Figure 51 shows the interface used for creating lists of collocation candidates.

Figure 51. Interface for creating collocation lists

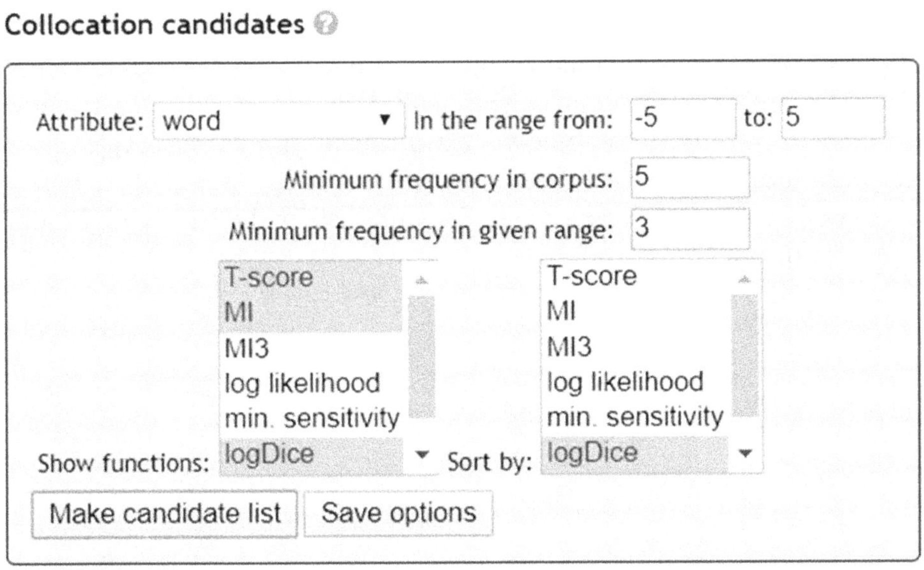

It is possible to choose the attribute for which user want to create a list. In the drop-down menu, the following attributes can be chosen: word, lemma, lempos, lc, lema_lc and tag. The range for defining the collocate's position is from -5 to 5, meaning that the collocate can be up to five places on the left from the node (-5) and up to five places on the right (5), but the range is customizable and can be changed depending on the user's requirements. The next option applies to defining the criterion of the collocations' frequency, where the necessary requirement is that a collocation with a certain frequency appears in the corpus or in the given range. The last two options apply to the way certain measures are displayed and to setting criteria for sorting results. logDice, MI and T-score are most commonly used to show statistics, while the list is most often sorted according to descending logDice value, due to previously mentioned reasons. All those settings can be saved for future searches if the user doesn't want to change them often.

To conclude, sorting candidates-collocates according to descending logDice coefficient is very useful for studying collocational relations of words, whereas sorting the candidates according to descending frequency is very useful for studying colligations.

Word Lists

One of the tools that can be used in all corpora in NoSketch Engine and it is the option for creating word lists. This allows us to create different lists of words that are based on their frequency within a corpus. The lists can be defined according to these attributes: word, lemma, tag, lc, lemma_lc and lempos or according to the type of text included in a corpus. Apart from that, word lists can be created based on the subcorpus user choose. Figure 52 shows the basic interface for creating word lists in the NoSketch Engine system for the ukWaC corpus.

Figure 52. Interface for creating word lists in ukWaC

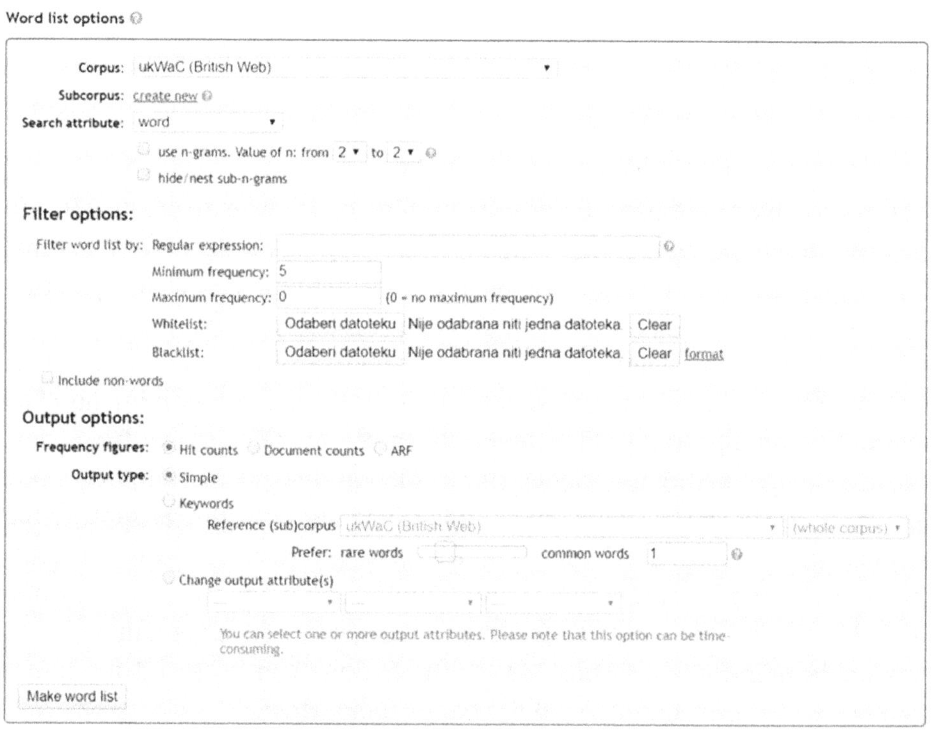

Figure 53. View of first page results for the most frequent word in ukWaC

Word list

Corpus: **ukWaC (British Web)**
Total number of items: **1,442,224**
Total frequency: **1,794,186,861**

Page 1 Go Next >

word	frequency
the	94,567,973
of	55,387,442
and	53,718,451
to	49,261,034
a	35,413,182
in	31,337,936
is	20,597,181
for	18,968,515
that	15,093,332
on	13,987,398
The	13,962,244
with	12,608,473
be	12,018,973
are	10,647,326
as	10,219,490
by	9,482,514
it	9,435,023
you	9,213,895
I	8,777,722
was	8,738,257
at	8,716,214
or	8,382,276
from	8,301,894
have	7,837,689
this	7,262,815
will	6,856,587
an	6,195,270
not	6,144,625
which	5,384,750
has	5,278,063
can	4,824,744
we	4,569,534
all	4,473,750
their	4,420,882
your	4,406,425
but	4,353,826
they	4,038,118
more	3,823,526
been	3,592,097
one	3,431,819
were	3,373,014
his	3,262,390
his	3,262,390
This	3,209,991
about	3,178,164
he	3,157,150
It	3,105,058
who	3,100,184
had	3,076,596
also	3,044,847
do	2,965,510
A	2,908,427
our	2,872,885
up	2,866,862
out	2,856,330
would	2,825,069
there	2,735,220
other	2,713,715
In	2,617,703
if	2,603,368
so	2,571,670
time	2,554,818
new	2,553,236
any	2,527,689
its	2,457,039
n't	2,414,020
people	2,404,236
some	2,401,302
into	2,300,680
when	2,248,075
We	2,208,122
may	2,191,440
work	2,190,837
them	2,147,034
what	2,081,134
only	2,074,090
my	2,072,392
than	2,071,945
should	2,052,937
information	2,032,401
no	1,978,655
over	1,893,457
first	1,885,017
use	1,842,866
these	1,842,129
very	1,785,875
such	1,783,451
If	1,765,797
two	1,738,732
then	1,672,816
like	1,670,783
now	1,599,649
most	1,573,248
years	1,572,058
how	1,566,949
where	1,564,243
just	1,561,300
could	1,544,343
year	1,543,888
through	1,540,091
many	1,535,957

Page 1 Go Next >

Figure 54. View of first page of results for most frequent lemma in ukWaC

Word list

Corpus: **ukWaC (British Web)**
Total number of items: **1,325,745**
Total frequency: **1,799,585,199**

Page 1 Go Next >

lemma	frequency
the	108.435.381
be	65.058.247
of	55.913.315
and	54.814.846
to	49.261.303
a	38.008.948
in	34.074.132
for	20.370.116
have	17.758.568
that	15.561.501
on	14.605.881
with	13.079.401
it	12.721.463
as	11.124.675
you	10.621.338
this	10.423.331
by	9.916.058
at	9.299.831
I	8.785.377
from	8.731.770
or	8.514.454
will	7.556.659
we	6.796.268
an	6.676.309
not	6.443.026
do	6.275.134
which	5.462.744
but	5.289.199
can	5.210.331
all	5.044.482
they	4.985.657
your	4.762.653
their	4.551.679
he	4.451.994
use	4.405.865
if	4.390.677
more	4.224.872
make	3.867.697
make	3.867.697
one	3.631.230
work	3.612.730
his	3.566.806
other	3.438.183
about	3.325.692
our	3.308.516
who	3.279.695
year	3.277.030
also	3.257.269
so	3.100.984
time	3.087.071
up	2.964.709
take	2.930.425
out	2.914.133
when	2.856.775
would	2.829.467
there	2.797.582
good	2.784.662
some	2.778.884
any	2.701.519
new	2.672.683
say	2.600.477
its	2.594.655
people	2.580.882
get	2.550.216
see	2.508.800
these	2.484.368
include	2.439.010
n't	2.414.023
no	2.412.420
my	2.385.876
go	2.357.541
into	2.311.112
need	2.273.146
only	2.215.984
may	2.191.652
them	2.170.865
information	2.137.320
give	2.135.994
provide	2.135.593
what	2.105.811
than	2.080.484
should	2.053.292
well	2.042.393
over	2.027.473
find	1.992.273
first	1.988.524
service	1.919.841
then	1.887.671
now	1.885.377
such	1.876.576
very	1.839.046
like	1.827.308
where	1.787.347
most	1.775.925
two	1.739.809
just	1.736.568
day	1.730.014
know	1.705.133
after	1.664.287
come	1.661.784
way	1.658.156

Page 1 Go Next >

On the left side of the menu, there are additional options through which users can get the list of all words or lemmas contained in the corpus. They will be displayed according to their frequency within the corpus. Figure 53 shows the first page of results for the "All words" option, with all the words in the ukWaC corpus being listed according to frequency, whereas Figure 54 shows the first page of results for the "All lemmas" option, where user can see all the lemmas contained in the ukWaC corpus, also listed according to frequency.

Figure 55. Frequency for word "knjiga" in hrWaC

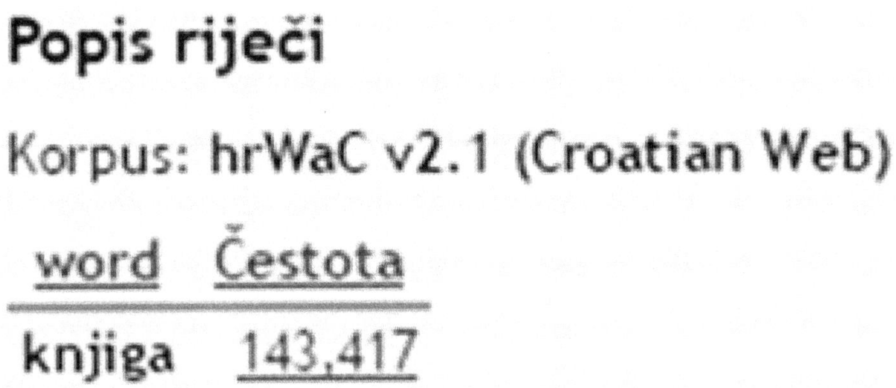

Under the option which allows us to choose the attribute user wants is the option for searching corpora according to n-grams. An n-gram is a continuous sequence of two or more words (Kilgarriff, 2014). It is possible to choose a sequence of up to six words in the menu. A sequence of two words is called a bigram, if it has three words it's trigram, for four it's tetragram (quadrigram) etc. Connections between the words don't necessarily have to have a specific meaning: for example, trigram ''pa je zato'' (eng. "therefore it is") has no specific meaning, whereas trigram ''kupiti bijeli kruh'' (eng. "buy white bread") has collocational meaning. Not every n-gram is considered a collocation, but every collocation is an n-gram (Kilgarriff, 2014). If user want to create a word list according to an n-gram, user need to select the checkbox and choose the number for the sequence whose frequency list user wants to get. This type of search does not require inputting the attribute's value.

Apart from creating lists according to a given attribute, it is also possible to additionally filter the search options in the "Filtering options" section which offers three options for filtering search results. In the ''Regular expression'' option, user input a value (word, expression or term) which user want to find

Figure 56 .Results of word list for words which have 3 characters/letters

word	Čestota
što	5,272,390
sam	4,482,063
kao	4,060,438
ili	3,730,821
ali	3,559,683
sve	3,036,627
jer	2,770,192
još	2,069,723
smo	2,017,123
ima	1,856,191
već	1,766,432
kad	1,753,756
bio	1,747,278
ako	1,675,900
bez	1,247,384
dok	1,139,984
oko	1,085,370
kod	1,061,979
nas	1,008,050
nam	977,419
taj	876,377
oni	817,513
dva	807,494
svi	801,109
Ako	769,907
ove	749,206
sto	709,823
pod	701,775
tri	686,451
sad	684,536
ono	676,044
ovo	656,386
ona	650,883
dio	648,356
čak	603,991
dan	593,161
baš	592,147
put	587,862
vam	582,461
ste	577,834
tko	565,137

in accordance with the chosen attribute in the "Search for attribute" field. For example, if user need information concerning the frequency of the word *''knjiga''* (eng. book) in the hrWaC corpus, then the chosen attribute will be "word", and its value will be *''knjiga''*. Figure 55 shows the frequency for the word *''knjiga''*, i.e. for nominative singular of the lemma "*knjiga*", not for all its forms in all grammatical cases.

It is possible to create a frequency word list based on the number of letters (characters) those words have. If user wants to find the most common three-letter words, the attribute will be ''word'' and its value three consecutive full stops without any spacing, which denote any three letters. The full stops substitute one character (letter), so it is possible to adjust the search according to our own preferences. If user wants to find the most common words with, for example, five letters, user will use five full stops etc. Figure 56 shows the first part of the search results when author searched for three-letter words.

The search can also be conducted according to the first letter of the word, its prefixes or its endings. If user wants to get the list containing the most frequent words starting with the letter "*ž*", then user need to input the parameter ''ž.*'' after which the list of the most frequent words starting with "*ž*" in the hrWaC corpus will be created (Figure 57). It is important to mention that the parameters for inputting value in the ''Regular expression'' option are the same as those for the CQL queries needed to create concordances. The only difference is that there is no need to put the value in quotation marks and that it cannot be define more than one search criterion.

The next two options are arbitrary and apply to defining the lowest and highest word frequencies in a corpus, with the value for minimum frequency being 5, which means that the word we are searching for has to appear at least five times in the corpus in order for it to be displayed in the search results. The maximum frequency is set to 0, meaning that there is no upper limit, which is a useful solution because it provides a complete display of frequency in the whole corpus.

The option "Word search" allows us to upload our own document with a word list, and based on that we can then conduct a frequency analysis of the desired words in a corpus, whereas the option "Exclude words" applies to our own list of words we want to exclude from the results. The documents we upload have to be stored in the .txt format (plain text), cannot contain any formatting and have to be coded in UTF-8 format, with every word being written in a separate line. Also, the list has to match the attribute according to which we want to conduct a search.

Figure 57. Most frequent word in hrWaC which stared with letter "ž"

lemma	Čestota
željeti	1,200,846
život	1,157,584
žena	675,696
živjeti	556,971
županija	314,630
želja	235,865
žrtva	170,596
ženski	163,603
životinja	157,412
životan	154,127
županijski	142,886
živ	127,327
župa	86,014
žalost	70,067
žaliti	69,027
žao	64,609
žut	62,468
župan	55,997
župnik	50,896
župni	46,446
živac	43,162
žestok	39,372
žalba	33,602
žiri	31,839
žica	29,066
željeznički	28,790
židovski	28,614
židov	28,428
želudac	26,881
životinjski	26,120
žanr	25,747
življenje	25,057
žlica	23,280
žila	20,961
žalosno	20,741
željan	20,598
željeznica	20,403
željezo	20,277
žrtvovati	18,618
žestoko	17,947
živa	17,799
živčan	17,566
žuriti	16,654
žitarica	16,165
ž	14,135
živo	14,107
žalostan	13,176
živcirati	12,879
žar	12,375
ženiti	12,210

So, if we are searching according to the attribute ''lemma'', then the document has to contain lemmas, and if we are searching according to the attribute "word", then the list can contain a word in any of its morphosyntactic form. Figure 58 contains an example of a correctly written and stored document with a prepared list of words whose frequency we want to check by using

Figure 58. Prepared word list in .txt format which is ready for upload to hrWaC using option Search words

the option ''Search words'' based on the "word" attribute. The list shows the declination of the nouns *''kravata''* (eng. a tie), *''penkala''* (eng. pen) and *''Vegeta''* (a name of a product) in singular form. Figure 59 contains a prepared word list with words we want to exclude from the search results for the search from Figure 59, those words being nominatives singular of the three aforementioned nouns. After both documents have been uploaded to the hrWaC corpus, we get the frequency of our desired vocabulary, as shown in Figure 60. It can be seen that the search results do not include nouns in nominative singular because this is what we have defined in the document uploaded in the "Exclude words" option. It is important to stress that the "Search words" option can be used on its own, without combining it with the "Exclude words" options, if we simply do not wish to exclude anything from the search, whereas the "Exclude words" option can only be used in combination with the first option and not on its own.

Figure 59. Prepared word list in .txt format which is ready for upload to hrWaC using option Exclude words

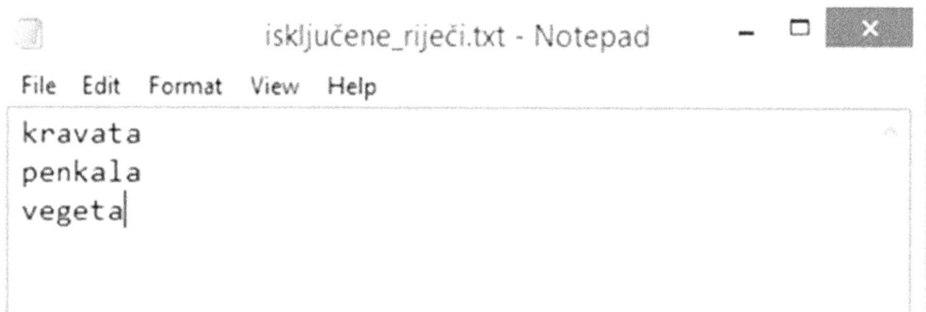

An additional option can be found in the "Filtering options" section, and it allows us to include non-words in the search, things like punctuation marks.

The next section is focused on adjusting additional options for displaying search results and is called "Display options". Two main categories can be adjusted, and they both concern determining frequency values and the way search results are displayed. When selecting frequency values, it is possible to select one of three options – "number of results", "number of documents" and "average relative frequency" (ARF). Selecting the first option will provide us with the frequency of the word we searched for. For example, Figure 61 shows the frequency for the word *''zima''* (eng. winter)[8] in the hrWaC corpus.

Figure 60. Results for word frequency which are uploaded through option Search words and Exclude words

Word list

Corpus: hrWaC v2.1 (Croatian Web)

word	Freq
kravate	2,672
kravati	581
kravatom	840
kravatu	2,052
penkale	245
penkali	20
penkalo	56
penkalom	95
penkalu	157
vegete	851
vegeti	44
vegetom	284
vegetu	458

Figure 61. Frequency for word "zima" using option "number of results"

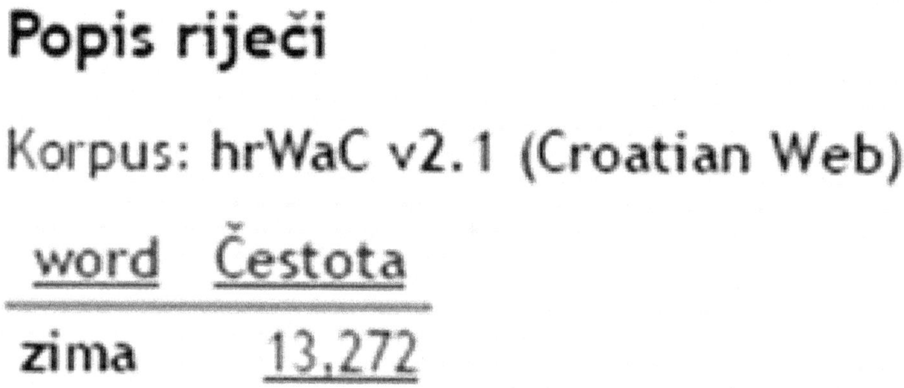

If we select the ''number of documents'' option, the number of documents in the hrWac corpus in which the word "*zima*" appears will be shown (Figure 62). The last option applies to average relative frequency which displays the

Figure 62. Frequency for word "zima" using option "number of documents"

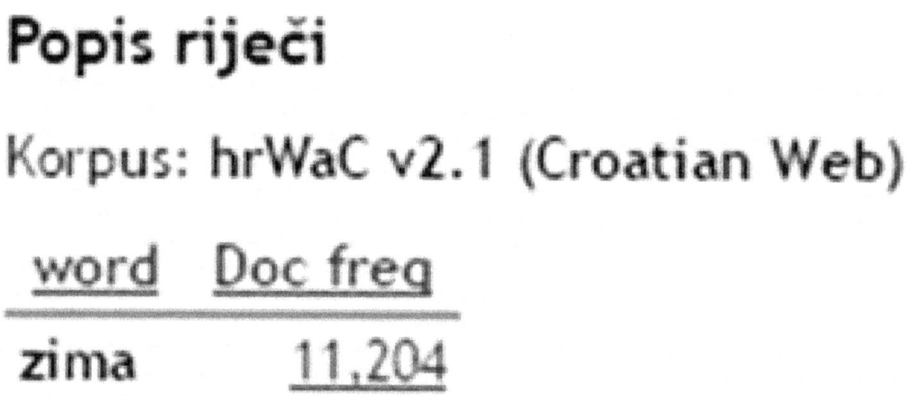

frequency of occurrence of the word in all documents, but with multiple occurrences of the same word in one document being excluded (Kilgarriff, 2014). For example, Figure 63 shows the ARF *''zima''*.

Figure 63. Frequency for word "zima" using option "ARF"

Popis riječi

Korpus: hrWaC v2.1 (Croatian Web)

word	Prosječna relativna čestota (PRČ)
zima	7,191.6

Figure 64. Results for frequency of word "kultura" in hrWaC and slWaC

Popis riječi

Korpus: hrWaC v2.1 (Croatian Web)

Referentni korpus: slWaC 2.0 (Slovene Web, Version 2)
Switch focus and reference (sub)corpus

	hrWaC v2.1 (Croatian Web)		slWaC 2.0 (Slovene Web, Version 2)		
word	Prosječna relativna čestota (PRČ)	Prosječna relativna čestota (PRČ)/mill	Prosječna relativna čestota (PRČ)	Prosječna relativna čestota (PRČ)/mill	Rezultat
kultura	19,082.1	13.7	11,956.1	9.5	1.4

The second category deals with the way the word list we are looking for is displayed. The first option, set as default, is called "Simple" and provides the classic display of a word's frequency as described and seen in Figure 65. The "Keywords" option is used when we are looking to compare the

Figure 65. Frequency for word "nova" by attributes "tag" and "word"

	word	tag	Freq
P | N	nova	Agpfsny	123,028
P | N	nova	Agpnpay	24,616
P | N	nova	Agpmsgn	12,385
P | N	nova	Agpnpny	9,837
P | N	nova	Ncfsn	4,109
P | N	nova	Agpnsgn	965
P | N	nova	Ncfpg	344
P | N	nova	Agpmsgy	40
P | N	nova	Xf	18
P | N	nova	Ncmpg	16
P | N	nova	Agpnsay	11

frequency of occurrence of the given word in the hrWaC corpus and some other available reference corpora or subcorpora. Figure 64 shows the result for the word *''kultura''* (eng. culture) according to the "Keywords" option for hrWaC and slWaC (Slovenian web corpus). In this example is used Slovenian web corpus because in Croatian and Slovenian language word *culture* has the same spelling.

The last option is ''Change output attribute(s)'' and it allows us to create word lists based on three levels. In other words, it is possible to create a list which will contain a display of frequency for multiple attributes (word, lemma, lempos, lc_lemma, lc, tag). The way this option is used will be shown on several examples in the following text.

If user wants to get the display of the word ''nova'' (eng. "new"), i.e. of its tokens in a corpus, then we need to define the search criteria in the following way: the attribute will be set to "word", the value will be "*nova*", whereas for the option ''Change output attribute(s)'' in the first drop-down menu we will have to choose the attribute ''word'' and in the second menu ''tag'' in order to get the frequency list of all morphosyntactic tags assigned to that token. In other words, we want also to be able to identify different word classes for that token and different grammatical cases that form encompasses (to be more specific, we want to know if "*nova*" is an adjective, is it in genitive or accusative, to which gender it applies, if it's in singular or plural or if it's an adnoun). The results based on those settings can be seen in Figure 65.

The second example concerns creating word lists based on the "lemma" attribute. If we want to find the most common forms of the verb *''zaposliti''* (eng. "to hire"), then we need to define the search criteria as follows: the attribute will be ''lemma'', the value will be "*zaposliti*", whereas in the ''Change output attribute(s)" option we need to select the attribute "word" in the first drop-down menu in order for the words to be displayed, and the attribute "tag" in the second menu to get a frequency display of morphosyntactic tags next to that lemma. Figure 66 shows the frequency list for that exact search.

Apart from creating frequency lists for individual words and their forms, it is possible to get a list of the most frequent word classes in a corpus. For example, if we want to create a list of the most common nouns in the hrWaC corpus, we will need to choose the attribute "tag", input the morphosyntactic tag for nouns (N.*) as the value and adjust the first level of display so that it shows the attribute "lemma". Figure 67 shows the first page of the list of the most frequent nouns in hrWaC. If we want to get the list pertaining to some other word class, we only need to change the morphosyntactic tag as the value, with everything else remaining exactly the same.

Figure 66. Frequency for word "zaposliti" by attributes "lemma", "word" and "tag"

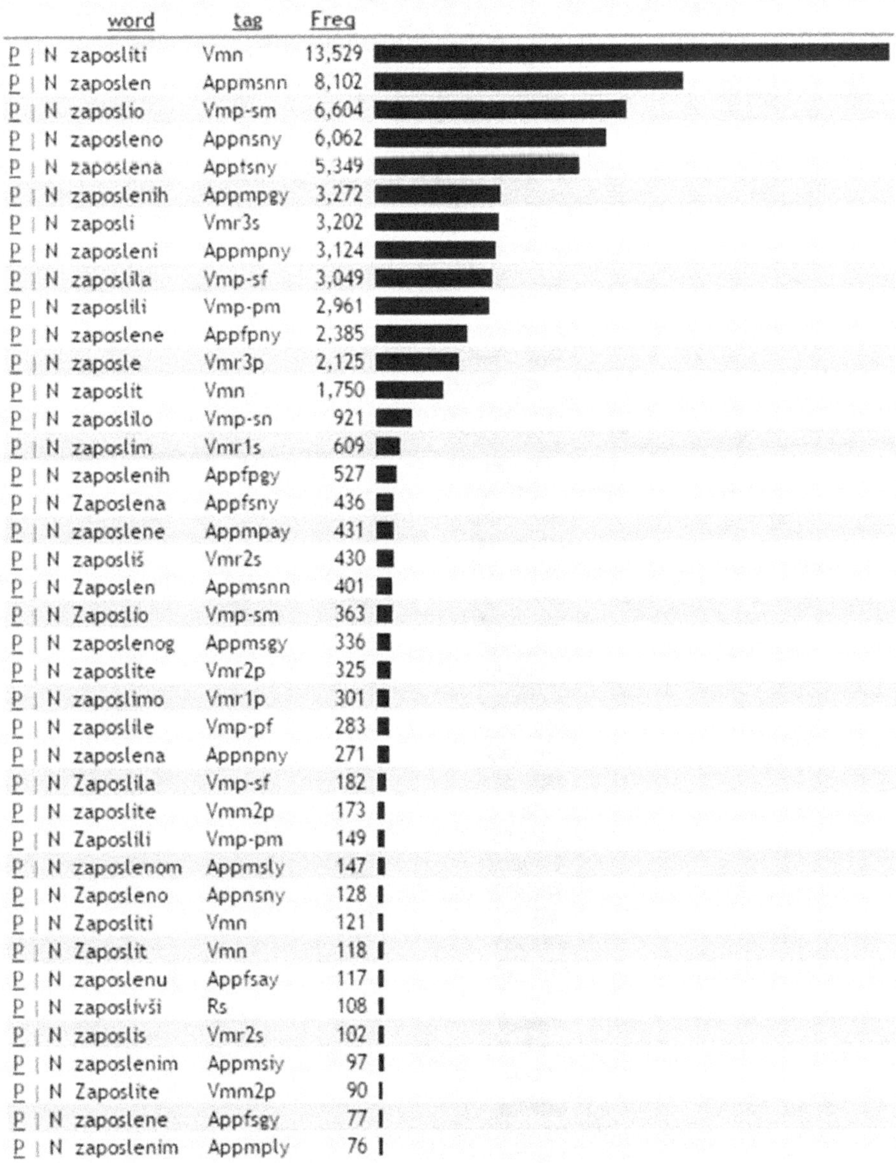

	word	tag	Freq
P | N	zaposliti	Vmn	13,529
P | N	zaposlen	Appmsnn	8,102
P | N	zaposlio	Vmp-sm	6,604
P | N	zaposleno	Appnsny	6,062
P | N	zaposlena	Apptsny	5,349
P | N	zaposlenih	Appmpgy	3,272
P | N	zaposli	Vmr3s	3,202
P | N	zaposleni	Appmpny	3,124
P | N	zaposlila	Vmp-sf	3,049
P | N	zaposlili	Vmp-pm	2,961
P | N	zaposlene	Appfpny	2,385
P | N	zaposle	Vmr3p	2,125
P | N	zaposlit	Vmn	1,750
P | N	zaposlilo	Vmp-sn	921
P | N	zaposlim	Vmr1s	609
P | N	zaposlenih	Appfpgy	527
P | N	Zaposlena	Appfsny	436
P | N	zaposlene	Appmpay	431
P | N	zaposliš	Vmr2s	430
P | N	Zaposlen	Appmsnn	401
P | N	Zaposlio	Vmp-sm	363
P | N	zaposlenog	Appmsgy	336
P | N	zaposlite	Vmr2p	325
P | N	zaposlimo	Vmr1p	301
P | N	zaposlile	Vmp-pf	283
P | N	zaposlena	Appnpny	271
P | N	Zaposlila	Vmp-sf	182
P | N	zaposlite	Vmm2p	173
P | N	Zaposlili	Vmp-pm	149
P | N	zaposlenom	Appmsly	147
P | N	Zaposleno	Appnsny	128
P | N	Zaposliti	Vmn	121
P | N	Zaposlit	Vmn	118
P | N	zaposlenu	Appfsay	117
P | N	zaposlivši	Rs	108
P | N	zaposlis	Vmr2s	102
P | N	zaposlenim	Appmsiy	97
P | N	Zaposlite	Vmm2p	90
P | N	zaposlene	Appfsgy	77
P | N	zaposlenim	Appmply	76

Another way we can use the ''Change output attribute(s)'' option can be seen in the example in which we are trying to find the most common form of the auxiliary verb ''*biti*'' (eng. "to be") in hrWaC. In this example, the given attribute is "lemma", its value is the verb "*biti*", while on the first level of the ''Change output attribute(s)'' option we need to select the attribute ''word''.

Figure 67. First page for results of most frequent word in hrWaC

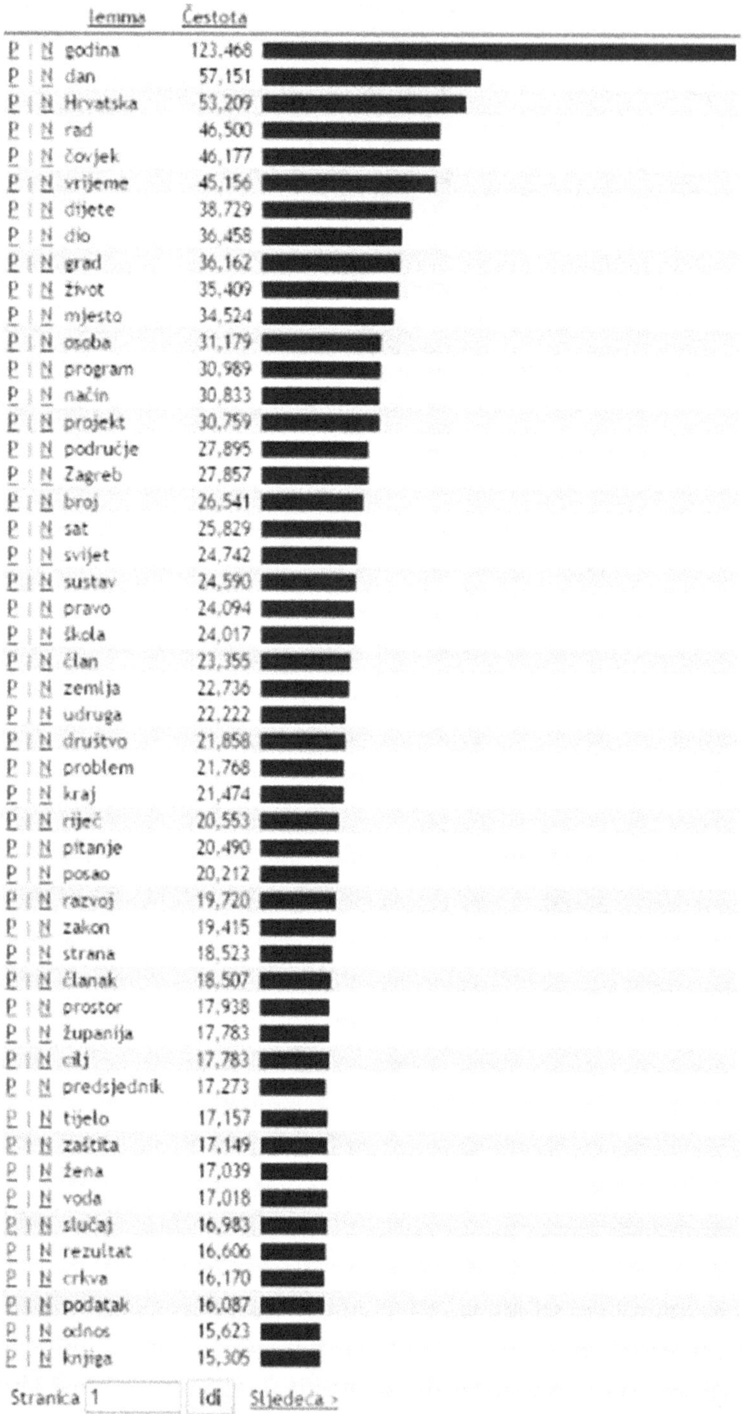

	lemma	Čestota
P | N	godina	123,468
P | N	dan	57,151
P | N	Hrvatska	53,209
P | N	rad	46,500
P | N	čovjek	46,177
P | N	vrijeme	45,156
P | N	dijete	38,729
P | N	dio	36,458
P | N	grad	36,162
P | N	život	35,409
P | N	mjesto	34,524
P | N	osoba	31,179
P | N	program	30,989
P | N	način	30,833
P | N	projekt	30,759
P | N	područje	27,895
P | N	Zagreb	27,857
P | N	broj	26,541
P | N	sat	25,829
P | N	svijet	24,742
P | N	sustav	24,590
P | N	pravo	24,094
P | N	škola	24,017
P | N	član	23,355
P | N	zemlja	22,736
P | N	udruga	22,222
P | N	društvo	21,858
P | N	problem	21,768
P | N	kraj	21,474
P | N	riječ	20,553
P | N	pitanje	20,490
P | N	posao	20,212
P | N	razvoj	19,720
P | N	zakon	19,415
P | N	strana	18,523
P | N	članak	18,507
P | N	prostor	17,938
P | N	županija	17,783
P | N	cilj	17,783
P | N	predsjednik	17,273
P | N	tijelo	17,157
P | N	zaštita	17,149
P | N	žena	17,039
P | N	voda	17,018
P | N	slučaj	16,983
P | N	rezultat	16,606
P | N	crkva	16,170
P | N	podatak	16,087
P | N	odnos	15,623
P | N	knjiga	15,305

Stranica 1 Idi Sljedeća ›

Figure 68. First page results of most frequent form of the auxiliary verb "biti" in hrWaC

	word	Čestota
P | N	je	4,859,447
P | N	su	1,591,636
P | N	bi	575,158
P | N	nije	470,674
P | N	sam	423,938
P | N	biti	316,158
P | N	smo	280,497
P | N	bio	208,963
P | N	bilo	180,001
P | N	bila	141,773
P | N	nisu	137,899
P | N	bili	95,634
P | N	ste	77,027
P | N	si	71,172
P | N	nisam	59,511
P | N	bih	51,422
P | N	bude	49,626
P | N	bit	43,875
P | N	Nije	33,644
P | N	jest	30,844
P | N	bile	30,632
P | N	nismo	26,308
P | N	bismo	23,646
P | N	budu	17,184
P | N	biste	14,036
P | N	Bilo	13,951
P | N	Je	12,637
P | N	jesu	12,573
P | N	Nisam	12,023
P | N	nisi	11,985
P | N	Bio	11,679
P | N	niste	11,598
P | N	Bila	6,921
P | N	JE	6,817
P | N	jeste	5,352
P | N	Bit	5,269
P | N	Nisu	4,897
P | N	budemo	4,789
P | N	jesam	4,739
P | N	budem	4,452
P | N	Jeste	4,445
P | N	jesi	3,709
P | N	Bili	3,653
P | N	Nismo	3,594
P | N	jesmo	3,203
P | N	Biti	2,829
P | N	bijaše	2,774
P | N	budete	2,726
P | N	Jesu	2,721

After that, a frequency list of the most frequent forms of the auxiliary verb "*biti*" will be displayed (Figure 68).

REFERENCES

Bartolec, B., Ivanković, I. (2013). Ispred, iza, u i oko–gdje sve mogu doći prijedlozi. *Rasprave: Časopis Instituta za hrvatski jezik i jezikoslovlje, 39*(2), 361-376.

Bekavac, B. (2001). *Primjena računalnojezikoslovnih alata na hrvatske korpuse*. Faculty of Humanities and Social Science, Department of Linguistics.

Bennett, G. R. (2010). *Using corpora in the language learning classroom: Corpus linguistics for teachers*. University of Michigan Press. doi:10.3998/mpub.371534

Blagus Bartolec, G. (2012). Kolokacijske sveze prema drugim leksičkim svezama u hrvatskom jeziku. *Fluminensia, 24*(2), 47-59.

Borić, N. (2002). Leksikografska prezentacija kolokacijskih sklopova. *Strani jezici, 31*(1-2), 56–63.

Burnard, L. (1996). *Introducing SARA: An SGML-Aware Retrieval Application for the British National Corpus*. Paper Presented at the *Second Conference on Teaching and Language Corpora*.

Donesch-Jezo, E. (2013). Using language corpus in teaching foreign language vocabulary. *International Multidisciplinary e-Journal, 2*(1), 11-25.

Evert, S. (2014) *The Statistics of Word Cooccurrences: Word Pairs and Collocations* (Unpublished Ph.D. dissertation). University of Stuttgart.

Hunston, S. (2002). *Corpora in applied linguistics*. Ernst Klett Sprachen. doi:10.1017/CBO9781139524773

Hunston, S. (2010). *Corpus approaches to evaluation: Phraseology and evaluative language*. Routledge. doi:10.4324/9780203841686

Ivir, V. (1992). Kolokacije i leksičko značenje. *Filologija, 20*(21), 181–189.

Johnston, T. (2008, June). Corpus linguistics and signed languages: no lemmata, no corpus. *3rd Workshop on the Representation and Processing of Sign Languages*.

O'Keeffe, A., McCarthy, M., & Carter, R. (2007). *From corpus to classroom: Language use and language teaching*. Cambridge University Press. doi:10.1017/CBO9780511497650

Petrović, B. (2007). Razvijanje kolokacijske kompetencije u hrvatskome kao stranom i drugom jeziku. *Strani jezici, 36*(1), 31-38.

Pritchard, B. (1998). O kolokacijskom potencijalu rječničkog korpusa. *Filologija*, (30-31), 285-304.

Reppen, R. (2011). Using corpora in the language classroom. *Materials development in language teaching*, 35-51.

Rječnik korpusne lingvistike. (n.d.). http://www.hnk.ffzg.hr/bb/definicijekl.doc

Rychlý, P. (2008, December). *A lexicographer-friendly association score.* RASLAN.

Sinclair, J. (1991). *Corpus, Concordance, Collocation.* Oxford: Oxford University Press.

Stojić, A., & Murica, S. (2010). Kolokacije–teorijska razmatranja i primjena u praksi na primjerima iz hrvatskoga i njemačkoga jezika. *Fluminensia: časopis za filološka istraživanja, 22*(2), 111-125.

Tadić, M. (2009) New version of the Croatian National Corpus. In After Half a Century of Slavonic Natural Language Processing. Masaryk University.

ENDNOTES

1 A lemma is defined as the abstraction from a set of wordforms belonging to the same word class. Thus, WALK indicates walk, walks, walking and walked (but not the noun walk) (Hunston, 2010, p. 9).

2 Headword refers to a different word form which appears in corpus, e.g. house, houses are headwords of lemma house.

3 Lemmatisation is the classification or identification of related word forms under a single label or lemma (the equivalent of headwords or headsigns in a dictionary)—is central to the process of corpus creation (Johnston, 2008).

4 http://www.hnk.ffzg.hr/bb/definicijekl.doc

5 http://www.hnk.ffzg.hr/bb/definicijekl.doc.

6 A simple search for the word "letjeti" (eng. "to fly") provides a concordance. After that, by clicking on the Collocations, we open the menu called Collocation candidates where the range is set from 0 to 5. Everything else is set as default before we click the "Create list" button.

7 Taken from: Rychlý, P. (2008). A lexicographer-friendly association score. Proceedings of Recent Advances in Slavonic Natural Language Processing, RASLAN, 6–9.

8 The frequency shown in Figures 56, 57 and 58 applies to the word ''*zima*'' in nominative singular alone.

Chapter 4
Methodology and Research

ABSTRACT

This chapter will give insight to used methodology and analysis for interpretation of conducted in-depth interviews with language teachers in primary and secondary schools in Croatia. This research is a case study about perceptions, attitudes, emotions, knowledge, and suggestions about use and implementation of computer corpora in teaching language learning in primary and secondary schools. In-depth interviews were conducted with four teachers who explore their existing knowledge about corpus linguistics and computer corpora. The research is based on language teachers' thoughts and experiences of how computer corpora can be incorporated into the teaching process of language learning. Results are implications (e.g., advantages and obstacles) for inclusion of corpus-based teaching in primary and secondary schools.

INTRODUCTION

Research was based on in-depth interviews with teachers from primary and secondary schools in Croatia. For the purpose of the research 20 schools were contacted to participate in the research. Schools which were contacted participated in the European project CRISS Horizon2020[1] where main goal was to acquire, evaluate and certified digital competences of students in primary and secondary schools. Teachers from this schools were digitally competent, they frequently used ICT in their teaching and therefore were contacted and invited to participate in the research. Additional, only language teachers from

DOI: 10.4018/978-1-7998-3680-3.ch004

these 20 schools were asked to participate in the research. Out of 20 schools only 4 of them accepted invitation, more accurately just 4 language teachers from 4 different schools (2 from primary and 2 from secondary school) decided to participate in the research. Intention was to have the same, equal number of primary and secondary school teachers in the research. Due to the lack of interest in participating in the research the sample of participants is small, but they give valuable insight into teachers' motivation, attitudes, knowledge and perceptions about the use of computer corpora for teaching language subjects in primary and secondary schools. This is not quantitative research in which results can be calculated and compared, this research lies exclusively on teachers' thoughts, emotions and process of preparation and learning about computer corpora and exploring possibilities for including this type of language learning tool and methodology into primary and secondary schools. In research participated two primary school teachers and two secondary school teachers. Two teachers are teaching Croatian as first language and literacy (one in primary school and one in secondary school) and other two teachers are teaching English as second language in secondary school (one in primary school and one in secondary school, with exception that one teacher teaches additionally and German as second language).

Research was conducted in second half of school year 2018/2019. Structure of questions for conducting in-depth interviews was taken form doctoral theses of John D. Bunting from 2013 by the name An Investigation of Language Teachers' Explorations of the Use of Corpus Tools in the English for Academic Purposes (EAP) Class at Georgia State University. Questions from aforementioned dissertation were in come matter altered so they correspond to target group of participants and topic of this research. The method of in-depth interviews was chosen because it "is a technique designed to elicit a vivid picture of the participant's perspective on the research topic; the researcher's interviewing techniques are motivated by the desire to learn everything the participant can share about the research topic; this is an effective qualitative method for getting people to talk about their personal feelings, opinions, and experiences; it is also an opportunity to gain insight into how people interpret and order the world" (Milena, Dainora, Alin, 2008, p. 1279). Additionally, this method can provide insights to indirect and direct use of corpora "by analysing learners' attitudes and representations about corpus use; learners' behaviour and processes in corpus use. effects of corpus use as a learning aid; effects of corpus use as a reference resource" (Boulton, 2017, p. 485)

In-depth interviews were divided into three parts. First part is dedicated to gaining background information about participants (teachers) knowledge, education, views, attitudes and perception about corpus linguistics and corpora. Second part of in-depth interviews correlates with preparation process for class in which teachers would use computer corpora for preparing teaching materials or working directly with students on corpora. This part of research was not obligatory so teachers could choose not to do it if they do not feel competent or insecure in the process. Just two teachers felt motivated and confident to participate in this part of the research and decided to prepare teaching materials using corpora. Other two teachers did not what to participate in this segment of the research due to their insufficient knowledge about use of computer corpora for teaching and the lack of time they had for preparation. Third part of in-depth interviews was about teachers' experience, satisfaction and process of teaching with corpus-based materials. Complete list of in-depth interviews can be found in Appendix A.

The main goals of the research was to explore in which measurement language teachers are educated about corpus linguistics and computer corpora, would they use computer corpora for preparing teaching materials, would they use computer corpora directly in classroom with students and what are teachers perceptions, motivation and emotions about using computer corpora for teaching languages in primary and secondary schools. All questions from in-depth interviews are equally important because they provide answers about why teacher would or would not use computer corpora in their workflow. Their background information (where they did work, which type of learners did they teach, what is their experience as language teachers, etc.), activities in conferences, additional educations, workshops, etc, are important information which have influenced on their perception of computer corpora and how they see advantages or disadvantages in education system. Additionally, there is no comparison between involved teachers because this study aims to show teachers emotions and attitudes about implications of corpus-based language teaching.

Aim of the research was to explore and see what is teachers motivation and perception of using computer corpora in their work (teaching language subjects), is it appropriate for primary and secondary school students and for what part of teaching language will be most suitable (e.g. grammar, vocabulary, literacy, etc.). To gain perspective and insight to teachers' knowledge, motivation, perceptions, needs and attitudes in-depth interviews were conducted. This methodology was used to get explanation why "despite the affordances of corpora, the reality is that they are still rarely used by language teachers" (Ebrahimi, Faghih, 2016, p. 121). Main vision of this research was to examine what is the reason for that and in-depth interviews provided insights into teacher perspective.

Qualitative method was used for analysing and interpreting research results gained through in-depth interviews with language teachers. Main goal of this research method was to give an answer or the explanation, can computer corpora be incorporated in primary and secondary education within language subjects, if so how and in which measurement are the language teachers motivated for such a task.

One of the participants in this research (teacher AP) incorporated computer corpora directly in his classroom where students used and individual searched corpora. This was great opportunity to explore students' perceptions of computer corpora because this was the first-time students from primary school have heard of it and used it for learning L1 language. This part of the research was analysed using quantitative method (online survey). To see what was students perception of the learning materials and computer corpora, after the held class students have filled in the online survey with 10 question about how they experienced this class, what do they think about computer corpora, was it helpful and interesting and would they use it again for learning language. Main goal of this part of the research was to explore are students in the age of 14 motivated to use computer corpora for language learning during the school class. Complete list of question which were included in online survey can be found in Appendix B.

The research sample is small because the process of conducting in-depth interviews is comprehensive and it can be conducted with a small group of people. Involved teachers have given an insight to teachers' inner state regarding their work with students in primary and secondary schools in Croatia, computer corpora, corpus linguistics, motivation, DDL approach, corpus tools, students need, teaching process and indirectly and directly use of corpora for purpose of teaching first and second language subjects.

Analysis and interpretation of in-depth interviews and online survey conducted with students of primary schools will be elaborated in chapters Using computer corpora in primary schools and Using computer corpora in secondary schools. These two chapters will give insight into teachers' perceptions, attitudes and knowledge about computer corpora and corpus linguistics. All conclusions will be presented in the final two chapters Implication of computer of computer corpora in primary and secondary education and Conclusion and Further Research.

REFERENCES

Boulton, A. (2017). Corpora in language teaching and learning. *Language Teaching*, *50*(4), 483–506. doi:10.1017/S0261444817000167

Bunting, J. D. (2013). *An Investigation of Language Teachers' Explorations of the Use of Corpus Tools in the English for Academic Purposes (EAP) Class* (Doctoral dissertation). Georgia State University.

Ebrahimi, A., & Faghih, E. (2017). Integrating corpus linguistics into online language teacher education programs. *ReCALL*, *29*(1), 120–135. doi:10.1017/S0958344016000070

Milena, Z. R., Dainora, G., & Alin, S. (2008). Qualitative research methods: A comparison between focus-group and in-depth interview. *Annals of the University of Oradea. Economic Science Series*, *17*(4), 1279–1283.

ENDNOTE

1 More about project can be find here: https://www.crissh2020.eu/criss-project/

Chapter 5
Using Computer Corpora in Primary School

ABSTRACT

This chapter will provide information and data about primary schools and its teachers who participated in the research. The chapter will show in-depth interviews with teachers from two primary schools in Croatia. The purpose of the in-depth interview is to research and analyze teacher needs, opinions, attitudes, values, and knowledge about computer corpora in general. The second goal is to explore in which way teachers in primary schools would use computer corpora for creating teaching materials, exams, or language exercise. The aim of this chapter is to investigate if computer corpora can be implemented in primary schools for teaching language subjects and in which way and for what students/grades it would be most eligible.

USING COMPUTER CORPORA IN PRIMARY SCHOOL

This chapter will provide detailed information about use of computer corpora in primary education level for creating educational materials for students from age 10 to 14.

Education and teacher training agency[1] in Croatia on their official website has published official document[2] in which is explained Croatian educational system for primary and secondary schools. According to Education and teacher training agency Croatian educational system starts with first grade of primary school which is mandatory for all children. Primary school is for

DOI: 10.4018/978-1-7998-3680-3.ch005

children between 6 and 15 years of age and it lasts for eight years. During this period students are acquiring knowledge and abilities for continuing education in secondary school.

It is divided into two parts, lower primary school which lasts for four years (from 1st grade to 4th grade) and high primary school which lasts for another four years (from 5th grade to 8th grade). Student age in lower primary school is between 6 and 9 years and in high primary school the age is between 10 and 15 years. This research was conducted with two teachers who are working with students in high primary level school and their students age is approximately between 10 and 15 years.

After students finish primary school they have possibility to continue their education in secondary school which are not mandatory. All students have equal rights to enrol in the first grade of secondary school in line with number of enrolment places which is determinate by the decision of Ministry of Education, Science and Sports in Croatia. Secondary schools in Croatia are divided to gymnasium, vocational and art schools. Gymnasium school lasts for four years and it ends with final state test. In vocational schools education last between one and five years and it ends with term paper which student have to elaborate. Students who finish vocational school can take state test and gain higher level of qualification. Gymnasium prepare their students for continuing their education (to enrol to university), vocational school train their students for labour market and art schools provide students with knowledge, capabilities and creativity in different art fields.

In research participated two teachers, one teacher teaches Croatian as first language and literacy, second teaches English as second language. Teachers did not use computer corpora in their line of work, and they did not search them before this research was conducted. During this research they were introduced with available corpora through user interface NoSketch Engine where they search, and filter concordance lines based on their quires. They used Croatian National Corpus, Croatian Web Corpus and British Web Corpus.

Identity of the involved teachers will be protected, and they will remain anonymous. When describing their thoughts, citations and all relevant materials they will be referred as teacher AP and teacher BP. Teacher AP teaches Croatian as first language and literacy in primary school Horvati in Zagreb (capital city of Croatia) and teacher BP teaches English as second language in primary school Ksavera Šandora Đalskog in Donja Zelina . This chapter is divided into two main section, first section is named Case 1 and refers to teacher's AP experience working with computer corpora, attitudes toward teaching process, working in primary school, students' attitude and motivation for learning Croatian language and using computer corpora in classroom, corpus linguistics, etc. Second section is named Case 2 and refers to teacher's BP experience and attitudes about computer corpora, teaching process, working in primary school, students' attitude and motivation for learning English language, corpus linguistics, etc. It is important to mention that teacher AP used and worked with computer corpora during this research, he also introduced computer corpora to his students and they worked with it during the two school classes in total duration of 90 minutes (one school class in Croatian schools lasts for 45 minutes). He introduced computer corpora with two groups of students from 8th grade (names of classes are 8A and 8B). After two classes at which students used computer corpora, they fill out online survey about their experience, level of satisfaction and motivation about use of computer corpora directly in classroom. Complete survey with all questions is available at the end of the book in separate section named Appendix B.

On the other hand, teacher BP participated just in the in-depth interview, he did not develop corpus-based teaching materials for his students and did not introduced corpora to his students. But his contribution to this research is also valuable because of the insight to teachers' attitudes and motivation for incorporating new teaching methodology and tools into the process of learning English language in primary schools.

All questions which were included in the in-depth interviews can be seen at the end of the book in separate section named Appendix A.

CASE 1: USING COMPUTER CORPORA FOR TEACHING CROATIAN AS FIRST LANGUAGE IN PRIMARY SCHOOL

General Background Information About Teacher AP

Teacher AP is a professor of Croatian language in primary school Horvati (Zagreb, Croatia) where he works with students from 5th to 8th grade (ages 10 to 15). Before this research he had heard about corpora but had not used it for preparing teaching materials nor in a classroom.

Teacher AP has master's degree in Croatian language and literacy from Faculty of Humanities and Social Sciences from University Zadar. Last 11 years teacher AP is working as teacher of Croatian as first language. Majority of his work is related with teaching in primary schools, but he has experience in working with older students from secondary schools. His love for books and reading in early age steer his ambition to become professor and teacher of Croatian language and literacy.

The main differences between working in primary and secondary school due to teacher AP is in educational curriculum and learning materials. He states:

In primary schools the emphasis is put on learning language structures like grammar and vocabulary and learning outputs are repeating and sometimes expending in every grade. In secondary schools learning fields are almost the same as in primary schools with exception of media culture which we cannot find in secondary level education. In secondary schools' emphasis is mostly put on learning and analysing literacy. (Teacher AP, 2019)

Another difference between primary and secondary approach to education according to teacher AP is social diversity of students. Student diversity in primary school is greater than in secondary, "you have gifted students and students with disabilities in learning in the same class" (Teacher AP). On the other hand, in secondary school's student abilities and competences are more balanced and homogenous. Also, the difference is in the teaching methods and educational strategies which are used for teaching.

Teacher AP is open minded about using and incorporating new and modern learning methods in classroom and for preparing teaching materials for his students, like including information and communication technologies in educational process. He has affinities towards creative ways of teaching extracurricular activities like film arts, literary creation and media content. When teaching language, he prefers educational content which is related to morphology and syntax of Croatian language.

Teacher AP has preferences regarding grades and students he teaches, he prefers to work with students in 7th and 8th grade (age 12 to 15) because they are more mature, and they are used to more divers learning activities. Additionally, they have good background knowledge of Croatian language. Learning materials and themes are more difficult in higher grades and for him as a teacher that presents challenge, how to find the best way how to present these materials to the students.

Negative aspects and frustrations of being a teacher in primary school for teacher AP presents a social perception of teacher's work which is from year to year more negative and that negativity is transferred to students and parent's relation toward every segment of school and what it stands for. Another negative side of teaching in primary school for teacher AP is related to financial side, he thinks that teachers in primary education are underpaid for their work because their job do not end when school class is over.

Teacher AP regularly participates on Regional professional meeting, upscaling his skills and knowledge through different kind of national level education and trainings. Often, he participates on national congresses which are related to teaching Croatian language with use of information and communication technologies (ICT) as part of Erasmus+ KA1[3] programmes. His fields of research are related to contemporary ways of teaching and working with children with disabilities, student relation to school and similar. In his research work he had worked with different primary schools, universities and institutes for social research.

Teacher AP thoughts and attitudes toward structure of language class in primary school for learning Croatian language is as follows:

I would give teachers more autonomy in decision making about what and how to teach, adjust curriculum so that part of teaching outcomes is facultative, for certain classes I would define clearer teaching outcomes. Also, I would adjust curriculum to social surroundings and approach them with examples from actual and real-life situations.

Teacher AP emphasis that major issues in teaching are lack of motivation on all levels, teaching materials which are in some areas too comprehensive and in some areas too poor, lack of national strategies for development of educational system and poor material conditions in the schools.

Teacher AP thinks that the most useful way for teaching first language in primary school is for students to work on text with concrete and specific examples, conducting conversational exercise with students, encourage collaborative learning which is base for creating critical opinion with students.

His teaching methods are combination of traditional approach with contemporary teaching methods where he aspires to establish optimal weight. Relevant need in his teaching process is feedback about student progress in learning and comprehension of learned materials.

Teacher AP has wide knowledge about using information and communication technologies and his opinion about integration of contemporary methods and approaches into a process of learning language is positive. He thinks that diversity in teaching has positive influence both on teachers and students.

He thinks that use of technologies is needed in every aspects of learning process when its use is pedagogically and didactyly justified. Additionally, he points out that technology can rise level of student's motivation for learning and for the teachers it can improve and facilitate their teaching and preparation process for the classroom.

Teacher's AP Knowledge and Attitudes Towards Corpus Linguistics and Computer Corpora

Teacher AP until now did not use or search computer corpora. He did hear about corpus linguistics and his opinion is that corpus linguistics is "one of fields of science about conducting language analysis using computer language databases and statistical processing of found data" (Teacher AP, 2019).

Until now teacher AP did not have any contact with computer corpora but during one of congresses he did hear about term corpus. In this research teacher AP was for the first time introduced with terms corpus linguistics, corpus, computer corpora and corpus tools.

Based on definition of corpus tools which states that they represent different ways how corpus data can improve learning process and language acquisition, teacher AP is aware of hrWaC corpus and Riznica but he does not have enough knowledge about corpus tools, e.g. concordance lines, frequency lists, collocations, etc. This is the first time he worked with computer corpus and its tools.

Based on introduction to corpus and its tools teacher AP thinks that this type of tools can have wide area of use in language teaching, for example "it can be used for learning vocabulary which belong to different functional styles, for learning different word structures and forms like verbs and forms of a noun, adjective, or pronoun that express the semantic relation of the word to other words in the sentence – case, for learning word formation like prefixes and suffixes" (Teacher AP, 2019).

Teacher's AP Attitudes About His Experience Working with Computer Corpora

For the purpose of the research teacher AP used NoSketch Engine interface where he individually conducted searches on three corpora for Croatian language, HNK, hrWaC and Riznica. Teacher AP individually conducted search of corpora but in some areas of searching methods and result interpretation he needed additional help. He needed help with CQL query and where/how to find morphosyntactic tags which are used for CQL search in Croatian corpora. The interface for corpus search was very clear and simple to comprehend and teacher AP did not have any problem with initial approach of using and searching corpora.

Problematic part, when working with computer corpora, for teacher AP was procedure and correct use of CQL query and tags from MSD summary. He thinks that use of hrWaC corpus is not suitable for primary school students because of its diverse content. Great deal of content consists of web blogs, forums, chats and comments from social networks which contains unappropriated language for younger students. Regarding that he would not use it directly in classroom with students, but he thinks that is good language database for language research.

Teacher's AP Attitudes About Integration of Computer Corpora Into Primary School Curriculum

Teacher AP thinks that integration of computer corpora within primary school education would be useful and welcomed both by teachers/schools and students like for all other tools which have well organized structure for its use and represents refreshment in teaching and learning process.

Teacher AP thinks that main problem with integration of new teaching methods into educational process is when they appear ad hoc without additional time for teachers to prepare and adjust to them. Integration must be conducted progressively providing additional education for the teachers, for example in a form of workshops. It must provide clear examples how corpus tools are used in teaching process and what is their purpose in teaching language subjects. Teacher AP states that integration of computer corpora and its tools would have positive impact on teaching process, and it would revitalize teaching materials which can be helpful for teaching linguistic rules.

Teacher AP states that computer corpora can be used both by teachers and students. He thinks that teachers would not be motivated to individually search computer corpora but with well-prepared materials and tutorials for searching and using corpora. With these educational materials teachers would use them for creating teaching materials and in the classroom with their students. On the other hand, students are always motivated for using and experimenting with new ICT tools, but their motivation rapidly falls if teaching activities are not well prepared and conducted or if they (students) do not see the purpose of those tools.

For his teaching class teacher AP would use referent corpus which has large number of tokens and represents standard language. He would use it for teaching grammar like verbs with emphasis on aorist and imperfect in Croatian language.

Teacher's Attitudes About Process of Educating Teachers About Using Computer Corpora

Teacher AP thinks that education about computer corpora and its use must be integrated into formal education for language teachers, not just for Croatian language but for all languages which can be studied in higher education level. His attitude about educating teachers how and what corpus and its tools are must me part of regular classes in higher education for students which are studying language. According to his opinion those subjects must provide students with lots of examples how to use corpus tools in theory and practise. He points out that students would learn about different use of corpus and its tools through variety of different examples in different countries and with different language subjects, through analysing science researches. Additional education in the form of different type of workshops about use of computer corpora would be welcomed for the teachers who did not have corpus linguistics during their studying period. In this type of education teacher AP would include examples of good practice in classroom.

Description of Students and Class Groups Which Participated In The Research

Teacher AP orally provided the information about his students in school year 2018/2019 during the in-depth interviews. He stated that in school year 2018/2019 he worked with 4 groups/classes of students. Two groups were in the 6th grade (age 12 and 13) and two groups were in 8th grade (age 14 and 15). These were mixed classes with approximately same numbers of male and female students. Majority of his students were interested and motivated for learning Croatian language, “about 10% of students have poor results and grades but other 90% have excellent grades (A)” (Teacher AP, 2019). Accordingly to the Teacher AP students have most issues with learning and understanding grammar especially if they did not mastered lesson materials from previous years, “based on students abilities this generation of students is similar to previous years, but they are learning less at home, they are not ready for collaborative learning, they are ambitious and they are too confident about their abilities and knowledge” (Teacher AP, 2019) .

Teacher AP as states that the biggest challenge in working with this groups of students is how to train them for collaborative learning, critical thinking and problem solving, but according to him these are problems on school level not just for one or two classes.

Additional, Teacher AP claims that student activity in classroom is good but the lack of their activity at home, doing their homework is a big issue. Also, they do not use online resources for learning and expanding their knowledge database.

Strengths and Challenges in Teaching For Teacher AP

His strength in teaching and working with students is ability to recognize students’ needs and that he can easily adjust to the different situations. He can easily manage his classroom, and students respect him and his teaching methods.

The biggest challenge in teaching, for teacher AP, is effort to make students aware of their invested time and acquired competences. Also, big challenge is to provide acknowledgement to students regarding their abilities, e.g. if they are gifted, average or have difficulties with learning and comprehending presented materials.

For his teaching class teacher AP used textbooks and workbooks which are approved and provided for by law (Ministry of Education, Science and Sport in Croatia). On daily base he is creating and preparing his own teaching materials, texts for exercise, homework, exams, etc. Teacher AP is developing his own exams for students and regularly is upgrading and changing them. He thinks that there is a need for online repository which would include diverse multimedia and interactive materials and examples of good practice.

Teaching outcomes for every school year are defined in advanced by HNOS[4] and teacher AP or any other teacher cannot modify them except in the field of extracurricular activities. He states that most important outcomes are those which are related to language competences and less with literacy.

The operationalization of teaching outcomes is arbitrary, and teachers can conduct in their own way. He uses different kind of summative and formative evaluation, like dictations, written exams, homework, etc. He points out:

I am trying to develop formative evaluation because this kind of evaluation lays on continuous progress with regular guidance. (Teacher AP, 2019)

Preview of Held Class for Croatian As First Language Using Computer Corpora

Teacher AP decided to conduct research directly in classroom with his students to see which effect direct use of corpora in classroom would have on his students and how they would respond to using corpus tools in the classroom. In this research participated students from two classes, grade 8A and grade 8B. They have had two classes in which they used corpus tools on computers. Each class lasted for 45 minutes so in total they worked with computer corpora for 90 minutes. Additionally, they had third class in which they presented their results and solutions of exercise in front of the teacher and other classmates.

Teacher AP did not use or search computer corpora before he decided to participate in this research. He was provided with explanation of what corpus is but he individually stared to research how to search and use corpus tools. After familiarizing with corpus material, he created working tasks and exercise for his students. He decided to work with HNK and hrWaC corpora. He states that for teaching and working with students it is better to use HNK because it is referent corpus but, in the end, he gave opportunity to his students to work on both HNK and hrWaC corpus. Exercises which he prepared was connected to the lesson about idioms and etymology, workload was 90 minutes and methodology used was project-based teaching.

At the beginning of the class teacher AP presented to his students what corpus is and how can they conduct simple searches and get results. He also explained KWIC view, what are concordance lines and how they can get additional content if they need it for language analysis.

He used Google Drive folder to share his teaching materials and hyperlinks to students in the classroom. In shared document teacher AP put two hyperlinks, one for HNK and one for hrWaC corpus. Exercise consisted out of 5 tasks which students had to resolve using one of the computer corpora for Croatian language (example of exercises is available in Appendix C).

In the first task students were asked to analyse and search synonyms[5] for words which are taken from foreign language. For example, in Croatian language word computer has two terms. Croatian word for *computer* is *računalo* and loanword from English language is *kompjutor.* Students searched for both words to see frequency of each word in the corpus. Based on their research they saw which word is more frequent in language use. Teacher provided his students whit set of 7 pairs of synonyms which students had to search through corpus. Here is the list of word:

- Noun: *barcode*, defined by Cambridge dictionary a small rectangular pattern of thick and thin black lines printed on a product, or on its container, so that the details of the product can be read by and recorded on a computer system[6] (Croatian term is: *linijski čitač*, and loanword from English is: *barkod*)
- Noun: *computer*, defined by Cambridge dictionary is an electronic machine that is used for storing, organizing, and finding words, numbers, and pictures, for doing calculations, and for controlling other machines[7] (Croatian term is: *računalo*, and loanword from English is: *kompjutor*)
- Adjective: *educational*, defined by Cambridge dictionary - providing education or relating to education[8] (Croatian term is: *obrazovni*, and loanword from English is: *edukacijski*)
- Noun: *laptop*, defined by Cambridge dictionary - a computer that is small enough to be carried around easily and is flat when closed[9] (Croatian term is: *prijenosno računalo*, and loanword form English is: *laptop*)
- Noun: *event*, defined by Cambridge dictionary anything that happens, especially something important or unusual[10] (Croatian term is: *događanje*, and loanword from English is: *event*)
- Noun: *experiment*, defined by Cambridge dictionary a test done in order to learn something or to discover if something works or is true[11] (Croatian term is: *pokus*, and loanword from English is: *experiment*)
- Noun: *screen,* defined by Cambridge dictionary is a flat surface in a cinema, on a television, or as part of a computer, on which pictures or words are shown[12] (Croatian term is: *zaslon*, and loanword from French is (a Gallicism): *ekran*)

In this task students learn some new words and saw frequency of loanwords versus Croatian terms in authentic language use. They analyse frequency of tokens to see which word form is commonly used in Croatian language. In this task students used simple search for querying corpus. Figure 1 shows solution for task 1 which teacher AP give to his students. This student choose to search for loanwords *computer*, *event* and *laptop*. On slide student presented

Figure 1. Example of student exercise for task 1

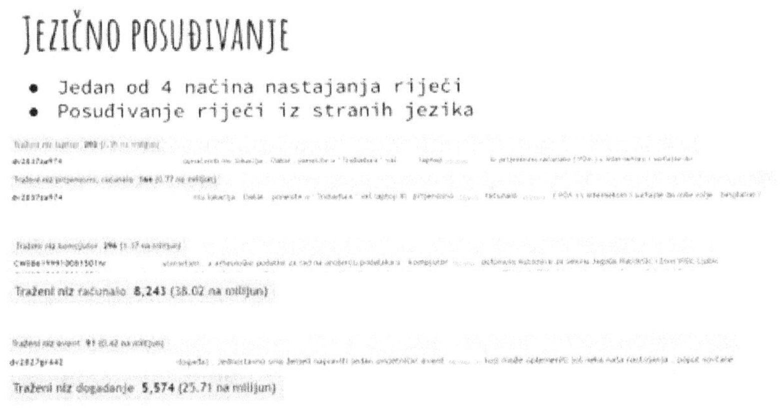

Figure 2. Example of student exercise for task 2

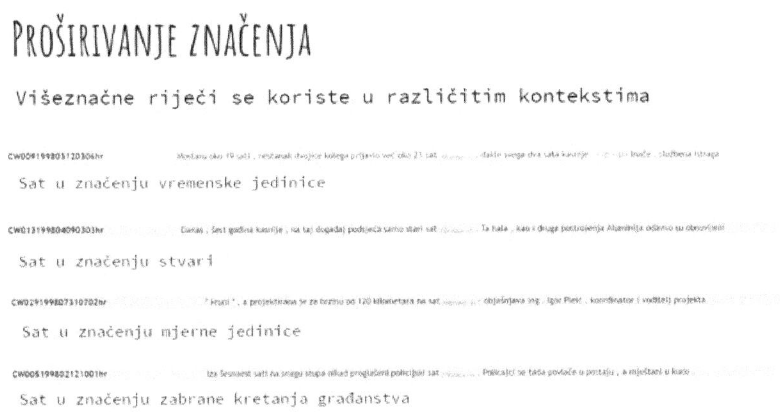

information about frequency of these words and one example of concordance line for each example in which the word is used.

In task 2 (Figure 2) students learned about homonyms, words which have same spelling but different meaning depending on context in which they are used. In this task teacher gave students example of homonym for Croatian word *kolo/kola* (engl. wheel). In Croatian language this word has several different meanings depending on contexts which surrounds her. All meanings of word *kolo/kola* are as follows:

- a circular object connected at the centre to a bar, used for making vehicles or parts of machines move[13]
- type of dance in which participants (dancers) form a circle[14]
- to be connected or join on the base of similar characteristics[15]
- name of Croatian literary magazine[16]
- sequence of sport competitions in certain time period[17]
- transport vehicle (car, coaches, animal drawn vehicles)[18]

Using and presenting these examples teacher explained his students what homonyms are and how to find them. In this task students used simple search for querying corpus.

In this task teacher AP has formed exercises about polysemous words. In semantics polysemy occurs when a word form carries more than one meaning.[19] Emphasis in this exercise was put on analysing content in which polysemous word is occurring because surrounding content defines meaning of a word. Word which teacher AP give to his students was *sat* (eng. hour). In Croatian language this word has more than one meaning and the task of students was to find as much as possible different meanings of word *hour* based on corpus search. Student used simple search and from the KWIC view they gone through concordance lines until they found at least three different meaning. They individually and in the groups analyse KWIC view and concordance lines from which they read examples with different meaning of the word. They analyse use of tokens taking into consideration surrounding context in which token was found. After analysing corpus results, they took screenshot of example sentence and put it to their presentation. Figure 80 shows successfully resolved task from one of the students. In this example student has found four different meaning of word *hour.*

First result which is showed on Figure 2 refers to the time measurement (e.g. it is approximately 21 o'clock). Second example which student has find refers to the object (e.g. sat/clock as item/device from which we can see or measure a time). Third example refers to measurement unit (e.g. 120 kilometres per hour). Fifth example refers to police hour, time in which citizens have restricted movement (e.g. all residents from one part of city must me in their houses until 9 pm).

In third task teacher AP asked students to search corpus for words *veselo* (eng. *happily)* and *misleći* (eng. *think*). In Croatian language these words can have a different role as part of speech depending on contexts in which they are used. For example, these words can be used as adverb and adjective in a sentence. Figure 3 shows in which way student resolved task 3. Student

Figure 3. Example of student exercise for task 3

found two different use of word *veselo* and *misleći*, in the first example words are used as adverbs and in the second example they are used as an adjective.

Students used simple search and from the KWIC view they gone through concordance lines until they found different part of speech for given word.

In task 4 (Figure 4) teacher AP asked students to search corpus for sting *-pis-*, this is a root of word which remains the same no matter of affixes (prefixes and suffixes). Based on mentioned string students task was to find different examples of prefixes and suffixes which can be used with this root. For this task students use search query character which allows to search tokens

Figure 4. Example of student exercise for task 4

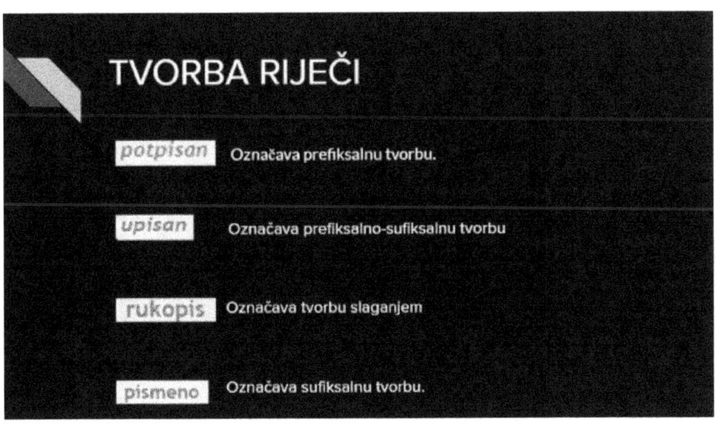

in corpus that have given string of characters no matter where this string is placed in the word (in the middle, beginning or the end of the word). From KWIC view students analysed concordance lines with different prefixes and suffixes which appears with root *-pis-*. Another task for student was to find different word formation based on root *-pis-*.

Figure 4 shows one of the examples of student solution for task 4 where they searched corpus with base *-pis-*. First line shows example of prefixal formation which forms word *potpisan* (eng. *signed*). The second line shows example of prefixal-suffixal formation which forms word *upisan* (eng. *enrolled*). Third line shows word formation based on prefixal-suffixal formation. This example shows word *rukopis* (eng. *manuscript*). The last, forth, line shows example of suffixal formation. The word is *pismeno* (eng. *writing*).

In fifth task teacher gave students exercise about idioms, a group of words in a fixed order that have a particular meaning which is different from the meanings of each word on its own.[20] Another characteristic of idioms is that order of words from which a phrase is composed is always the same. Teacher AP give students three idioms which are characteristic for Croatian language. He did not give them a hole idiom just the first part of the phrase. The task of students was to search for idioms which teacher AP give to them and from search results find whole, complete idiom. After that they conducted analyse of content/context in which idiom appears. Based on analysis they conclude in which context where idioms used and what is their meaning. Students used simple search and from KWIC view and concordance lines they wrote their explanation of idioms they found. The idioms which teacher AP gave to his students are following:

1. kadija te tuži…
2. nešto je trulo…
3. čovjek se veže…

Full phrases of idioms are:

1. Kadija te tuži, kadija ti sudi.
2. Nešto je trulo u državi Danskoj
3. Čovjek se veže za riječ, a vol za rogove.

The meaning of listed idioms:

1. Idiom is used when we want to express our disappointment or dissatisfaction with situation in which there is no justice and outcome of situation is depending on the will of person who has more power in his/hers hands. This idiom is connected with Ottoman Empire where *kadija* was local judge.[21]
2. Idiom taken from William Shakespeare's play Hamlet (eng. *something is rotten in the state of Denmark)* refers to when something is corrupted or wrong.
3. It is Latin idiom (Verbea ligant homines, taurorum cornua funes) and it refers to promises which people make to each other. It means that promise must be fulfilled.

Figure 5. Example 1 of student exercise for task 5

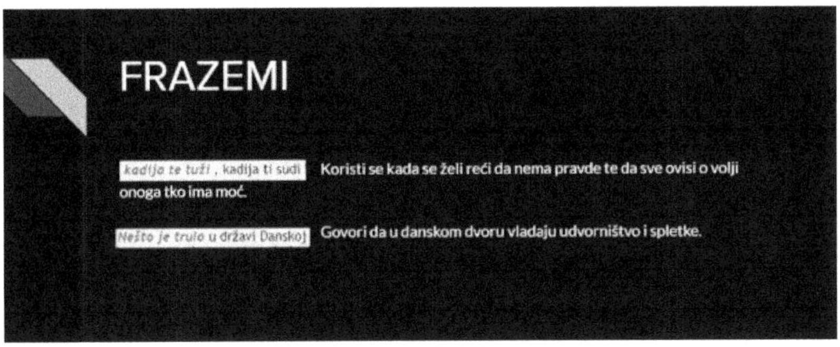

Figure 6. Example 2 of student exercise for task 5

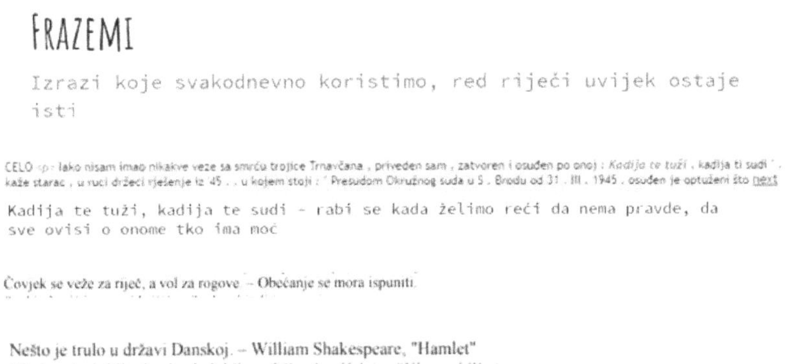

Figure 5 and 6 shows student's examples of corpus search for mentioned idioms with their explanations. All results are correct and students successfully finished their tasks.

Analyse of Students Motivation for Using Computer Corpora in Classroom

Teacher AP used corpora directly in classroom with his students for learning Croatian as first language. He worked with two class groups who are in there last year of primary education. After two classes in which students learn Croatian language with corpora on computers and one class in which students presented their results both classes took online survey in which they expressed their degree of satisfaction with corpus tools used in classroom. Survey consists of 15 questions about age, gender, degree of satisfaction with presented materials, exercise, corpus and self-assessment about the level of their knowledge of Croatian grammar. Complete survey with all included questions can be seen at the end of the book in Appendix B. Analyse of the survey was conducted with program SPSS (Statistical Package for the Social Sciences). In research participated 35 students from two 8th grades (last year of primary educational level), 8A and 8B class groups from which

Figure 7. Gender of students

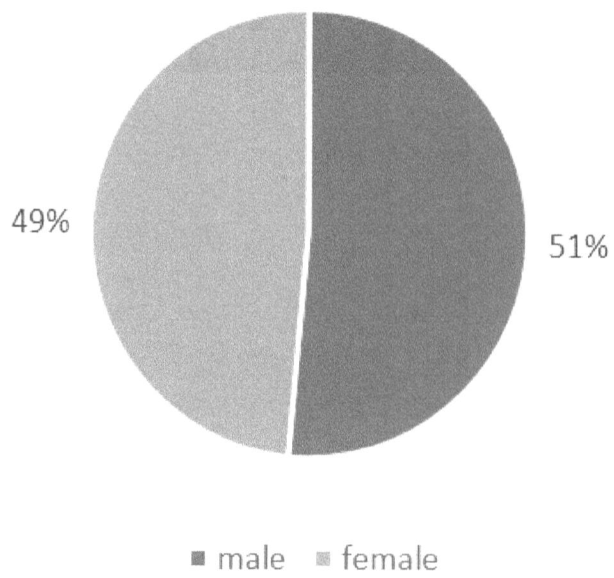

Figure 8. Age of students

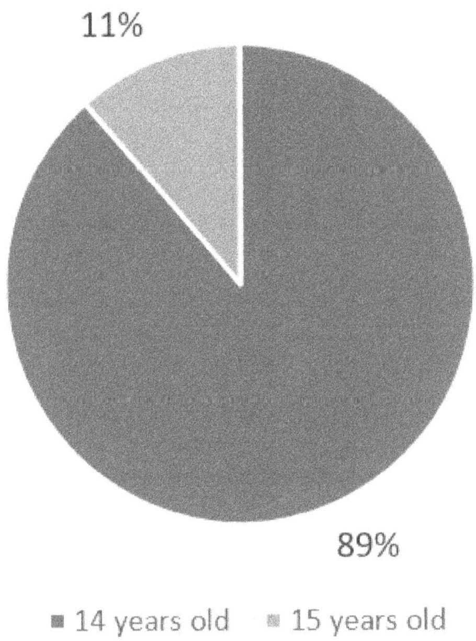

were 51% male students and 49% female students (Figure 7). Majority of students from both classes are 14 years old (89%) and 11% are 15 years old (Figure 8). Students were asked to self-assessed their knowledge of Croatian as first language and majority of students (42,9%) assessed it as very good, 37,1% assessed it as good and 20% of them assessed it as excellent. No one did assess their knowledge of language as bad. This data is corresponding to teacher AP remark in which he claims that in these two classes majority of students are A-Graders.

Students were asked to give their opinion on the matter of increased knowledge of Croatian grammar after held corpus-based lesson in their classroom. Majority of students (85,7%) thinks that lesson increased their grammar knowledge and 14,3% of students thinks it did not.

Overall, students were satisfied with presented materials and curriculum which was corpus-based materials, 54% students were satisfied, 31% were very satisfied, 12% were extremely satisfied and 3% were dissatisfied (Figure 9).

Students were asked to give their assessment about apprehension of presented materials in relation to previous classes where they used traditional teaching methods, e.g. using textbook. Majority of students (89%) understood

Figure 9. Students satisfaction with curriculum

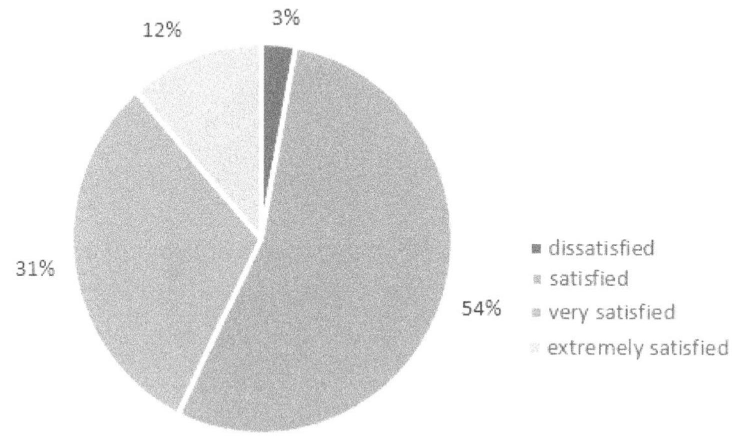

and completely understood presented materials, 3% did not understood it and 8% did not see the difference in relation to previous classes.

Additionally, students think that the method of transferring knowledge in classroom using computer corpora for learning Croatian grammar was excellent and very good (74,1%) and 28,6% students thought the method was good. No one thinks it was a bad teaching method.

Figure 10. Level of apprehension of exercise

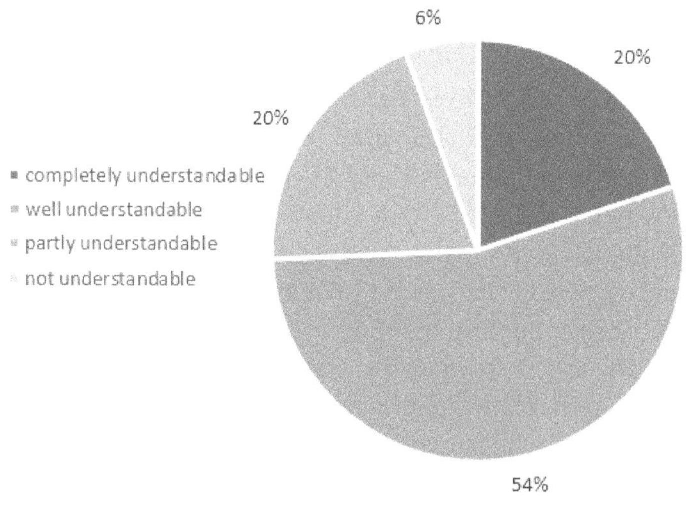

Figure 10 shows level of students' apprehension of corpus-based exercise which teacher AP prepared for them to solve it during the class. For 74% of students exercise was completely or well understandable, 20% of students partly understand exercise and 6% of students did not understand it at all. Majority of involved students understood exercise and solve it without any problems.

Level of satisfaction with corpus-based exercise in their class was high, 29% of students were extremely or very satisfied, 3% were dissatisfied and 68% were satisfied. With their current teaching materials 45% of students are extremely or very satisfied, 52% are satisfied and 3% are dissatisfied.

Comparing these two statements shows the same number of students (3%) are dissatisfied with both corpus and traditional materials. Higher percentage of students (45%) is extremely or very satisfied with traditional materials rather than corpus-based exercise but higher percentage of students (68%) states that they were more satisfied with corpus-based exercise than with traditional ones. Based on this author assumes that student will be open to incorporate this kind of teaching materials and exercise directly into classrooms.

Students opinion about integration of information and technology communication tools like computer programs and applications for learning language and use of internet in classroom is divided. Half of students (57,1%) thinks than integration of internet and applications for learning language will not make their process of learning Croatian language easier but 42,9% students thinks it can help them to master Croatian grammar easier in the classroom.

Figure 11 shows students attitude about best ways to learn Croatian language and grammar in classroom. For 57,1% of students best way for learning Croatian language and grammar is through writing and communication exercise, 42,9% of students thinks that the best way is through listening,

Figure 11. Students opinion about best ways to learn Croatian language and grammar

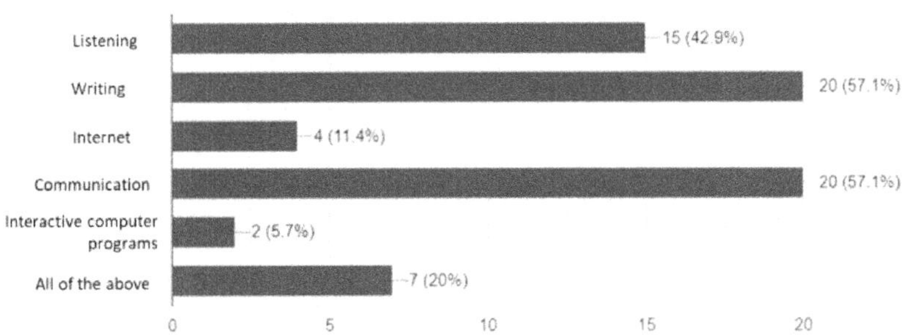

20% of students thinks that the best way to learn language is combination of all listed elements: writing, listening, communication, interactive computer programs and internet. Smaller number of students 11,4% of them thinks that the best way for learning language is through internet and only 5,7% of them thinks that interactive computer programs will help them to better master Croatian language and grammar.

Figure 12 shows results of students' interest in certain topics through which they can learn language in classroom or at home. When learning Croatian language students are most interested in reading articles about actual topics (45,7%) from everyday life in journals, internet, web portals and social networks. Second topic which students choose is reading Croatian literature (37,1%) e.g. books. Another significant data is that 31,4% of students are interested in writing essays when it comes to learning language. Students

Figure 12. List of topics and tasks for learning language

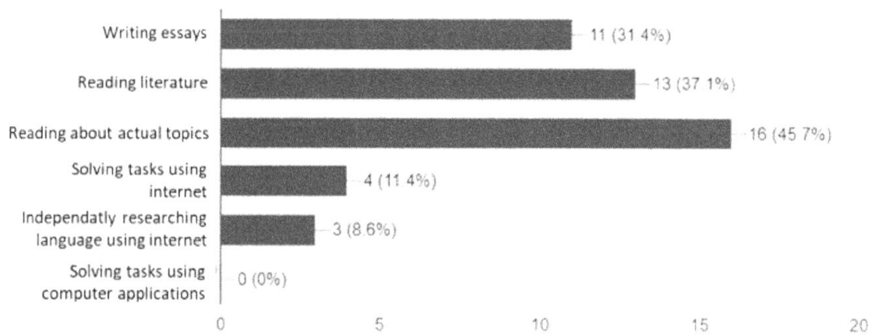

are less interested in solving tasks using internet (11,4%) and individually researching language using internet (8,6%). Interesting data is that none of the students choose solving tasks and language exercise using computer applications.

Most of the students are confident in their capabilities to use individually corpus and its tools for learning Croatian as first language (85,7%) and only 14,3% of students thinks that they cannot use corpus tools independently for learning. Also 60% of students stated that they would like to use corpus again in their classroom for learning Croatian as first language and 40% of students stated they don't want to use it again for learning Croatian language.

It is interested to see that students do not want to use computer applications for learning language and minority of them (8,6%) wants to use internet for individual language research but still majority of students (60%) would use again corpus for learning language. Result of this research maybe lies in fact that students did not completely understood what corpus tools are and because they used it in just two classes. Also, second fact is correlated to short period of time which teacher AP had to introduce corpus to his students. Research results could be different if students used corpus for longer period, e.g. one school semester or a whole year. In that chase we could tested their results and have had different data. It is important to emphasise that this survey analyse students degree of satisfaction and motivation to use new computer tool, corpus tool for learning Croatian language. The conclusion of this part of research is that students which are at their last year of primary school education are motivated and interested in using computer corpora for learning Croatian language. They are capable independently use corpus tools with initial guidance by teacher. Also, there is possibility of including corpus and its tool directly into the classrooms not just for preparing teaching materials which teacher AP had proved within this research.

Teacher's AP experience working with corpora

Teacher AP never has worked with computer corpora before participating in this research. He on his own (individually) search corpus and get familiar with it. For his lesson preparation, teaching materials development and class organization he used hrWaC and HNK Croatian corpora. He has prepared the teaching unit about word formation and idioms. It was in a form of repetition. Student have already learned about the topic in previous classes. Teacher AP emphasis that corpus-based teaching has many advantages for teachers and for students. He states:

Advantages of developing teaching materials and exercise using computer corpora are in possibilities which they offer to teachers and students, for example: providing a better opportunity for collaborative work, possibility of adapting language content / curriculum, accurate view of language facts, increased motivation for learning with students, possibility to combine digital and language skills in learning process. Use of corpus and corpus tools emphasis focus to the individual/student supported with teacher mentoring. I would also like to point out that it provides various opportunities for adapting teaching process and work with children with disabilities and provides the possibility of extending tasks for children with special needs. (Teacher AP, 2019)

In his reflection on held class where he used corpora with students he points out that the disadvantages of developing teaching materials and exercise using computer corpora are exclusively technical nature. Technical conditions need to be fulfilled before the integration of corpus tools into direct teaching with students. Lack of technical equipment is a major obstacle and the possibility of using only one computer classroom in the school where students can work on computers during the classes is a big problem.

Teacher AP is satisfied with the possibilities which this type of teaching provides, especially for teaching units dealing with the word formation, morphology and syntax in the Croatian language. Also, it is positive that language units can be analysed on authentic texts and on texts which belongs to different functional styles in Croatian language.

He would repeat this type of teaching because modern type of teaching requires the use of different methodological approaches and contributes to the modernization and diversity of the teaching process. He wouldn't change anything just expand the use of the corpus to other language content and material.

Teacher AP states:

I will use corpora and corpus tools again because they have proved as effective and useful in the teaching process. The current changes in the curriculum at the national level in Croatia presupposes the introduction of digital content in teaching and I see computer corpora as one of the information and communication tools which can help to motivate and improve quality of students learning process in language teaching. (Teacher AP, 2019)

Regard to the search methods which NoSketch Engine offers, teacher AP has used simple, lemma, phrase, character and word search type for his preparation. His students in the class have used simple, phrase, character and word search type. Teacher AP and his students did not use CQL query because teacher AP did not feel confident enough to use it because of the lack of knowledge how to correctly compose query. Also, he thought that this type of search is too advanced for students who are for the first time encountering with computer corpora and corpus tools. He states:

Simple types of search have worked great (like simple, lemma, phrase, character and word), but I did not use more complex or advanced search types (such as CQL queries) due to insufficient knowledge of how they work. Also, students are not sufficiently trained for a more demanding tasks which include search of the corpus. They have for the first time use corpora and they needed teachers (my) assistance. If students and teachers were more educated about the whole process of using and searching the corpora, I would use them in everyday teaching with the students. (Teacher AP, 2019)

He hadn't had any problems during the preparation of materials nor in the classroom. Everything was done well because of good planning and relative simplicity of the process. Due to that the objectives for the teaching unit have been fully carried out. He did not depart from his curriculum, only in the sense of the subject approach. All segments of teaching and using corpora in the classroom worked just fine. He wouldn't change anything in his teaching unit with corpora because he has include all segments of language unite and managed to finished all tasks with his students during the class.

Additionally, teacher AP thinks that the students were satisfied with class and that corpus-based approach helped them to understand learning materials and teaching unit, improving their systematization of the learned material which is abstract to them.

In relation to the traditional teaching approach which includes using textbooks and grammars in the classroom teacher AP point out that students were more motivated for learning and that corpus tools help them to better understand materials. He states:

Students have much better understood and comprehend language unit by using corpus approach rather than traditional approach (which implies the use of textbooks, grammar and workbooks) because of vivid illustration of the procedure and the method. (Teacher AP, 2019)

Regarding corpus methodology teacher AP has positive attitude and he thinks it can be easily incorporated into learning process of Croatan language in primary schools. His opinion about it is:

Corpus methodology can help meet the needs of language learning in different levels of teaching, for example it can be used as a data source for developing exercise and teaching content, as a language template for analysing texts from different perspectives, examining language facts in different contexts, for linguistic and sociolinguistic reflections, for the research of language conventions, etc. (Teacher AP, 2019)

During this research teacher AP has used only concordance, KWIC and frequency list because of insufficient knowledge of corpus tools and analysis offered by corpus. Additionally, he states that these corpus tools have simple and clear presentation of corpus results and are not problematic for primary school students. This is very important, especially for students and teachers who are for the first-time encountering corpus tools. Advanced search methods he did not use because he was not well informed about them.

He would like to learn more about advanced corpus search methods and analysis and how it can be used for teaching purpose. He points out:

If I would have opportunity for additional education or training about the use of corpus tools, I would certainly use other available tools, methods of analysis and search. (Teacher AP, 2019)

His prediction for corpus-based learning approach is bright and he will use them again with all of his students. He points out:

In the future, I think corpus-based language teaching will be used more often because of the recommendation in the national curriculum, but the recommendation for now applies only to secondary schools, while there is still no national recommendation for primary schools. But I think that it can be used in primary schools because primary school language learning materials represents the overall section of the grammar of the Croatian language, which is only slightly expanded in secondary school. (Teacher AP, 2019)

Preparation of class or teaching materials using corpus tools in comparison to traditional preparation with textbooks and manuals is more demanding and requires more detailed planning, it implies giving clear and unambiguous instructions to students how and what to do inside corpus. It implies more work and preparation by teacher because teachers do not have the teaching materials which they could use to implement this teaching method. It is missing simple manual for using corpus tools. Teacher AP concludes his remarks about process of preparation with thoughts:

If I had more knowledge and if I continued using the corpora to prepare the lessons then preparation would be faster. (Teacher AP, 2019)

Teacher AP believe that computer corpora can be included into direct classes with students from 5th to 8th grade (high levels of primary school). According to him limitations are only of a technical nature and insufficient or non-existent education of the teachers. On the other hand, he states that the advantages of using corpus in direct teaching with students provide teacher with the ability to use the method for preparing project teaching tasks and developing students' competencies which implies a critical component. He points out that corpus-based approach is suitable for a collaborative learning approach but also corpora and corpus tools can also be easily used for teaching literature and creativity, language and communication, culture and media. It can be applied in all categories of Croatian language subject in primary schools. He see the great use and purpose for teaching grammar and language analysis.

Teacher AP successfully implemented corpora and corpus tools into curriculum of primary school for learning Croatian as first language. His experience and experience of his students were positive and motivated. It is remarkable fact that teacher and students for the first time used corpus and its tools for language learning and that there were no problems, no resistance, no frustrations and no negative comments and thoughts about whole process. Use of computer corpora had positive impact on teacher's cognitive process about teaching Croatian language, it has opened up new teaching methods and tools for refreshing his teaching skills and upgrade the level of motivation for students. Based on his experience with corpora and corpus tools in classroom and outside of it, author can conclude that corpus-based approach can be implemented into regular process of teaching Croatian language in primary schools.

CASE 2: USING COMPUTER CORPORA FOR TEACHING ENGLISH AS SECOND LANGUAGE IN PRIMARY SCHOOL

General Background Information About Teacher BP

Teacher BP is teaching English as second language in primary school as well in secondary school. He studied English language at Faculty of Humanities and Social Sciences in Zagreb, University of Zagreb. During the study years he knew he would work as teacher of English language. He has been working in this profession for five years and he mostly teaches English in primary school, but he had worked in secondary school as well. He states that working in secondary school is more demanding, the materials are at a much higher level and in vocational schools mostly have disciplinary problems.

His advantages as teacher of English language are authoritative attitude, toughness and strictness as well as clear instructions and goals towards the students, which they can appreciate. On the other hand, empathy and understanding, individual approach to students and a dynamic teaching style. He prefers topics familiar to the students, because then their motivation is high. Also, he stats that youth, approach, communication, empathy, discipline, professionalism, consistency are his strengths in teaching and working with students and the biggest challenge in teaching is to rise motivation of students for learning and comprehending English language.

About working with different grade levels and different age students he states following:

The worst thing for a teacher is to struggle with a boring and inapproachable topic. I have taught all eight grades of grade school, first and third grades of high school and grown up speakers. I like 7th and 8th graders the most and first graders the least, because it is more kindergarten than class. (Teacher BP, 2019)

As source of frustration in his work teacher BP states that he is dissatisfied with teacher salaries and work conditions, lack of understanding from the principals, poor textbooks, unnecessary bureaucracy that no one reads because it is done just for satisfying form without purpose or use, many colleagues who after a number of years become fachidiots and cannot see further than their own subjects.

Teacher BP describes his view how teaching process of English language should look like:

English language has a steady position as the most important foreign language, and it will stay that way. As much as we like to say that our teaching is flawed, it is still above average concerning other countries. If you meet an Italian, German or a French, they will probably know English less than an average Croatian and that tells a lot about our approach. There is always room for improvement but there are a lot of teachers here doing a very good job. In the learning process I would remove the emphasis from grammar to creative writing and language use. The problem with children is that they use language too one-dimensional. Better students listen to it online and the worst ones study the rules without understanding them. Neither of these methods are best. Language needs to be converted from passive to active, from listening to speaking and writing. (Teacher BP, 2019)

The most effective ways to teach English language in primary school teacher BP see in working on a relevant, interesting and interactive texts. He states this is the base of foreign language teaching. Also, he thinks that texts which students read must cover various themes. Only, he would shorten the texts because students often get everything served on a platter with teacher's command "learn it". He thinks that the best way to encourage active use of language is to give students only half of a text and let them finish it, analyse it and use the language.

Strengths and Challenges In Teaching For Teacher BP

His teaching process and relation with students describes as dynamic because he tries to "get out" of textbook materials as often as possible and give his students broader picture of content. Atmosphere in is classroom is relaxed because he often jokes with his students because he believes that a relaxed (not too relaxed tough) atmosphere is a good base for active communication and it can reduce the fear of a foreign language at students.

The most important need in teaching process and working in classroom with students for teacher BP are active students and good teaching material. His thoughts about teaching materials used in his school in school year 2018/2019 are:

At this moment I am working with very bad textbooks and I have worked with better ones previously, it is like driving a Fiat after a Mercedes. (Teacher BP, 2019)

Teacher BP is open to try new teaching methods and approaches but the thinks it sold be critical in choosing the right one for himself. His thoughts about integration of new teaching methods and approaches in teaching English language in primary school are summarized in the following way:

One must not blindly follow all of the new approaches but try them and test them. If it works, great. If not, toss it aside. No method is perfect, that is why there are so many them. For example, playing in the classroom, for a long time the experts have been saying this is the best method, especially for younger pupils. But I have found it goes either way. Pupils have fun while they play and speak English, but they remember little outside of that activity, which means that activity is it's own purpose without a lot of pedagogic use, at least in my experience. (Teacher BP, 2019)

Teacher BP thinks that use of technology has a significant and big role in today's educational system. He states that in education like in anywhere else we should have boundaries and recognize quality of presented materials, programs and ICT tools. Use of technology in education especially teaching language subjects without question can provide new forms, activities and new dimensions for learning where multifunctionality can unlock hidden potential in students.

Teacher's BP Knowledge and Attitudes Towards Corpus Linguistics And Computer Corpora

Teacher BP knows what corpus linguistic is because he used corpus as a student at the university as part of computer linguistics class where we used Croatian corpora in order to analyse certain language segments and based on analysis produce statistics. He has also used COHA corpus for writing his master's degree thesis. The first thing that come to his mind when talking about corpus linguistics are scientific researches based on use of corpora, discourse analysis, targeted term searching with goal of getting insight into certain hypothesis and analyse of search results as base for confirming or disconfirming certain hypothesis. It is interesting that teacher BP had subject from corpus linguistics during his study and he knows what corpus is, but he isn't familiar with any corpus tools. He thinks that role of corpus tools is to provide a deeper understanding of language, synonyms, context, grammar, discourse, style, changes in language etc. Because he has experience with searching corpora and analysing corpus results, he thinks that results of corpus search are well presented, and he does not see any problems with interpretation.

Teacher BP thinks that the method of using corpus in class is completely marginalized some extra training would be enough in a form of a workshops.

Teacher BP conclude his thoughts about use of corpora and corpus tools in learning English language with remark that he for the time being, do not have the need for corpus use in his classes but he states that:

Corpus could be useful for finding new examples for learning vocabulary, but it would not be my first choice for the search. There are millions of good materials online, with already prepared lessons and good examples. That is why I think it is not necessary for primary school to go deeper into the semantics and examples, the subject matter is hard enough as it is. (Teacher BP, 2019)

Teacher's BP Attitudes About Integration of Computer Corpora Into Primary School Curriculum

Integration of corpus tools in primary level education by the opinion of teacher BP hasn't bright future because of teacher's resistance. He states:

Sincerely, I haven't thought about it because I think corpus analyse is a higher degree of research so I don't see it would have a direct use in classroom. Knowing my colleagues and seeing how even the smallest changes cause fear, overwork, and rejection, I am almost certain that the majority would have a negative reaction to this proposal. (Teacher BP, 2019)

Additionally, he states if corpus tools would be integrated into curriculum of language subjects at the beginning only teachers could use them. Students on the other hand could use them in classroom after teacher's detailed explanation to the students how it works.

Advantages and use of corpus should be clearly explained to students. If they understood it and accepted it then corpus tools and corpora could provide students with a new dimension of language analyse and they might accept it. Teacher BP also reflects on his experience as teacher in primary school and states:

Then again, speaking from experience students accept new things with disapproval because as much as we tell them something is useful, to them it's hard and boring and they cannot see direct usefulness of integrating new teaching methods or tools in classroom. (Teacher BP, 2019)

In schools year 2018/2019 he teaches 1st, 4th, 5th and 8th grade in primary school. Learning objectives are different and adjusted to age and prior knowledge of students. They are defined beforehand, but teacher can choose and modify them by certain level. He thinks the most important objective is written knowledge of language. To him it is more important that a student writes essay better then he solves a task about conditional tense. The reason for this, he states, is because use of language in its natural purpose is one thing and assigned content that needs to be learned is another, foreign language cannot be learned only by learning the rules but using different forms of learning. Currently he is teaching 7th grade students and his class group is heterogenous, it has male and female students. Their interest and dedication to English class is individual, so he has students who are highly motivated and the ones who have contact with the English language through internet and video games. Students learn to speak English easier than they learn spelling and grammar. He hasn't been working so long that he could compare different generations and their level of motivation and success in learning English language.

There are certain problems and challenges regarding the teaching materials for learning English in primary school. Teacher BP thinks textbooks are low quality, he would change publisher of textbooks. He often on his own finds online materials which are more helpful to him then official literature. There are always some students which are problematic in classroom but in isn't nothing that cannot be worked out. Motivation and student activity in classroom could always be better, especially with students who have problems with learning. Classes are very different concerning the level of activity, some are inactive, others very active.

Teacher BP has experience with use of corpora and corpus tools because of his formal education at University of Zagreb where he had corpus linguistics and it is familiar with it. Due to lack of time he did not prepare teaching unit nor use computer corpora during this research. His attitude towards using computer corpora in primary school is somewhat neutral because he thinks that corpora can be used for conducting linguistic researches or language analysis in higher education, e.g. universities, language institutes, etc. Corpus-based approach according to teacher BP can be integrated into learning English language in primary school but he is concern that other teachers would not be supportive to that idea and that this filed is too hard for primary level students.

REFERENCES

Cambridge Dictionary. (n.d.). Available at: https://dictionary.cambridge.org/dictionary/english/

Croatian National Educational Standard. (n.d.). Available on: http://hud.hr/wp-content/uploads/sites/168/2014/11/vodic-kroz-hnos.pdf

Education and teacher training agency in Croatia. (n.d.). Available on: https://www.azoo.hr/images/AZOO/Ravnatelji/RM/Hrvatski_obrazovni_sustav.pdf

Hrvatski jezični portal. (n.d.). Available at: http://hjp.znanje.hr/

Lexico dictory. (n.d.). Available on: https://www.lexico.com/en/definition/synonym

Proleksis enciklopedija online, Leksikografski zavod Miroslav Krleža. (n.d.). Available at: http://proleksis.lzmk.hr/29580/

ENDNOTES

1 Official website of Education and teacher training agency in Croatia: https://www.azoo.hr/

2 Document is available on: https://www.azoo.hr/images/AZOO/Ravnatelji/RM/Hrvatski_obrazovni_sustav.pdf

3 Erasmus+ is the EU's programme to support education, training, youth and sport in Europe. The aim of Erasmus+ is to contribute to the Europe 2020 strategy for growth, jobs, social equity and inclusion, as well as the aims of ET2020, the EU's strategic framework for education and training. Erasmus+ also aims to promote the sustainable development of its partners in the field of higher education, and contribute to achieving the objectives of the EU Youth Strategy. Detailed description is available on: https://ec.europa.eu/programmes/erasmus-plus/about_en

4 Croatian National Educational Standard - The standard refers to a holistic approach to the educational process and includes the aimes of education,

educational content, suggestions of teaching methods, expected learning outcomes and teaching environments. It is available on: http://hud.hr/wp-content/uploads/sites/168/2014/11/vodic-kroz-hnos.pdf

5 Based on Oxford dictionary synonym is a word or phrase that means exactly or nearly the same as another word or phrase in the same language, for example shut is a synonym of close. Definition is available on: https://www.lexico.com/en/definition/synonym

6 https://dictionary.cambridge.org/dictionary/english/bar-code?q=barcode

7 https://dictionary.cambridge.org/dictionary/english/computer

8 https://dictionary.cambridge.org/dictionary/english/educational

9 https://dictionary.cambridge.org/dictionary/english/laptop

10 https://dictionary.cambridge.org/dictionary/english/event

11 https://dictionary.cambridge.org/dictionary/english/experiment

12 https://dictionary.cambridge.org/dictionary/english/screen

13 https://dictionary.cambridge.org/dictionary/english/wheel

14 http://hjp.znanje.hr

15 http://hjp.znanje.hr

16 http://hjp.znanje.hr

17 http://hjp.znanje.hr

18 http://hjp.znanje.hr

19 https://dictionary.cambridge.org/dictionary/english/polysemy

20 https://dictionary.cambridge.org/dictionary/english/idiom

21 http://proleksis.lzmk.hr/29580/

Chapter 6
Using Computer Corpora in Secondary School

ABSTRACT

This chapter will provide information and data about secondary schools and its teachers. The chapter will show in-depth interviews with teachers from secondary schools. The purpose of the in-depth interview is to research teacher needs, opinions, attitudes, values, and knowledge about computer corpora in general. The second goal is to explore in which way teachers in secondary schools would use computer corpora for creating teaching materials, exams, or language exercise. The aim of this chapter is to investigate if computer corpora can be implemented in secondary schools for teaching language subjects and in which way and for what students/grade it would be most eligible.

USING COMPUTER CORPORA IN SECONDARY SCHOOLS

This chapter will provide detailed information about use of computer corpora in secondary education level for creating educational materials for students from age 15 to 19[1]. In research participated two teachers, one teacher teaches Croatian as first language and other teaches English and German as second language. Teachers did not use computer corpora in their line of work, and they did not search them before this research was conducted. During this research they were introduced with available corpora through user interface NoSketch Engine where they search, and filter concordance lines based on

DOI: 10.4018/978-1-7998-3680-3.ch006

their quires. One teacher used British Web Corpus (ukWaC), German Web Corpus (deWaC), EU DGT-UD: German, EU DGT-UD: English and SkELL for research purpose while second teacher did not used any corpora. Secondary school in Croatia lasts for maximum of 4 years and there are different types of secondary schools. This research was conducted with two teachers who are working with students in secondary schools and their students age is approximately between 15 and 19 years.

Identity of the involved teachers will be protected, and they will remain anonymous. When describing their thoughts, citations and all relevant materials they will be referred as teacher AS and teacher BS. Teacher AS teaches Croatian as first language in secondary school Bedekovčina in Bedekovčina (place near Zagreb) and teacher BP teaches English and German as second language in secondary school Ugostiteljsko-turistička school (School for Tourism and Hospitality) in city Osijek. This chapter is divided into two main section, first section is named Case 1 and refers to teacher's AS experience and attitudes about computer corpora, attitudes toward teaching process, working in secondary school, students' attitude and motivation for learning Croatian language and using computer corpora in classroom, corpus linguistics, etc. Teacher AS is working in secondary school where teaching activities are conducted through three different courses: agricultural school, medical school and architecture/construction school. This school has three- and four-year programs. Teacher AS participated just in the in-depth interview, he did not develop corpus-based teaching materials for his students and did not introduced corpora to the students. But his contribution to this research is also valuable because of the insight to teachers attitudes and motivation for incorporating new teaching methodology and tools into the process of learning English language in secondary schools.

Second section is named Case 2 and refers to teacher's BS experience working with computer corpora, experience and attitudes about computer corpora, teaching process, working in secondary school, students' attitude and motivation for learning English and German language, corpus linguistics, etc. It is important to mention that teacher BS worked with computer corpora during this research. She prepared teaching unit using British and German corpora for her students. Because of the lack of time and insufficient equipment of classrooms she did not introduced computer corpora to her students. But she gave valuable information about preparation process of teaching materials for learning English and German language in secondary schools. This school has three- and four-year programs. Three-year program includes following professions: waiters, chefs and confectioners. Four-year program includes following professions: sales manager for tourism and hotels and technician for tourism and hotels.

Research was conducted through in-depth interviews with involved teachers in second half of school year 2018/2019. Structure of questions for conducting in-depth interviews was taken form doctoral theses of John D. Bunting from 2013 by the name An Investigation of Language Teachers' Explorations of the Use of Corpus Tools in the English for Academic Purposes (EAP) Class at Georgia State University. Questions from aforementioned dissertation were altered so they correspond to target group of participants and topic of this research. All questions which were included in the in-depth interviews can be seen at the end of the book in separate section named Appendix A.

CASE 1: USING COMPUTER CORPORA FOR TEACHING CROATIAN AS FIRST LANGUAGE IN SECONDARY SCHOOL

General Background Information About Teacher AS

Teacher AS is professor of Croatian as first language in secondary school where he works with students age 14 to 19. Before this research he had heard about corpora but did not use them for preparing teaching materials nor in classroom. It has to be pointed out that teacher AS did not use or prepare teaching materials based on corpus search for his students during this research due to tight teaching schedule and lack of time, he just gave his opinion about corpus linguistics and computer corpora in a field of secondary education. Teacher AS has master's degree in Croatistics at the Faculty of Humanities and Social Sciences of the University of Zagreb. He states that he become teacher of Croatian language because he loves to read books and that he is not a fan of STEAM (Science, Technology, Engineering, Arts and Mathematics) subjects. Last 19 years he works as teacher of Croatian as first language. In this time, he worked also in primary education. His first year of teaching he spent at a primary school. Main difference between primary and secondary school for teacher AS is:

I believe working in an elementary school is more challenging and stressful because of the emphasis on the pedagogic component of work. The students need to be guided through grade school education and the basis of language needs to be established with them. (Teacher AS, 2019)

In his teaching experience he worked with 7th and 8th grade classes in primary school and in secondary school with all grades (three- and four-year programs), where he held lessons for vocabulary and grammar.

As his strengths in teaching and working with students he emphasis that he does his best to teach the children something new, help them with what they don't know and prepare them for what comes next after they've finished school. He is also completely dedicated to preparation for class and teaching and in this process, he always tries to make the subject matter interesting for the students so they can see the usefulness of what they do, practice and learn.

Also, he sees his language teaching approach in a certain way and he states:

It should be connected with real and everyday situations, one should show the importance of language in everyday life. Metalinguistic learning should be discarded to gain motivation and make language learning interesting. I try to implement it to everyday situations. I use many examples and repetitions. (Teacher AS, 2019)

He thinks that Croatian school system is full of frustrations, from needles and complicated administration to other colleague's lack of understanding, unmotivated students and teachers as well as inadequate working environment. This is useful insight into teacher's perspective and level of motivation in his workplace and one of the reason way teachers do have time for exploring different tools. Level of frustration do not motivates teacher to incorporate for example computer corpora because they are overwhelmed with their obligations.

His teaching needs are related to availability of different texts that are teachable, with meaningful and appropriate context for students of different ages. Teacher AS thinks that integration of new teaching methodologies and approaches in teaching language subjects would be useful if there would be proof of their usefulness in everyday situations and if they will get students interested and motivated to learn more. As for the role of technology in teaching language subjects, in his case Croatian language, he states that technology can be a useful tool for teaching a language, but it cannot replace direct communication which is very important in language learning either first or second languages.

Teacher's AS Knowledge and Attitudes Towards Corpus Linguistics and Computer Corpora

Teacher AS is familiar with term corpus linguistics and he states that corpus linguistics researches appearance and frequency of words in large language databases which consist of large amount of texts. He states that teachers rarely or never encounter corpus linguistics in their work, and he thinks it is maybe similar to teaching lexicography, but it is not mentioned in that context at all. Although he knows about corpus linguistics and corpora he isn't familiar with corpus tools and he did not used and worked with any of them. For corpus tools teacher AS think that they could be useful for teaching frequency of words. Educating language teachers about use of corpus tools is first step to use it in their work. Teacher AS thinks that an additional education would be enough for teachers to learn about what they are, where they can find them and how to use them especially if that education would include examples of good practise in teaching language subjects in classroom with students. He thinks that integration of corpus tool and changes which accompanied that integration would cause a negative reaction among teachers but with good structure of education workshops and a lot of examples of use and implementation in classroom would have benefits. He thinks that it's all about utility. Corpus tools could be implemented in class if they would be presented in an interesting way and with clearly explained usage in everyday speaking practice. Also, he states that corpus tools could be used for studying the frequency of words and syntagma appearance, for example phraseme or rhyme. Additionally, he thinks it could be used for teaching some parts of lexicography with students who are in higher classes in secondary schools. Before he would get into searching and using corpus tools for creating corpus materials for his students or in his classroom with direct corpus approach, he thinks it would be interesting to see examples of corpus tools use in class.

Outcomes and Challenges in Teaching Croatian as First Language

The teaching outcomes are defined by the Croatian language curriculum which is determined by the Croatian Ministry of Education, Sports and Science. The most important outcomes are those connected with concrete assignments and real-life situations. Assignments which students worked with must be associated with situations that students face or could face in their everyday lives, that is why the activities need to be as various as possible. Evaluation, on the other hand, is determined beforehand based on what we want the students to do or practice and we use summative and formative evaluation (grades are from 1 to 5 where 1 is F and 5 is A).

In this school year (2018/2019) he had mixed student groups, female and male aged fifteen to eighteen. His thought about his students are following:

Not a lot can interest them these days due to lack of concentration. Most of them put in the least amount of dedication to class and studies and are satisfied with barely a pass. Learning is also connected with that: they adopt only the things that are interesting for them at that moment. It has nothing to do with what is necessary for them to learn. (Teacher AS, 2019)

The biggest challenge in working with his students in secondary education is getting today's generations interested in school and studies as well as trying to pass on to them all the useful knowledge they will need in life. There are different challenges when it comes to working as language teacher in secondary schools and all depends on the situation, different needs, knowing the students, simplicity of presentation, gravity of the subject matter, high demands put on teachers and the appeal of what is being learned.

CASE 2: USING COMPUTER CORPORA FOR TEACHING ENGLISH AND GERMAN AS SECOND LANGUAGE IN SECONDARY SCHOOL

General Background Information About Teacher BS

Teacher BS is professor of English and German as second language in secondary school Ugostiteljsko-turistička school in Osijek and she works with students age 14 to 19. She works with all grades in secondary school, but in this research she prepared learning materials for first and second year of secondary school.

Teacher BS has a master's degree in English and German Language and Literature for translator at Faculty of Philosophy in Osijek where she later passed additional exams from pedagogical and psychological field so she could work in primary and secondary school. She works in the teaching profession for 9 years. Before this job as an English and German teacher in secondary school she worked also in primary school.

Teacher BS believe that she is good in process of transferring knowledge to her students and she manages to establish a good communication with them. She likes to teach grammar and provides help to the students so that they can learn it easier. So far, she has been teaching all grades of primary and secondary school. But mostly she likes to work with higher grades of secondary school and adults because she also works as a lecturer of foreign languages in a school for learning foreign languages.

Source of teacher BS frustrations in her everyday work in secondary school is mostly connected to the administration process and student's behaviour and attitudes toward school, learning and professors. She states:

Main thing which frustrates me is about administration and paperwork, because it is all about appearance and what looks good on paper, it doesn't have anything to do with a real situation. Second source of frustration is about the attitude of students towards school, professors and education in general. I believe that teachers should be better educated to deal with aggressive and frustrated students. (Teacher BS, 2019)

Teacher BS attitudes about teaching English and German language in secondary school is following:

I believe that process of teaching English language in secondary schools is well designed both in theory and practice and that students generally respond positively to teaching and learning. German language on the other hand is harder to teach due to the low pre knowledge of students, too little contact with language in everyday life and the dislike of students for language. (Teacher BS, 2019)

She thinks that teaching process of learning English and German language as foreign languages in secondary schools should consist of equal representation of listening and reading with comprehension, speaking and writing exercise. Additionally, students should be more involved in the teaching process.

Teacher BS needs in teaching process are focused on student's behaviour during the language class. She would like for students to regularly bring their textbooks, notebooks and workbooks to the teaching class and to have more serios approach to learning materials. Also, teacher BS emphasis that availability of the computer and projector during the class would help greatly in the teaching process. Her teaching approach is combination of frontal, group and collaborative work.

Teacher BS opinion about integration of new teaching methods and approaches in teaching process of English and German language as secondary language is positive, but she points out that they must be previously educated about the changes and must be provided with demonstration how to successfully integrate these methods into the teaching process. Regarding the role of information and communication technologies in teaching language subject especially English and German language she has positive attitude and states it can make learning more fun and interesting for students and it can motivate them to learn more.

Teacher's BS Knowledge and Attitudes Towards Corpus Linguistics and Computer Corpora

Teacher BS is not familiar with the term corpus linguistics and the first thing which come to her mind is technology and computers. She didn't have any experience with corpulent linguistics until this research and she did not use any of corpus tools during her study, in classroom, for research or preparation of teaching materials. After initial explanation what corpora and corpus tools are, she formed attitude and opinion about it. For role of corpus tools in teaching English and German language she states that they could me interesting for students to use them in learning process because it provides them with context in which situations can some words appear. Also, she points out they are good for learning collocations in language.

Teacher's BS Attitudes About Integration of Computer Corpora Into Secondary School Curriculum

She thinks that teachers are not enough or at all familiar with corpus tools, and how and when they can be used or why they could be useful to them for teaching language subjects. Attitude of her school about integration and use of corpus tools in classroom is neutral, she states if administration would see need and usefulness of corpus tools in teaching process, they would integrated them in regular curriculum with condition they are free to use or not to expensive.

Teacher's Attitudes About Process of Educating Teachers About Using Computer Corpora

Teacher BS thinks that education is a form of workshops would not be enough for teachers to learn how to use corpus tool in education and that it should be integrated into the formal education of teachers at universities.

She points out that changes would not be welcomed among teachers in her school which would cause interaction of new teaching methods and tools. She states:

I think that only a small group of the teachers would welcome the integration of corpus tools in teaching process, while most of them would consider this to be a burden because of small amount of hours they have with students and a large volume of material they need to go through. Older teachers would not welcome it with open arms because most of them are not sufficiently IT literate or do not like changes. (Teacher BS, 2019)

About the motivation of students for using computer corpora and corpus tools for learning and in the classroom teacher BS points out that the biggest problem whit her students and colleges is motivation factor, she fears that, nor students nor teachers are motivated enough for this:

I think teachers could use corpus tool in the classroom only if they present the corpus results to the students because the schools are still not equipped with computers for students. I also think that the use of corpus tools in a classroom with students would take to much time from class, and the students are not motivated enough to do it alone at home. Because of this discouragement and unmotivating of students, the great number of teachers would also be unmotivated to use it. (Teacher BS, 2019)

Description of Class Groups and Learning Outcomes for Prepared Teaching Unit Using Corpora

Learning outcome for this school year for teacher BS are following: students can distinguish and apply linguistic legality and vocabulary for developing language skills at the appropriate level to achieve written and oral communication; distinguish details and specific information from the text; identify the main thoughts from talking about familiar topics they regularly encountered in school and in their spare time; translate simple meal recipes; communicate in simple situations; connect sentences to describe events and their experiences or to express their opinions; recognize the similarities and differences between the culture of the country in which they live and the country of the target language (language which they are learning); to perceive the need for tolerant behaviour with people from other cultures; to achieve communication and cooperation with different people and groups in well-known conditions while respecting diversity and multiculturalism.

In teacher BS school the outcomes are partially determined by the curriculum, and partially compiled by board of foreign languages in her school.

In her opinion, the most important thing is for students to learn to communicate in everyday situations.

The structure of students is heterogenic in teacher BS school and depends on the directions which student is attending (e.g. waiter, chef, confectioner, tourist-hotelier and hotel-tourist technician). Some directions have larger number of male students, like waiters, and other directions have larger amount of female students like confectioners. In other directions, there are almost the same number of male and female students. Interest of students are different, but a large number of students do not see the importance of language for their profession even though their languages are very important for their future jobs. Students interest for language learning is getting smaller and smaller from generation to generation.

Strengths and Challenges in Teaching for Teacher BS

Teacher BS advantages in teaching English and German language are establishing good communication with her students and clarifying the grammatical structures for students in an understandable way for them. The biggest challenge in teaching and working with students for teacher BS is how to motivate students to do more, learn more and how to spark their interest in learning language, especially German language.

Issue and problems in her line of work are connected with available teaching materials and students attitude towards teachers, learning and school in general. She states:

Some of the teaching materials for German language we currently use are outdated and the topics are not close or connected to students' interests. It would be of great help if there were more interactive online exercises and tests to accompany the textbook. (Teacher BS, 2019)

Lack of students' motivation for learning teacher BS see in overload of students with large number of hours they must spent in school/classrooms, with comprehensive curriculum and learning materials which they must overcome and learn and with practical education. She summed it up:

Students are overloaded with a number of hours a day which they must spend in school, curriculum, and practical instruction, so it is difficult to motivate them to solve their homework and learn at home. It is often the case that students do not work and do not learn anything at home, so teachers have to do their best to remember the lesson in the classroom. (Teacher BS, 2019)

Preview of Corpus-Based Teaching Materials for English Language

For lesson in English language teacher BS used learning materials for first grade of secondary school and for lesson in German language she used learning materials for second grade of secondary school. In following chapter there will be explained and described her corpus teaching materials which teacher BS prepared for her students. The name of the lesson is "On the Road" and it is about learning future tense and verb phrase *going to*. Lesson is combining reading, listening and writing exercise and materials. At the beginning of the class students are watching picture from textbook and answering to teacher question about what they see. The topic of prepared class are holidays and traveling. Aim and learning outcomes for this class is for students to future tense in communication and writing. Teacher BS states that by the end of the class, students will learn when and how to use Going to Future when talking about future and intentions. They will also be able to ask and answer questions about their future and intentions. In this class students are working on 6 different tasks regarding *going to* verb phrase.

In first exercise students are communicating and writing down their answers about pictures from textbook (Figure 1). In second exercise students are listening to audio recording and in writing and oral give their remarks to students. Third task is writing exercise in which they must recognize a correct definition of *going to* verb phrase. Fourth task is based on student research of a question and a negative sentence with *going to.* Fifth task is based on audio recordings and communication between students and teacher in which exercise can be conducted oral or written. Students are listening to audio recording and after they are answering questions. In sixth task asked

Figure 1. Picture from textbook for first grade of secondary school for learning English as second language

to construct sentences using verb *going to* to describe what they will doing in future.

Descriptions of Tasks From Textbook

Task 1: Students are looking at the photos, reading the text and answering the questions.

1. What do the following numbers stand for? 2, 10, 18, 200, 1000
2. How do you win the race?
3. Which team from the photos do you think is going to win? Why?
4. Would you like to take part in a race like this? Why/Why not?

Task 2: Students are listening to a news reporter interviewing a member of one team and correcting five mistakes in the dialogue.

Task 3: Students are underlining all the verb phrases with *going to* in the dialogue. Then they are choosing the correct definition below.

We use (be) going to + verb to talk about:

a something we are doing now

b something we plan to do in the future

Task 4: Students are looking for an example of a question and a negative sentence with *going to* in the dialogue.

Task 5: The reporter is interviewing a member of another team. Students are completing the dialogue with the correct forms of *going to* where appropriate. Then they are listening to the dialogue and checking.

Task 6: Students are using the ideas in the box and making a list of things they are going to do. After that, they are asking and answering questions.

- this evening
- next weekend
- next year when you leave school
- in ten years' time

Based on this textbook tasks' teacher BS created corpus-based exercise using corpus tools. In her research she used two different two online corpora for composing additional exercises for her students. Teacher BS used ukWaC and SkELL.

Box 1.

do some homework	buy a motorbike	work in another country	be famous	get a job	see a film

Corpus Based Exercise

Task 1

Students search for different type of races through ukWaC corpus. First, they will type *race* in simple query type and analyse results. Their task is to write five different type of races they found in search results and verbally explain them in front of the class.

Task 2

Students are searching corpus for verb phrase *going to* using phrase query type. Their task is to analyse corpus search results and find five different sentences in which *going to* is used to describe some activity which will happen in future.

Task 3

Students are searching corpus for verb phrase *going to* using phrase query type. Their task is to analyse corpus search results and find five different sentences in which *going to* is used in negative sentence.

They need to write down their findings and discuss them with their classmates and teacher.

Task 4

Students are searching corpus for verb phrase *going to* using phrase query type. Their task is to analyse corpus search results and find five different sentences in which *going to* is used as predictions about future (note to students: predictions are based on evidences, e.g. *The sky is full of dark clouds. It is going to rain.*).

They need to write down their findings and discuss them with their classmates and teacher.

Task 5

Students are provided with corpus-based exercise which they need to solve. Exercise consists of sentences with blanks which students needs to fill in. It includes all materials which students used in today's class and are related to verb phrase *going to* and vocabulary about different type of races. Among these sentences' students need to recognize which sentences are related to prediction and which are negation. Those sentences students need to underline or mark it with different colour.

Fill in the Missing Words

In the ____ have a showing of the French film 'Les Choristes ' in the drama studio at 7 pm. (evening)

On the ____ hear some DJs who will use laptops set up alongside their decks. (weekend)

Next ____ visit London to find university to study. (year)

This ____ start growing vegetables. (year)

This was the first ____ be able to actually relax under the sun, have a stroll down the beach, walk in the sand, etc. (day)

I asked them to review their decision, months later they came back and said they had but they ____ change their mind.
He loved cars and motorbikes and drove a red MG Midget. He ____ take his motorbike test and was already deciding which bike he buy.
It ____ snow again tomorrow.
Also, it ____ rain a bit, but with some sunny intervals.
The boy is from a wealthy and noble family. She ____ lead a happy and luxurious life.

Teacher BS developed corpus-based materials for her English class which she would give to her students if she could have time. During her preparation she worked with parallel corpora EU DGT-UD: English, British corpus (ukWaC) and SkELL. Query type that she uses for searching corpus were simple, lemma, phrase, word and CQL query. In SkELL she used all available options.

Specifically, for creating task 5 teacher BS used following CQL query:

[word="evening|weekednl|year|day"] [] {0,4} [word="going"] [word="to"] [word="going"] [word="to"] [] {0,4} [word="snow|rain|happy"]

Second CQL query teacher BS used to find example sentences in which verb phrase *going to* is used for predictions.

Preview of Corpus-Based Teaching Materials for German Language

For her second class with students who are learning German as second language teacher BS prepared teaching unit *Intelligenz und Gedächtnis* for second grade of secondary school students. In this unit students are learning how to properly use time expressions, which preposition, adverb and which grammatical case is used with certain time expression. Unit also covers theme of different kind of intelligence such as music, logical-mathematics, interpersonal, bodily-kinesthetic, linguistic intelligence, intra-personal and spatial intelligence.

Learning outcomes for this lesson are improving communication and writing skills with students and by the end of the class, students will be able to talk about different types of intelligence. They will also be able to recognize and use time expressions properly.

Topic: Intelligenzen haben eine Geschichte; Intelligenzen im Alltag; Zeitangaben (eng. Intelligences have a story: Intelligences in everyday life)

Description of Tasks From Textbook

Task 1: Students are reading the sentences and deciding which situation and intelligence corresponds to which person (a writer, a politician, an actor).

- *Musical intelligence (sound smart)*
- *Logical-mathematical intelligence (number/reasoning smart)*
- *Interpersonal intelligence (people smart)*
- *Bodily-kinesthetic intelligence (body smart)*
- *Linguistic intelligence (word smart)*
- *Intra-personal intelligence (self-smart)*
- *Spatial intelligence (picture smart)*

Task 2: Students are completing the table with the underlined time expressions from the task ***(mit fünf Jahren, jeden Abend, meistens, abends, dann***) and with other time expressions that are offered in the task b.

Zeitangaben (eng. times)

Box 2.

letzten Sommer zuerst dann zu Ostern am Ende im Mai um zehn Uhr von Montag bis Freitag
übermorgen (=in zwei Tagen) abends zu Weihnachten
vorgestern (=vor zwei Tagen)

Task 3: Students are listening to a conversation and trying to conclude which intelligences Marko and Vanessa are talking about.

Task 4: Students are listening to the conversation again. Then they are matching sentence halves and making sentences out of them, e.g.

1 *seit meinem dritten Lebensjahr* B *Zahlen lieben*

Seit seinem dritten Lebensjahr liebt Marko Zahlen.

Task 5: Students are making notes and telling a story. The story needs to correspond to one intelligence. The partner needs to guess the intelligence.

Box 3.

mit Präposition (Preposition)	**mit Akkusativ (Accusative)**	**als Einzelwort (Adverb)**
am Montag (eng. on Monday) (=nächsten Montag) (eng. next Monday)	**jeden** Montag (eng. every Monday) **nächsten** Montag (eng. next Monday)	**montags** (eng. Mondays) (=jeden Montag (engl. every Monday); auch (engl.also): Sonntag (eng.Sunday), samstags (eng. Saturdays), morgens (eng. mornings)...)

- Urlaub in Kroatien
- surfen
- tauchen, schwimmen, in der Disco tanzen
- Volleyball spielen
- Wassergymnastik
- ...

Corpus Based Exercise

Task 1

Students are reading the sentences extracted from corpus and matching them with corresponding person (a writer, a politician, an actor).

- *Musical intelligence (sound smart)*
- *Logical-mathematical intelligence (number/reasoning smart)*
- *Interpersonal intelligence (people smart)*
- *Bodily-kinesthetic intelligence (body smart)*
- *Linguistic intelligence (word smart)*
- *Intra-personal intelligence (self smart)*
- *Spatial intelligence (picture smart)*

Box 4.

Letzten Sommer war ich... Im Juli... Vor einem Jahr... Dann... Schließlich... Zuletzt...

Task 2

Students must search corpus with word *intelligence* and based on search results write down minimum of five different sentences which are in relation to five different intelligence from Task 1. They will use simple search query and analyse concordance.

Task 3

Based on given context students must recognize and write to which intelligence sentence is referring.

1. Meine Hobby sind: schwimmen, Tischtennis spielen und Basketball spielen.
2. Er vereint physische Stärke, ist talentiert und genau der Typ, den der moderne Fußball braucht.
3. Die Angie's Band - Mr. Erwin Spinger am Piano, Drummer Jo Schneider, Frauenschwarm Melvin Poole an der Gitarre und der virtuose Bassist Arnie G - heizen den Gästen ein und unterstützen die Gastsänger des Abends.
4. Bei allen Kursen steht der kommunikative Aspekt im Vordergrund, Sprechen und Verstehen der spanischen Sprache hat vorderste Priorität.

Task 4

Students must fill in the blanks with corresponding terms, e.g. with prepositions, adverbs and accusative.

1. Im Haushalt, der ____ Montag abend vom Stadtrat verabschiedet wird, findet sich kein Zuschuß mehr für das Haus der Jugend.
2. Spätestens ____ nächsten Montag sind, wie der Volksmund so schön sagt, die Batterien wieder aufgeladen und es kann mit neuer Kraft daran gehen, unsere Welt etwas schöner und lebenswerter zu gestalten.
3. Das wird sich schon ____ nächsten Montag zeigen - und in den kommenden Wochen erst recht.
4. In der Finanzrubrik finden Sie ab sofort ____ Montag im wöchentlichen Wechsel eine exklusive Kolumne von unserem stellvertretenden Chefredakteur Dr. Bernhard Jünemann und von mir.

5. Hier findet ____ Montag ein Wochenmarkt statt.
6. Er kommt ____ Montag mit zum Schwimmen.
7. Dann kann man ____ Sonntag noch ins Stadion!
8. Gegen 8 Uhr ____ kam Frau Wills und wir gingen gemeinsam zur Schauwand neben dem Rektorat und betrachteten die Landkarte.
9. Im Jahr der Technik lohnt es sich ____ früh aufzustehen, denn die Uni bietet Technik ____ Samstagmorgen.
10. Die Fotoausstellung ist bis 22. Dezember, ____ Montag ____ Samstag in der Zeit von 8 bis 17 Uhr und Sonntags von 8 bis 12 Uhr zu besichtigen.
11. So kann man ____ Dienstag ____ Freitag beispielsweise bereits ab 6 Uhr in die Fluten springen.
12. Diese Empfehlungen wurden ____ Mai 2004 vorgestellt.

Task 5

Students must connect mixed parts of sentences into meaningful content.

Solution of the Exercise

A-5: Auf dem Unifest gab es viele multikulturelle Angebote aus dem Bereich Musik: wir konnten afrikanische Musik hören bis hin zu Tango tanzen.

B-1: Ich spiele übelst gerne Volleyball und ansonsten geh ich gern mit meinen Freunden weg und feier bis zum Umfalln!
C-4: In seiner Freizeit geht Tim Patrick gerne schwimmen, zeichnet und hört dabei Musik.
D-6: So können Sie auch in der Freizeit viel Englisch sprechen.

Table 1.

A	Auf dem Unifest gab es viele multikulturelle Angebote aus dem Bereich Musik: wir	1	meinen Freunden weg und feier bis zum Umfalln!
B	Ich spiele übelst gerne Volleyball und ansonsten geh ich gern mit	2	war Mathematik.
C	In seiner Freizeit geht Tim Patrick	3	ein beliebtes Ziel für Wassersportler.
D	So können Sie auch in der Freizeit	4	gerne schwimmen, zeichnet und hört dabei Musik.
E	Segeln und Surfen auf dem Speichersee Nördlich von Lingen liegt der Geester See	5	konnten afrikanische Musik hören bis hin zu Tango tanzen.
F	Mein Lieblingsfach	6	viel Englisch sprechen.

E-3: Segeln und Surfen auf dem Speichersee Nördlich von Lingen liegt der Geester See, ein beliebtes Ziel für Wassersportler.

F-2: Mein Lieblingsfach war Mathematik.

Task 6

Based on six word clouds from the picture (Figure 2) students need to identify which word could refers to which type of intelligence and write them down.

Figure 2. Word cloud with key words for different type of the intelligence

Teacher BS developed corpus-based materials for her German class which she would give to her students. During her preparation she worked with parallel corpora EU DGT-UD: German, German corpus (deWaC) and SkELL. Query type that she used for searching corpus were simple, lemma, phrase, word and CQL query. In SkELL she used all available options.

Specifically, for creating task 3 teacher BS used simple query in which she wrote key word which is related to different type of intelligence. After going through concordance lines, she selected the sentences which are related to her teaching unit and included them to her exercise.

For task 4 teacher BS used CQL query in order to prepare exercise with blanks in which students need to recognize in which sentences they must use preposition, adverb or accusative using different days in week or different time of day. Following CQL query were used:

```
[word="am" & tag="Sp.*"] [word="Montag"]
[word="auch"] [word="Sonntag"]
[word="nächsten"] [word="Montag"]
```

[word="jeden"] [word="Montag"]
[word="samstags"] [word="Montag"]
[word="morgens"] [word="Montag"]

For task 5 teacher BS used CQL query to create exercise in which students need to match right halves of sentences. She searched deWaC for sentences and when she found them, she split them in two and mixed them. For this type of exercise teacher BS used simple and phrase query to find suitable sentence examples which correspond to her teaching unit.

Task 6 teacher BS developed using SkELL and its option to create word clouds with similar words. She conducted the search based on key word which describes different types of intelligences. Based on key words she generated word clouds and used screenshots for creating exercise. Aim of this exercise is for students to recognize which words are referring to which intelligence. Also, through this exercise students are expanding their vocabulary and learning new words.

Teacher's BS Experience Working With Corpora

During this research teacher BS worked with five different corpora. Preparing teaching materials or English class she searched ukWaC, EU DGT-UD: English and SkELL and for German class she searched geWaC, EU DGT-UD: German and SkELL. Teacher BS prepared teaching unit for the first grade of secondary school (English as second language) and teaching unit for the second grade of secondary school (German as second language). Teacher BS prepared and developed two teaching units, she did not use them with her students due to lack of time and insufficient technical equipment (in school where she teaches there is just one informatic classroom with computers that students can use and it is problematic to organize class in it). Before this research teacher BS did not use or worked with corpora, it was her first encounter with this type of open educational resource and technology for language learning. Before she started to use corpora, she had educational introduction to computer corpora and its functionalities through NoSketch Engine interface.

Advantages of using corpora and corpus tools for preparing teaching materials for language learning in secondary school based on teacher BS experience are new and interesting approach to teaching English and German language, new large educational resource for extracting language examples and free access to the tools and texts.

Disadvantages of using corpora and corpus tools for preparing teaching materials for language learning in secondary school are related to time, which is needed for preparation, large amount of content that teacher needs to read and go through in order to select appropriate sentences for students.

She points out:

Problem with searching and using corpora for preparing teaching unit is related with time. Process is very time consuming, the preparation process lasted much longer then usual. I had to put additional effort for creating exercises. There are a lot of diverse texts and some of it is not appropriate for students in secondary school. So, I had to read a lot of concordance line to get suitable examples for class.

Teacher BS will use corpora in her future work as teacher of English and German as second languages, not just for preparing teaching unites in secondary school but also on her other job where she teaches English and German language in the school for learning foreign languages for adults. She states that computer corpora are valuable educational resources which provide teacher with large amount of authentic language examples and language in use, it gives teacher and students insight to "real" language and teacher can in a just few mouse clicks get context, sentences and vocabulary for creating his teaching materials. She states:

I will use corpus tools again for preparing my own teaching materials or for checking some language fact.

Simple query types like word, lemma, characters, phrase worked well, and they were very easy to use but CQL query was very complicated because of its syntax. If she hadn't had help she do not know if she could successfully develop corpus-based materials. But on the other hand, CQL query indeed offers advanced and useful results if you know how to correctly use it.

Teaching outcomes for her units were successfully accomplished but she thinks that this type of methodology would be hard to incorporated into curriculum of secondary school because it requires a lot of preparation time and teachers do not have much of extra time to sparer. Teacher BS states that if there were some kind of workshops or educational materials available on Croatian language then teacher would easier overcome these obstacles.

Teacher BS attitudes about corpus tools and their advantages and disadvantages are diverse. During this research she used concordance lines, KWIC, CQL query search and similar words in SkELL.

For teacher BS parallel corpora EU DGT-UD: English and EU DGT-UD: German) were problematic for use because of too complex texts and examples which are not suitable for students in secondary school. This type of corpora are more suitable for students at universities who are studying languages. As a best solution for secondary school for teacher BS was SkELL because of its simplicity and possibilities to create word cloud which she thinks students would accept because of the graphical showcase of vocabulary. Also, SkELL was for her the best option because it has simplified view, content and examples and there wasn't to much options which were complexed. In her opinion SkELL is much better solution for learning German language because students in secondary school aren't motivated and interested enough for leaning German and SkELL could motivate them for learning. For learning English language in secondary school both ukWaC and SkELL are suitable because English is more popular with students and they have better knowledge because they are on daily base and in everyday life situations exposed to it through movies, music, internet, etc. Most of the time for preparing teaching materials for her unit she spent on analysing and reading concordance lines and KWIC in ukWaC and deWaC corpora because of a large amount of texts which are available in it and this is one of the disadvantages of preparing teaching materials using corpora.

Teacher BS points out that there are many more functionalities and options which computer corpora can provide both to teachers and students, but she did not have the time to explore all of them.

Direct use of corpora in classroom with students for teacher BS in not an option in this moment because of the school infrastructure, e.g. school is not adequately equipped with technology which is required to conduct this type of teaching. If students and teacher do not have available classrooms with computers or tablets this kind of teaching is not possible. Also, she points out that for student it would be problematic to search corpora with CQL queries because they are to complex for them and the time to explain students how to conduct the search would take too much of the time from class and this is something that teachers cannot afford.

Teacher BS states that this research process was informative, positive and valuable for her further development as a teacher of foreign languages because she learned something new, get additional knowledge which she will use and insight into new and free technologies for teaching English and German language.

ENDNOTE

1 Explanation of Croatian primary and secondary education is given in more details in chapter "Using Computer Corpora in Primary School."

Chapter 7
Implications of Using Corpus Tools in Primary and Secondary Education

ABSTRACT

This chapter will give a comparison of using computer corpora in primary and in secondary schools. It will compare information that was collected from primary school teachers and secondary school teachers about using computer corpora for language subjects on primary and secondary educational levels. Based on the given information, the chapter will provide an explanation of the advantages and disadvantages of using computer corpora in language learning on those two educational levels. The chapter will explore which educational levels have more possibilities for incorporating computer corpora in their teaching activities and how it can be used in the classroom with students.

INTRODUCTION

This chapter will give an overview of the implications of using corpus tools and computer corpora in secondary and primary schools based on in-depth interviews which were conducted with teachers who participated in this research. Structure of corpus-based examples of teaching materials are very similar to the examples found in textbooks but the content is not the same (Reppen, 2011).

DOI: 10.4018/978-1-7998-3680-3.ch007

It is important to emphasize that the majority of teachers who participated in this research did not want or have time to use corpus with their students in the classroom. Two teachers did not have time to create and use the corpus for preparing teaching materials for their students. The lack of time, small incomes, overload with obligations and curriculum are some of the segments which influenced teacher perspective of incorporating new tool for language learning in process of creating teaching materials, exams and exercises.

Before the teacher begins with the process of creating teaching activities for his students, it is very important that the teacher has an elaborate plan and clear goals what he or she wants to achieve with the unit. Reppen (2011) in the book "Using Corpus in the Language Classroom" lists several guidelines for the teachers which they should take into account before starting to create teaching materials and activities for their students. Guidelines include the following items:

- Teachers should have a clear idea of what they want to teach their students.
- They need to choose the corpus that is the best source of information for their teaching unit.
- They need to explore the corpus for the teaching matter they want to teach.
- Their guidelines for using corpus in the classroom should be complete and easy to follow.
- The examples that are being used should be directed to the teaching matter.
- They need to provide a variety of ways for students to interact with teaching materials.
- They need to use a variety of exercise examples.
- If teachers are using computers in a classroom session, there should always have an alternative plan or additional activity if there are technical difficulties or inability to use the computer.

Idrizi and Miftari (2018) stresses that teachers should consider two factors when they decide "to incorporate corpus in the class: (1) students should undergo adequate training in corpus use; and (2) a more balanced inductive/ deductive approach should be used to ensure all students cope with the corpus-based activities in the language classroom" (p. 1431).

McEnerym and Wilson (1997) are describing corpus based learning with four different learning approaches (p. 6):

1. Discovery learning - the students proceed through the data under their own impetus. They discover features about language for themselves.
2. Divergent learning - even with the most careful set of instructions, a key feature of corpus-based learning is divergence: different students take different paths through the data and find slightly different things. Consequently corpus based teaching often has a strong peer-based learning element: students must share experiences, and, in doing so, widen their understanding of a feature under examination.
3. Mediated learning - the corpus is not a source of didactic learning: rather, it is a medium through which learning may be achieved. Students learn through the process of interacting in some way with the corpus (e.g. via practical grammatical analysis), rather than from its explicit content. (Contrast the traditional textbook, where the students do learn directly from its contents.)
4. Directed learning - learning from a corpus is directed by the teacher, but not led. The teacher may point the general direction for the students, that is, tell them what points to examine and what questions to ask. But it is the students who lead themselves and one another through the learning process.

The preparation of teaching materials using the corpus includes two types of teaching activities. One refers to the activities where the teacher is bringing prepared corpus-based materials to the classroom and presents them to the students, while the other activity relates to the direct work of the students with corpora, where students are using computers for searching and using the corpus with the help of a teacher (Reppen, 2011). It is up to the teachers to decide which approach they will apply in their teaching process, which approach best meets teachers needs based on the type of language they are teaching and what structure of the student they are working with.

The corpus approach to language teaching places the emphasis on student exposure to a large number of language examples of authentic language (language in use) that are different from the language examples offered in textbooks and grammars where often are examples which are taken out of context and are quantitatively limited.

The role of corpus and corpus tools in language teaching can make it easier for teachers to teach the language to the students which can improve communication skills because it offers a large number of examples of authentic, useable language with which students will meet in communication with native speakers. Bergovec (2007) states that students should be exposed to a large amount of written and spoken material for them to expedite the number of lexical circuits which are available to them.

Reppen (2011) states that KWIC provides students with the opportunity to see the word or language structure in high concentration, i.e. expose them to a large number of language examples in a short time, which is an extremely powerful language learning tool. The teachers can always exclude language examples which they consider unsuitable for the certain level of the language knowledge or structure of students they teach and so adjust the content to their needs.

The frequency of vocabulary in the language is very important because based on its statistical data author gain insight into the representation of particular words or expressions in the language. For this reason, making frequency list with corpus can provide the teachers with guidelines what and when during the school year they will teach their students, or on which words and phrases in the language they will put the emphasis. Reppen (2011) points out that frequency lists can serve as a starting point for selecting the appropriate vocabulary to be taught, and students can use it to study prefixes and suffixes, learn new words and validate existing vocabulary skills or see what words are used more frequently one with another, e.g. what is the most frequent adjective with noun *hair*.

Chen and Bruncak (2015) emphasis that students could use corpora for learning vocabulary, e.g. wordlists because "those lexical items are likely to be encountered in real life as a result of their high frequency and corpus wordlists can therefore be of great use for vocabulary teaching and learning(p. 121).

Idrizi and Miftari (2018) are giving practical examples how corpora can be used for language teaching, e.g. "learners can be tasked to use a corpus as a supporting tool during the writing of their second or third draft of their essay or, they can be given a task in which they would be provided with an essay which contains deliberate errors" (Idrizi, Miftari, 2018, p. 1428).

Additionally, Ebrahimi and Faghih (2016) are describing how "teachers can use wordlists to establish vocabulary targets for learners at different levels, or they can employ corpora tools to analyze students' writing, as well as analyze the difficulty level of different instructional texts, corpora can also be used indirectly by language teachers for designing classroom activities or developing tests" (p. 132).

Besides wordlists, concordance are often used in language learning "as a method to help learners study corpora through a computer program, which presents concordance lines for language analysis, DDL is an approach in which concordance lines are implemented with an aim to help learners identify a particular language phenomenon" (Girgin, 2019, p. 3).

Huang (2017) is describing using corpora "at the phrasal level, one of the most common and easy ways to start exploring corpora is by using a concordancer to generate KWIC examples of how a chosen word or phrase is used in writing or in speech in a specific communicative context" (p. 13).

However, due to many above mentioned examples how corpora can be used in language teaching during this research it could been see that no one of involved teachers did used corpora indirectly or directly in their work. Meunier (2011) and Jantunen (2016) are listing four reasons why there is a still resistance of using corpora for language teaching, "(1) corpora, corpus methods and corpus studies have not reached teachers, or may be rejected, (2) using authentic data is only one pedagogical method, (3) the importance of frequency, i.e. are frequent items also useful to teach, (4) the lack of studies exploring the impact of corpus methods on language learning" (p. 98).

DATA DRIVEN LEARNING (DDL)

Data Driven Learning (DDL) is a type of teaching where students themselves are learning language with the help of a corpus. The role of the teacher is not excluded but has been modified so that the teacher helps the students and teacher is not in the focus of the student. The main purpose of this type of language learning is to develop students' autonomy so that students could better master the language skills and acquire new technological and informational skills.

The term DDL introduced Tim Johnes in 1991 for describing the language learning method in which students become researchers and independently explore the language (Boulton, 2011).

In the centre of the DDL approach, Johnes (1991) points out that there is the use of a machine or a computer, but not in the role of a surrogate or substitute professor but in the role of a special kind of informant whose role in teaching the language is passive because it is silent until the student askes question, i.e. student set the query based on which the informant provides the best possible answer after which the student tries to interpret the answer and understand its meaning and include it in the existing database knowledge of the language. The role of a professor in the DDL approach does not imply his exclusion from the teaching process, but the change of his role where from the center of teaching or transferring knowledge to students teacher becomes a moderator and mediator in the process of teaching the language. Boulton (2009) states that a typical DDL approach to language teaching involves exposing students to large amounts of authentic language data such as computer corpora, giving students a more active role in the process of language research and they are at the very centre of the teaching process and take up more responsibility for their own language learning in relation to the traditional approach in which their role is passive because they are taught by professors with certain rules.

RELEVANT FACTORS FOR USING CORPORA IN PRIMARY AND SECONDARY EDUCATION FOR LANGUAGE TEACHING: EMERGED FROM THIS RESEARCH

Factors emerged from this research which had an influence on teachers' decision to use or not use corpora and corpus tools for preparing corpus-based materials for teaching and introducing the direct use of corpora in the classroom based on this research are following:

- Time
- Finance
- School infrastructure and use of technologies in the classroom
- Fear of changes

Time

All teachers argue that the lack of time during the school year is a big problem because of the overloaded school curriculum which they must go through with their students. Additionally, time factor depends on the group of students' teachers have to work with during the school year. Same students are easy to work with and some students need more time to comprehend the materials apropos teachers need more time to explain them the lessons. Factors which influenced on the lack of time for teachers to prepare and/or incorporate their materials into the classroom is complex are: detail national curriculum, heterogenous students regarding their knowledge and abilities, low number of hours for teaching. One factor which influenced on teachers in this research is a "the number of corpus-based classroom materials is still limited and teachers have the responsibility to adjust them suitably to the classroom use, which presents an extra work with teachers" (Özbay, Kayaoğlu, 2015, p. 87). Due to these reasons teacher AS and BP did not work with corpus tools during this research and did not prepare corpus-based materials for teaching unite of their choice. Because "a fact that time constraints may hinder or discourage the use and integration of any innovation by teachers" (Ebrahimi, Faghih, 2017, p. 131).

Teacher BS stated that problem with introducing students with new teaching tool, i.e. corpus, which is not a part of curriculum is problematic to integrate into the classroom due to lack of teaching hours which she cannot spend on explaining to students how to properly use corpus tools for learning English and especially German language. Additionally, teacher BS points out that preparation of corpus-based teaching materials took more time than using traditional approach, i.e. textbooks and grammars. It can be concluded that for successful implementation of corpus based materials and classes it needs to be "consider the fact that designing corpus-based activities is time-consuming, more corpus based materials should be developed by materials developers to help teachers in this regard"(Ebrahimi, Faghih, 2017, p. 131). It can be concluded that "the inductive nature of the data-driven learning approach necessarily involves time and requires both teachers and learners to be patient during the early stages of familiarization, which often involves trial and error" (Huang, 2017 p. 17).

Finance

All teachers are united in the statement that they are underpaid and that this is major source of frustrations in their line of work. They point out that their work does not stops when they leave the classroom which is the most common misperception about the teaching work. They must on daily base develop and cerate new and updated teaching materials in order to refresh their teaching, create exams, homework, exercises and evaluate existing ones which they give to the students. In Croatia teachers are not appreciated in the way they should be. Students do not respect teachers and their relationship to the teachers is transferred to their parents. Many teachers because of the financial situation do not want to put additional effort to developing and upgrading their teaching habits and methods. They put on the resist towards integration of new technologies, methodologies and teaching tools into their teaching process because it means more work for the same monthly payment. Like teacher AP said during the in-depth interview "you get what you pay for". Nevertheless, there are always enthusiastic teachers (like this research has show) who do their best regardless the conditions, poor infrastructure, low incomes, problematic students, low quality teaching materials, lack of motivation, etc. Their motivation is love for the job, teaching and their students so they are trying to make things better, to change the process, motivate students and create better simulative learning environment. Till there are such individuals present in the schools, integration of new teaching methods and technologies, as corpora and corpus tools have bright future in primary and secondary schools.

Motivation is one of the factors which influence the teacher's decision would he or her use and incorporate corpus tools in their teaching practices as Bernaus, Wilson and Gardner (2009) states "teacher motivation is the most important variable because if teachers are not motivated the whole notion of strategy use is lost" (p. 29). In this research all the teachers have stated that poor payment is demotivating factor (Smithers, Robinson, 2003; Addison, Brundrett 2008) for them to take upon themselves more extra work for which they would not get payed. Additionally, to motivate teachers to use corpora and corpus tools directly in the classroom with students then they need to motivate their students and this relationship relays on motivating teacher's to motivate the students (Atkinson, 2000; Bemaus, Wilson, Gardner, 2009; Guilloteaux, 2013; Hettiarachchi, 2013)

School Infrastructure and Use of Technologies in the Classroom

Croatian schools do not have all classrooms in school equipped with computers, laptops or tablets. Commonly each school has one classroom with computers in which is held class for computer science, e.g. informatics. Additionally, computers in some schools are slow, break down, shut down, etc. so this presents a problem working and using technologies in classrooms because teachers and students must work on low quality equipment. Organization issue is another problem, all teachers needs to coordinate with each other's to use classroom for their class. This is one of the reasons why direct use of corpora in the classroom with students is problematic. As Ebrahimi and Faghih (2017) emphasis "the most disadvantageous aspect of using corpora was the necessity to have access to computers and the internet" (p. 132). Students cannot use corpora and corpus tools in the classroom on daily base because of the technical, infrastructural and organizational issues. On the other hand, students can use it occasionally for solving tasks or doing their homework. Teacher AP did prove that direct use of corpus tools during the school class is possible regardless the restrictions which other three teaches mentioned. Based on the research it can be concluded that all depends on the teacher's attitudes and motivation for doing something new and different in teaching, openness to new educational teaching methodologies and technologics and in the case of computer corpora teacher needs to have higher level of computer literacy. Also Azarfam and Jabbari (2012) are listing reasons why use of technology in classroom is problematic for teachers and schools as they claim "that the integration of computers into existing subjects is proceeding slowly, and even the persistence of traditional education in some educational settings due to the absence of professional training leads the researcher to the conclusion that it is necessary to train teachers about new technologies, so that the infrastructures to be put into place and the contents to be produced can be used we would add a lack of confidence in teachers' use of computers in school, and insufficient data concerning teachers' views of relevant professional development programs" (p. 455).

Fear of Changes

All teachers who participated in the research emphasis that a major problem with introducing new things, especially new technologies into teaching process is a fear of change which is present with their colleges (older colleges but younger are to putting resist to changes). This fear of changes can be connected with the term technophobia which is defined as "an irrational fear and/or anxiety that individuals form as a response to a new stimulus that comes in the form of a technology that modifies and/or changes the individual's normal or previous routine in performing a certain job/task. Individuals may display active, physical reactions (fear) such as avoidance and/or passive reactions(anxiety)such as distress or apprehension" (Khasawneh, 2018, p. 6). Author Khasawneh in his research *Technophobia: Examining its hidden factors and defining it* states that feeling which people with technophobia feels "can then translate into the behavior of avoidance, where users avoid using new technologies or minimize their interaction with it" (Khasawneh, 2018, p. 2). Rosen and Weil (1995) in their research *Computer Availability, Computer Experience and Technophobia Among Public School Teachers* explores the term technophobia among primary and secondary teachers as an explanation for low levels of computer utilization. In their research they conclude "that teachers do not hold a positive attitude and do not feel comfortable with computers. First and foremost, teachers are worded about using and dealing with the actual computer machinery in their school teaching job. Second, teachers are troubled about computer errors including both consumer type errors (billing, personal records) and problems with the computer and its operation (the computer is "down" and getting error messages from the computer). In essence, in all of these situations, the teacher is most likely feeling "victimized" by the computer" (Rosen, Weil, 1995, p. 26). Azarfam and Jabbari (2012) are describing how "technophobia can be the discouraging factor that obstructs the successful application of technology in any field" (p. 452) adding that among teachers "is the perception that computers cannot meet the students' needs" (p. 453) but also "some teachers express reluctance to use computers because they do not feel comfortable with the computer, yet some others who still have reservations admit seeing some benefits to using the computer" (p. 453). This can be one of the phycological factors/reasons why teacher resits to introduce new technologies such as corpora and corpus tools into classroom for data driven learning. Additionally, low level of computer literacy can be a second reason for not using computer corpora with their students because use of computer corpora implies an advanced level of knowing and using computer software, applications and tools. In this research participated exclusively language teachers and level of computer literacy they gain individually not as a part of the formal education. In their research Azarfam and Jabbari (2012) have "found that effective computer-based education requires teacher access to computers, together with their confident and competent usage but at the same time, it is witnessed that teachers' decisions regarding technology use could be based not on fear but on personal views" (p. 455).

REFERENCES

Addison, R., & Brundrett, M. (2008). Motivation and demotivation of teachers in primary schools: the challenge of change. *Education,* 79-94. doi:10.1080/03004270701733254

Atkinson, E. S. (2000). An investigation into the relationship between teacher motivation and pupil motivation. *Educational Psychology*, *20*(1), 45–57. doi:10.1080/014434100110371

Azarfam, A. Y., & Jabbari, Y. (2012). Dealing with teachers' technophobia in classroom. *Advances in Asian Social Science*, *2*(2), 452–455.

Bergovec, M. (2007). Leksički pristup u nastavi stranih jezika s posebnim osvrtom na hrvatski. *LAHOR: Časopis za hrvatski kao materinski, drugi i strani jezik, 1*(2007), 53-66.

Bernaus, M., Wilson, A., & Gardner, R. C. (2009). Teachers' motivation, classroom strategy use, students' motivation and second language achievement. *Porta Linguarum: revista internacional de didáctica de las lenguas extranjeras*, *12*, 25-36.

Boulton, A. (2009). Data-driven Learning: Reasonable Fears and Rational Reassurance. *Indian Journal of Applied Linguistics.*, *35*(1), 81–106.

Boulton, A. (2011). *What data for data-driven learning? EUROCALL 2011: The CALL Triangle – Student, Teacher and Institution*. Nottingham, UK: University of Nottingham.

Chen, Y. H., & Bruncak, R. (2015, December). How can we use corpus wordlists for language learning? Interfaces between computer corpora and expert intervention. *Critical CALL–Proceedings of the 2015 EUROCALL Conference*. 10.14705/rpnet.2015.000320

Ebrahimi, A., & Faghih, E. (2017). Integrating corpus linguistics into online language teacher education programs. *ReCALL*, *29*(1), 120–135. doi:10.1017/S0958344016000070

Girgin, U. (2019). Perceptions of Turkish EFL Student Teachers towards Learning Phrasal-Prepositional Verbs through Corpus Based Materials. *Online (Bergheim)*, *2*(1), 1–19.

Guilloteaux, M. J. (2013). Motivational strategies for the language classroom: Perceptions of Korean secondary school English teachers. *System*, *41*(1), 3–14.

Hettiarachchi, S. (2013). English Language Teacher Motivation in Sri Lankan Public Schools. *Journal of Language Teaching and Research*, *4*, 1–11.

Huang, L. S. (2018). Taking Stock of Corpus-Based Instruction in Teaching English as an International Language. *RELC Journal*, *49*(3), 381–401. doi:10.1177/0033688217698294

Idrizi, E., & Miftari, I. (2018). Students'perceptions Of Using Corpora As Reference Tools In Essay Error Correction And Exploring Words With Affixes: A Pilot Study. *Knowledge International Journal, 23*(5), 1427–1432.

Jantunen, J. H. (2016). *Corpora, phraseology and dictionaries: How does corpus research intersect language teaching and learning?* Mémoires de la Société Néophilologique.

Johnes, T. (1991). Should you be persuaded - two samples of data-driven learning materials, Classroom Concordancing. *ELR Journal, 4*, 1–16.

Khasawneh, O. Y. (2018). Technophobia: Examining its hidden factors and defining it. *Technology, 13*, 60.

McEnery, T., & Wilson, A. (1997). Teaching and language corpora (TALC). *ReCALL, 9*(1), 5–14. doi:10.1017/S0958344000004572

McEnery, T., & Wilson, A. (2001). *Corpus Linguistics*. Edinburgh: Edinburgh University Press.

Meunier, F. (2011). Corpus linguistics and second/foreign language learning: Exploring multiple paths. *Revista Brasileira de Lingüística Aplicada, 11*(2), 459–477. doi:10.1590/S1984-63982011000200008

Özbay, A., & Kayaoğlu, M. N. (2015). EFL teacher's reflections towards the use of computerized corpora as a teaching tool in their classrooms. *Çukurova Üniversitesi Eğitim Fakültesi Dergisi, 44*(1), 85-104.

Reppen, R. (2011). Using corpora in the language classroom. *Materials development in language teaching*, 35-51.

Rosen, L. D., & Weil, M. M. (1995). Computer availability, computer experience and technophobia among public school teachers. *Computers in Human Behavior, 11*(1), 9–31. doi:10.1016/0747-5632(94)00018-D

Smithers, A., & Robinson, P. (2003). *Factors affecting teachers' decisions to leave the profession.* Academic Press.

Steinberger, R., Eisele, A., Klocek, S., Pilos, S., & Schlüter, P. (2013). *DGT-TM: A freely available translation memory in 22 languages.* arXiv preprint arXiv:1309.5226

Chapter 8
Conclusion and Further Research

ABSTRACT

The final chapter will give an overview of full research with its conclusions and implications of creating teaching materials, exercises, and exams with the use of computer corpora. It will explore future possibilities of using corpora and its tools in learning language subjects. The chapter will show research conclusions based on teacher experiences working with computer corpora and its tools to prepare their teaching units for language learning. This chapter will try to give an answer to the question, Does computer corpora have its future in language learning subjects in primary and secondary educational levels? Additionally, this chapter will present ideas for further research and existing limitations of this research.

INTRODUCTION

Corpus-based teaching has many implications not just in teaching language subjects in primary and secondary schools, but it is widely and more often used for teaching foreign languages, especially English. For large world languages (especially English) extensive studies have shown the importance of using the corpus as a tool for teaching the second and foreign language, as it provides students with practical training and first-hand experience in a natural context (Gavioli, Aston, 2001; Hunston, 2002; Boulton, 2010; Leech, 1997; Bennet, 2010). But the importance of the corpus is increasingly emphasized in the

DOI: 10.4018/978-1-7998-3680-3.ch008

field of computer lexicography, where big publishing houses such as Oxford University Press, Cambridge University Press, Collins and Macmillan in the UK, INL in the Netherlands, and Cornelsen in Germany are using corpus tools (like Sketch Engine) in their lexicographic work (Kilgarriff, Kovář, Rychlý, 2010). Consequently, dictionaries, grammars, glossaries, and manuals created for English, German and Dutch take into account the frequency of words, collocation, and phraseology, along with variations, lexis, and grammar. These newly-created dictionaries, grammars, textbooks, and manuals do not necessarily take into account only the original language corpora, but also the learner corpora (i.e., corpus generated by the collection of texts of students whom are adopting that language), which enables lexicographers and readers to take into account the mother tongue of students, and construct dictionaries that are not necessarily market-oriented but are oriented towards students (Hanks, 2008, p. 221; Kilgarriff; Vojtěch and Rychlý, 2010).

The goal of this research was to get insight to teachers needs and opinions about direct and indirect use of computer corpora in language teaching. Indirect use implies corpus-based materials which the teacher had prepared before and introduced them to students during the class, those materials are filtered and have just materials with which teacher wants to work with. Direct use of corpus implies that the teacher would work with computer corpora directly in the classroom with students where students with teachers guidance search and analyse computer corpora. The research findings are based on presumptions and opinions of four language teachers who are working in primary and secondary schools. Through in-depth interviews with teachers aim was to see their attitudes about the use of computer corpora in language teaching and can it be incorporated into a primary and secondary level of education.

Main questions of this research were directed to investigate and determine the teachers' needs and attitudes about:

- Use of free ICT tool (computer corpora) for preparing teaching materials for their students
- Perception and attitude towards using computer corpora and corpus tools for teaching language classes in primary and secondary schools
- Use of corpus tools directly in classroom with students (DDL approach)
- Education and knowledge about corpora and corpus tools
- Functionalities and possibilities of computer corpora and corpus tools in the field of language education at primary and secondary schools

This research gave insight into following questions and from it emerged advantages, disadvantages, obstacles, solutions and practical examples how to use corpora and corpus tools for preparing teaching materials, exercises and classes for students in primary and secondary schools. Additionally, this research gave insight into DDL approach with students from primary school thanks to teacher's AP enthusiasm, will, openness and dedicated work for trying to use new teaching tools in his classroom without any preconceptions.

All conclusions and statements in this book are based on in-depth interviews conducted with these four teachers and their experience with corpora and corpus tools. It is important to emphasise that just one teacher (Teacher AP) used corpora in classroom with students. Detail analysis was conducted with students from his class for the purpose of research level of students' motivation and satisfaction with direct corpus-based teaching in classroom. Furthermore, teacher BS prepared two language classes using corpus tools, but her students did not work with corpora directly in classroom. She prepared one teaching unit for English class and one for German class. Other two teachers, teacher BP and teacher AS did not prepare teaching unit using corpora and corpus tools due to lack of interest in matter and lack of time to explore new teaching methods. They just participated in first part of in-depth interviews and give their insight to their teaching methods and thoughts about corpus and corpus tools in general.

Use of Free ICT Tool (Computer Corpora) for Preparing Teaching Materials in Primary and Secondary Schools

These findings are based on in-depth interviews with two teachers (AP form primary and BS form secondary school) because they have worked with corpus tools and prepared teaching materials for their unit. Both proved that use of corpora for preparing teaching materials requires more preparation time. The reason for that maybe lies in the fact that these two teachers had never used corpora i.e. they had to put more effort to learn how to use corpus tools.

Teacher BS opinion about integration of new teaching methods and approaches in teaching process of English and German as second language is positive, but she points out that teachers must be previously educated about the corpora and must be provided with demonstration how to successfully integrate these methods into the teaching process. Regarding the role of information and communication technologies in teaching language subject, especially English and German language she has positive attitude and states it can make learning more fun and interesting for students and it can motivate them to learn more.

I think that only a small group of the teachers would welcome the integration of corpus tools in teaching process, while most of them would consider this to be a burden because of small number of hours they have with students and a large volume of material they need to go through. Older teachers would not welcome it with open arms because most of them are not sufficiently IT literate or do not like changes (Teacher BS, 2019).

Use of corpus tools for preparing teaching materials has it implication but due to lack of time or knowledge about use of corpus tools teachers are reluctant to use it. They rather use tools with which they are familiar with and that will not take much of their time for preparation. In most cases, they do not use corpus tools for teaching language except for internet as media for searching and exploring teaching materials.

Perception and Attitude Towards Using Computer Corpora and Corpus Tools for Language Teaching in Primary and Secondary Schools

Teacher AP states that computer corpora can be used by both teachers and students in primary school. He thinks that teachers would not be motivated to individually search computer corpora but with well-prepared materials and tutorials for searching and using corpora, the use of it would be much easier. With these educational materials, teachers would use them for creating teaching materials and in the classroom with their students. Teacher AP states that primary school students "are always motivated for using and experimenting with new ICT tools, but their motivation rapidly falls if teaching activities are not well prepared and conducted or if they (students) do not see the purpose of those tools" (Teacher AP, 2019).

Use of corpus tools in secondary school for teaching English and German language teacher BS states that they could me interesting for students to use them in learning process because they provide students with wider context in which some words appear. In addition, she points out they are good for learning collocations in English language.

Teacher BS thinks that teachers are not enough or at all familiar with corpus tools, and how and when they can be used or why they could be useful to them for teaching language subjects. Attitude of her school about integration and use of corpus tools in classroom is neutral, she states if administration would see need and usefulness of corpus tools in teaching process, they would integrated them in regular curriculum with condition they are free to use or not to expensive.

It can be concluded that corpus tools have potential for teaching language subjects in primary and secondary schools, but their integration depends not only on teacher attitudes and on knowledge but also on school administration, polices, finances and government especially ministries of education.

Use of Corpus Tools Directly in Classroom With Students (DDL approach)

Primary school teacher AP tested use of corpus tools in classroom with students who individually and in the groups searched corpora and interpret their results and finding. Based on what they found they made conclusions and gain language knowledge. DDL approach was applied during two school classes (in total of 90 minutes) of Croatian as first language. During these two classes students have for the first time heard about corpora and corpus tools and used them. At the beginning of the first-class teacher AP shared link to hrWaC and HNK corpora and in 10 minutes explained to them three query types (simple, phrase and character) that they will use till the end of the classes. He worked with two different classes but teaching unit was the same for both of them.

Overall, students were satisfied with presented materials and curriculum which were corpus-based materials, 54% students were satisfied, 31% were very satisfied, 12% were extremely satisfied and 3% were dissatisfied. Students were asked to give their assessment about apprehension of presented materials in relation to previous classes where they used traditional teaching methods, e.g. using textbook. Majority of students (89%) understood and completely understood presented materials, 3% did not understood it and 8% did not see the difference in relation to previous classes.

Additionally, students think that the method of transferring knowledge in classroom using computer corpora for learning Croatian grammar was excellent and very good (74,1%) and 28,6% students thought the method was good. No one thinks it was a bad teaching method.

For 74% of students exercise was completely or well understandable, 20% of students partly understand exercise and 6% of students did not understand it at all. Majority of involved students understood exercise and solve it without any problems.

Level of satisfaction with corpus-based exercise in their class was high, 29% of students were extremely or very satisfied, 3% were dissatisfied and 68% were satisfied. With their current teaching materials, 45% of students are extremely or very satisfied, 52% are satisfied and 3% are dissatisfied.

It could be concluded that the same number of students (3%) are dissatisfied with both corpus and traditional materials. Higher percentage of students (45%) is extremely or very satisfied with traditional materials rather than corpus-based exercise but higher percentage of students (68%) states that they were more satisfied with corpus-based exercise than with traditional ones. Based on this it can be assumed that students would be open to incorporate this kind of teaching materials and exercise directly into classrooms.

Most of the students are confident in their capabilities to use individually corpus and its tools for learning Croatian as first language (85,7%) and only 14,3% of students thinks they cannot use corpus tools independently for learning. Also 60% of students stated they would like to use corpus again in their classroom for learning Croatian as first language and 40% of students stated they do not want to use it again for learning Croatian language.

It is interested to see that students do not want to use computer applications for learning language and minority of them (8,6%) wants to use internet for individual language research but still majority of students (60%) would use again corpus for learning language. Result of this research maybe lies in the fact that students did not completely understood what corpus tools are and because they used it in just two classes. In addition, second fact is correlated to short period which teacher AP had to introduce corpus to his students. Further research could be done for longer period of the time in which students would be exposed to use of corpora for language learning.

It can be concluded that use of corpora and corpus tools can be implemented and has its implications with upper level primary school students for teaching Croatian as first language. Additionally, this is indicator that use of corpus tools in primary school can be applied on other languages not just Croatian. Attitudes of students implies fertile ground for implementing corpora into classroom. Additionally, for this kind of action teachers must be well trained and educated about computer corpora, corpus tools and their possibilities. They must be confident and have no fear about including new ICT tools in their interaction with students. Again, it is important to emphasis importance of educating teachers about computer corpora. For successful inclusion, education must be included in the formal education of language teachers. This reflects to all languages not just Croatian.

It can be concluded "that corpora are perceived positively by language learners and corpora seem to attract as well as motivate learners while doing language investigations in a more autonomous way" (Idrizi, Miftari, 2018, p. 1431). Another study did also examine motivation and perception of students using corpora directly in classroom and the results show positive attitude (Preradović, Posavec, Unić, 2019). This research has confirmed this statements because involved students had positive attitude during the lessons in which they individually use corpora and interpret results. Difference between above mentioned researches is that this one was conducted with primary school students not university students.

Education and Knowledge About Corpora and Corpus Tools

Just two teachers (teacher BP and teacher AS) heard about corpora before they participated in this research, but they did not used or searched them. It is interested to see that teachers (teacher AP and teacher BS) who did not heard about corpora till this research have more positive and open attitude towards using corpus tools for language teaching.

Teacher AP thinks that education about computer corpora and its use must be integrated into formal education for language teachers, not just for Croatian language but for all languages which can be studied in higher education level (at universities). In his statement about educating teachers how and what corpus and its tools are he states that learning about corpora must be part of regular classes in higher education for students who are studying language. According to his opinion those subjects must provide students with lots of examples how to use corpus tools in theory and practise. He points out that students would learn about different use of corpus and its tools through variety of different examples in different countries and with different language subjects and analysing science researches. Additional education in the form of workshops about use of computer corpora would be welcomed for the teachers who did not have corpus linguistics during their studying period. In this type of education teacher AP would include examples of good practice in classroom.

Teacher BS thinks that education in a form of workshops would not be enough for teachers to learn how to use corpus tool for language learning and that it should be integrated into the formal education of teachers at universities.

Educating language teachers about use of corpus tools is first step to use it in their work and teacher AS thinks that an additional education would be enough for teachers to learn about what they are, where they can find them and how to use them especially if that education would include examples of good practise in teaching language subjects in classroom with students. He thinks that integration of corpus tool and changes which accompanied that integration would cause a negative reaction among teachers but with good structure of educational workshops and a lot of practical examples, implementation in classroom would be positive. He thinks that it's all about utility. Corpus tools could be implemented in class if they would be presented in an interesting way and with clearly explained usage in everyday speaking practice. Before he would get into searching and using corpus tools in purpose of creating corpus-based materials for his class or in his class (DDL approach), he thinks it would be interesting to see examples of corpus tools use in class.

Further steps for inclusion of corpus tools in everyday work of language teacher is connected with formal education of teachers at university level. Successful implementation must begin as part of teachers' formal education. In that, way teacher will have more knowledge and skills about the use of corpus tools. Additionally, "teachers may not be aware of DDL if it is absent from their initial training, or may see it as a research activity confined to higher education "(Boulton, 2017, p. 483). This was the case with teachers involved in this research, they were not aware of possibility to use corpora for learning L1 or L2 language. As Breyer (2009) and Huang (2017) are stressing that "the best place to introduce language teachers to teaching and learning with corpora is when they are receiving their initial teaching education owing to such matters as limitations of time, the availability and suitability of resources or training to teach with corpora and so on" (p. 5).

Additionally, possibility of attending workshops or webinars is a good recommendation for rising awareness about use of computer corpora and its tools in language education. Teachers must be well trained before they could use it for developing teaching materials or for using corpora directly in the classroom with students. Huang (2017) points that for successful implementation of indirect or direct use of corpora into educational curriculum "lies in creating pedagogically driven corpora to meet instructional needs and curricular requirements with the need to develop teachers' knowledge and skills in corpus analysis and pedagogical mediation" (p. 17). Research has confirmed this statement because teachers to not use corpora in their work because it is not included in the national curriculum. As it was presented, some of newer textbooks suggests teachers' corpora as one of available tools to use but teachers are still not familiar with what corpora is and how they can use it for teaching.

Lack of education materials which will show teachers practical examples how corpora can be used in teaching language subject is another issue which must be addressed. Also, for teachers to know how correctly use corpora and interpret their results "there is a need for language teachers to learn how to evaluate the findings" (Özbay, Kayaoğlu, 2015, p. 86).

As Wallis, Cushing and Aarts (2019) are saying "a key missing element in applying corpora to teaching lies at the interface between students and corpus: the knowledge of schoolteachers" (p. 7). This is important factor which emerged during this research, big problem was to explain corpora to teachers and to describe them how they could use it with students. For corpora to be included in the classrooms teachers must undergo at least essential training about corpus functionalities and how to analyse and interpret corpus results. The main reason for that lays in the fact that "the language teachers can incorporate corpora and corpus tools into their teaching since they play significant roles in the process of introducing corpus work into the classroom and it is also the case that this experience with corpus tools must be broad and sufficient enough to enable teachers to integrate it to their teaching" (Özbay, Kayaoğlu, 2015, p. 87).

Major problem which many authors (Jantunen, 2016; Özbay, Kayaoğlu, 2015; Huang, 2017; Breyer, 2009; Wallis, Cushing, Aarts, 2019; Boulton, 2017) are emphasis and what this research has confirmed if lack of education about how to use of corpora for language teaching, either for learning first or second language. One of the solution is "before corpora and corpus methods can find their place in classroom interaction, corpus researchers must analyse corpus data and items and produce information that is relevant for teachers and language learners, this demands, first of all, close collaboration between teachers and corpus linguists" (Jantunen, 2016, p. 98).

Recommendation for all teachers who wants to include corpora in their teaching is to "become learners and experience corpus skills for themselves since they need to guide the learners for corpus based activities in the classroom" (Özbay, Kayaoğlu, 2015, p. 87).

Functionalities and Possibilities of Computer Corpora and Corpus Tools in the Field of Language Education at Primary and Secondary Schools

During this research all involved teachers gave their insights and provide their attitudes about advantages, disadvantages and all other possibilities which corpus tools can provide to primary and secondary school teachers who are teaching language subjects, i.e. Croatian, English and German language. They gave valuable insight into possibility to incorporate corpora and corpus tools in process of teaching language subjects. From this research emerged facts about teaching areas and unites in which corpora could be useful, for which group of students it can be suitable, is the DDL approach sustainable for students, can teachers use it for preparing teaching lessons and what are upsides and downsides of using computer corpora in primary and secondary education.

Teacher AP did the comprehensive research and his insight is very important part of this research. About advantages in using corpus tool for preparing teaching materials and DDL approach points out:

Advantages of developing teaching materials and exercise using computer corpora are in possibilities which they offer to teachers and students, for example: providing a better opportunity for collaborative work, possibility of adapting language content / curriculum, accurate view of language facts, increased motivation for learning with students, possibility to combine digital and language skills in learning process. Use of corpus and corpus tools emphasis focus to the individual/student supported with teacher mentoring. I would also like to point out that it provides various opportunities for adapting teaching process and work with children with disabilities and provides the possibility of extending tasks for children with special needs. (Teacher AP, 2019)

Teacher AP additionally states:

I will use corpora and corpus tools again because they have proved as effective and useful in the teaching process. The current changes in the curriculum at the national level in Croatia presupposes the introduction of digital content in teaching and I see computer corpora as one of the information and communication tools which can help to motivate and improve quality of students learning process in language teaching. (Teacher AP, 2019)

In relation to the traditional teaching approach which includes using textbooks and grammars in the classroom teacher AP point out that students were more motivated for learning and that corpus tools help them to better understand materials. He states:

Students have much better understood and comprehend language unit by using corpus approach rather than traditional approach (which implies the use of textbooks, grammar and workbooks) because of vivid illustration of the procedure and the method. (Teacher AP, 2019)

Regarding corpus methodology teacher AP has positive attitude and he thinks it can be easily incorporated into learning process of Croatan language in primary schools. His opinion about it is:

Corpus methodology can help meet the needs of language learning in different levels of teaching, for example it can be used as a data source for developing exercise and teaching content, as a language template for analysing texts from different perspectives, examining language facts in different contexts, for linguistic and sociolinguistic reflections, for the research of language conventions, etc. (Teacher AP, 2019)

He has positive predictions for corpus-based learning approach, and he will use them again with all his students. He points out:

In the future, I think corpus-based language teaching will be used more often because of the recommendation in the national curriculum, but the recommendation for now applies only to secondary schools, while there is still no national recommendation for primary schools. But I think that it can be used in primary schools because primary school language learning materials represents the overall section of the grammar of the Croatian language, which is only slightly expanded in secondary school. (Teacher AP, 2019)

On the other hand, teacher BP has slightly negative attitude towards corpus tools and their use in teaching English language in primary school:

Corpus could be useful for finding new examples for learning vocabulary, but it would not be my first choice for the search. There are millions of good materials online, with already prepared lessons and good examples. That is why I think it is not necessary for primary school to go deeper into the semantics and examples, the subject matter is hard enough as it is. (Teacher BP, 2019)

Additionally, he states if corpus tools would be integrated into curriculum of language subjects at the beginning only teachers could use them. Students on the other hand could use them in classroom after teacher's detailed explanation to the students how it works. Advantages and use of corpus should be clearly explained to students. If they understood it and accepted it then corpus tools and corpora could provide students with a new dimension of language analyse and they might accept it. Teacher BP also reflects on his experience as teacher in primary school and states:

Then again, speaking from experience students accept new things with disapproval because as much as we tell them something is useful, to them it's hard and boring and they cannot see direct usefulness of integrating new teaching methods or tools in classroom. (Teacher BP, 2019)

All teachers suggested that integration of computer corpora into teaching and learning process would be practical and interesting for them and the students. Despite their positive attitude towards computer corpora they did not have enough time to implement their materials into the classroom. Nevertheless, their contribution is also a valid source of information of how to incorporate corpus tools in teaching process on primary and secondary school level. Additionally, their contribution is important to see what are exiting obstacles for introducing corpus-based methodology into primary and secondary school classrooms as part of regular teaching units for language subjects.

For successful implementation of computer corpora and corpus tools into primary and secondary education in Croatian schools there are several factors which must be fulfilled before the integration process begin. Main factor is related to the low knowledge of teachers about what corpus is and how to use it for language teaching. Before using corpora, it would be useful to educate teachers about the subject through workshops, courses, online lessons, etc. In Croatia only universities have subject called Corpus linguistics where students which are studying languages can get information about corpora but they do not include much of practical examples and all is based more on theory then the practise and they use it to study and analyse language not to teach it.

Holdt, Kosem and Gantar (2017) are pointing that for "introducing corpus methodology and corpora as language resources to LI teaching in schools is one of the essential steps towards bridging the gap between real language use and student language problems, and language content in existing textbooks" (p. 106).

Özbay and Kayaoğlu (2015) are explaining that "efforts to incorporate corpus into the actual language teaching seem missing and the awareness towards corpus and corpus tools is very low and, in some cases, there is a resistance toward corpora from students and teachers" (p. 86)

Braun (2007) states that "corpora is still far from being part of overall teaching practice in the language classroom" (p. 48) what can be seen in research conducted at Faculty of Huminites and Social Science, University of Zagreb (Preradović, Posavec, 2019) which results shows that lecturers of Croatian as second or foreign language do not use corpora directly in the classroom nor for preparing teaching materials. Many of them use grammar books, dictionaries or internet as a source for creating teaching material.

Lack of corpus-based materials for teachers to use, lack of manuals in Croatian language for using corpora and corpus tools and lack of education about use of corpora with practical examples is a major issue why teacher do not use them in their work. Additional obstacle in implementing corpora in language teaching in Croatia is lack of teachers' motivation for using new technologies in classrooms due to low income (salary) and poor technical conditions e.g. equipment of classrooms with computers, laptops or tablets. But, it has been shown that computer corpora can be useful and powerful tool for rising student motivation for language learning and that students can comprehend it and master it as well as the teachers. Where is a will there is the way. Important factor for including corpora and its tools into primary and secondary education of students is to "clarifying expectations and encouraging openness to different learning pathways can go a long way in teachers' endeavours to exploit corpora for teaching and in learners' efforts to exploit them for learning" (Huang, 2017 p. 17).

Corpora is "offering a large number of authentic corpus examples, both as part of the explanations of the problems and in the exercises. Because many examples are taken from a corpus of student writing, it is likely that their content will be familiar to the (student) users" (Holdt, Kosem, Gantar, 2017, p. 106).

This research has showed that upper level primary students can use corpus and its tools in classroom and that DDL approach is suitable for this level of education. CQL query wasn't used because of the lack of time and knowledge but possibility of his use with primary school students cannot be excluded. With additional education of teachers in the field of corpora teachers could easily integrated it to their curriculum both for preparing teaching materials and direct use of corpora with students in classrooms. Based on analysis of students surveys it can be concluded that students are capable to individually search and use computer corpora during the class or from home doing their homework (1). Secondly, student's motivation for doing language tasks is increased with use of computer corpora (2) and third factor states that is possible regardless to lack of time, low finance/income of teachers, poor school infrastructure, lack of technologies in the classroom and fear of changes incorporated and include corpus tools into language teaching (3). Use of computer corpora directly in the classroom can motivate students to autonomisation in learning process (Boulton, 2010; Idrizi, Miftari, 2018; Preradović, Posavec, 2019; Warren, 2016), students can become more confident and independent while adopting new language knowledge and skills. Some author (Boulton, 2017; Wallis, Cushing, Aarts, 2019) are stressing that corpus results, examples of language can be too complex and inappropriate for primary and secondary students this research has proven otherwise. Based on research results primary school students did not have any problem with comprehend corpus examples, analysing concordances, interpreting results (KWIC) and adopting new language skills and knowledge.

Teacher BS proved that corpus tools can be used for preparing teaching unit for learning grammar and vocabulary based on use of KWIC, concordance, frequency, word could (similar word), all simple query types and CQL query. Teacher AS did not actively participate in research, because of the lack of time he did not use corpus tools during this research. Based on his knowledge about corpus linguistics teacher AS which teaches Croatian as first language in secondary school claims that corpus tools could be useful for teaching word frequency and some themes from lexicography in upper level secondary school. Also, he states that corpus tools could be used for studying the frequency of words and syntagma appearance, for example phraseme or rhyme.

Based on research results from primary school direct use of corpora in classroom is also possible for secondary school students because they are more mature, have wider range of technological knowledge and if primary students can do it there is no reason why secondary students could not do it. This hypothesis is not proven because the teachers from secondary schools which participated in this research did not use computer corpora in classrooms with their students. It can be stated that corpus tools are useful tool for preparing teaching materials for language class, e.g. language exercise, sentence examples, provide wider context for learning vocabulary and creating grammar examples for students.

There is more work to be done on different field as Boulton (2017) states "more longitudinal work is needed outside university classrooms: in autonomous contexts, in secondary education, in language schools, or in the workplace for 'genuine' life-long needs" (p. 485).

In terms of Croatian education system, the movements toward integration of corpora into secondary school education has been done in autumn of 2019 with new reform of national curriculum for primary and secondary schools. In national curriculum plan and program[1] on page 22 is proposed as one of the recommendations for achieving and acquiring pedagogical and educational goals for teaching secondary school students about frequency of words. This has been incorporated in textbook for first grade of secondary school, *Lica riječi 1*[2] (eng. Face of the words) which is used from school year 2019/2020 in all gymnasium and vocational school which lasts for four years.

FURTHER RESEARCH AND LIMITATIONS

This research has its limitations due to the time factor and the number of involved participants. Out of four language teachers just one of them used corpus in the classroom with his students and one of them prepared teaching materials using the corpus, and two teachers just provided their opinion and insight about the role of corpora in teaching language in secondary and primary schools. Furthermore, research was conducted during one school semester (from February till June in 2019) and it is based on teachers' attitude and insights about teaching process of language learning and corpus and its tools. Maybe the reason for low level of participants in this study can be find in local environment in Croatian education system. In 2019 primary and secondary school in Croatia were starting the new reform of national curriculum which did not have very positive effect on majority of teachers, they were overwhelmed with new obligations and programs.

Further research could be more focused on the direct use of corpora in just one level of education (primary or secondary). For example, it would be useful to measure student success in exams and exercises and level of comprehension of language materials which are corpus-based and those who are learning regularly using only textbooks. Further research could involve integration of direct use of corpora in classroom for one school semester or year which could give valuable insight into possibilities of corpus tools in language learning and teaching. Also, in this research teacher AP (form primary school) used only basic corpus quires but in next research it would be interesting to see how and in which language areas he could introduce CQL queries. Further research could examine DDL approach in which students would use corpus tools for language learning for a whole school year.

Also, it would be interesting to see would attitudes and teachers' opinions improve after they attend workshops and gain educative materials about using corpora and corpus tools.

It is important to emphasise that this research was conducted with Croatian teacher from two primary and two secondary schools in Croatia. Therefore, it is related to Croatian education system, laws and teaching curriculum which is specific to Croatia. But searching methods, functionalities, syntax of CQL query and all other corpus tools are the same regardless the country in which corpora and corpus tools are used. Because of that this research is valuable contribution to the field of computer corpora and corpus tools for learning, teaching, researching and analysing any of available languages through NoSketch Engine interface but also other systems because it explains how corpora is functioning and for what purpose it can be used in language teaching.

REFERENCES

Bennett, G. R. (2010). *Using corpora in the language learning classroom: Corpus linguistics for teachers*. University of Michigan Press. doi:10.3998/mpub.371534

Boulton, A. (2010). *Data-Driven Learning: On Paper, In Practise*. Academic Press.

Boulton, A. (2010). Data-driven learning: Taking the computer out of the Equation. *Language Learning*, *60*(3), 534–572. doi:10.1111/j.1467-9922.2010.00566.x

Boulton, A. (2017). Corpora in language teaching and learning. *Language Teaching*, *50*(4), 483–506. doi:10.1017/S0261444817000167

Braun, S. (2007). Integrating corpus work into secondary education: From data-driven learning to needs-driven corpora. *ReCALL*, *19*(3), 307–328. doi:10.1017/S0958344007000535

Breyer, Y. (2009). Learning and teaching with corpora: Reflections by student teachers. *Computer Assisted Language Learning*, *22*(2), 153–172. doi:10.1080/09588220902778328

Croatian National Curriculum. (n.d.). Available at: https://www.mvinfo.hr/file/articleAttachment/file/odluka-o-donosenju-kurikuluma-za-nastavni-predmet-hrvatski-jezik-za-osnovne-skole-i-gimnazije-u-republici-hrvatskoj.pdf

Gavioli, L., & Aston, G. (2001). Enriching reality: Language corpora in language pedagogy. *ELT Journal*, *55*(3), 238–246. doi:10.1093/elt/55.3.238

Hanks, P. (2008). *Mapping meaning onto use: a Pattern Dictionary of English Verbs*. AACL.

Holdt, Š. A., Kosem, I., & Gantar, P. (2017). Corpus-based resources for L1 teaching: The case of Slovene. In *Handbook on digital learning for K-12 schools* (pp. 91–113). Cham: Springer. doi:10.1007/978-3-319-33808-8_7

Huang, L. S. (2018). Taking Stock of Corpus-Based Instruction in Teaching English as an International Language. *RELC Journal*, *49*(3), 381–401. doi:10.1177/0033688217698294

Hunston, S. (2002). *Corpora in applied linguistics*. Ernst Klett Sprachen. doi:10.1017/CBO9781139524773

Idrizi, E., & Miftari, I. (2018). Students'perceptions Of Using Corpora As Reference Tools In Essay Error Correction And Exploring Words With Affixes: A Pilot Study. *Knowledge International Journal*, *23*(5), 1427–1432.

Jantunen, J. H. (2016). *Corpora, phraseology and dictionaries: How does corpus research intersect language teaching and learning?* Mémoires de la Société Néophilologique.

Kilgarriff, A., Kovář, V., & Rychlý, P. (2010). Tickbox lexicography. *eLexicography in the 21st century: New challenges, new applications*, 411-418.

Leech, G. (1997). Teaching and language corpora: a convergence. In A. Wichmann, S. Fligelstone, T. McEnery, & G. Knowles (Eds.), Teaching and Language Corpora, (pp. 1-23). Academic Press.

Özbay, A., & Kayaoğlu, M. N. (2015). EFL teacher's reflections towards the use of computerized corpora as a teaching tool in their classrooms. *Çukurova Üniversitesi Eğitim Fakültesi Dergisi, 44*(1), 85-104.

Preradovic, N. M., & Posavec, K. (2019). Advantages and Challenges of Using OERs in Teaching Less Commonly Taught Languages: Case Study From Croatia. In *Opening Up Education for Inclusivity Across Digital Economies and Societies* (pp. 73–96). IGI Global. doi:10.4018/978-1-5225-7473-6.ch004

Preradović, N. M., Posavec, K., & Unić, D. (2019). Corpus-Supported Foreign Language Teaching of Less Commonly Taught Languages. *International Journal of Instruction, 12*(4), 335–352. doi:10.29333/iji.2019.12422a

Sajko, N., Zrinjan, S., & Glušac, M. (2019). *LICA RIJEČI 1 - Udžbenik iz hrvatskoga jezika za prvi razred gimnazija i četverogodišnjih strukovnih škola (140 sati godišnje).* Zagreb: Hrvatska.

Wallis, S., Cushing, I., & Aarts, B. (2019). Exploiting parsed corpora in grammar teaching. *LiLT (Linguistic Issues in Language Technology), 18.*

Warren, M. (2016). Introduction to data-driven learning. Routledge handbook of language learning and technology, 337-347.

ENDNOTES

1 Available at: https://www.mvinfo.hr/file/articleAttachment/file/odluka-o-donosenju-kurikuluma-za-nastavni-predmet-hrvatski-jezik-za-osnovne-skole-i-gimnazije-u-republici-hrvatskoj.pdf

2 Sajko N., Zrinjan S., Glušac, M. (2019) LICA RIJEČI 1 - Udžbenik iz hrvatskoga jezika za prvi razred gimnazija i četverogodišnjih strukovnih škola (140 sati godišnje), Alfa, Zagreb, Hrvatska.

Appendix

APPENDIX A

Appendix A contains list of all questions which were included in the in-depth interviews with teachers from primary and secondary schools in Croatia. Results of Appendix A are shown and interpreted in Chapter 6 and 7.

IN-DEPTH INTERVIEW

Basic Beliefs About Teaching Croatian, English and German Language

(The aim is to identify the teacher's beliefs, the background and the teaching needs and to describe the group of students to whom this school year teachers teach and to share experiences and opinions about corpus tools).

ABOUT THE TEACHER

1. Formal education - Which faculty did you finish? How did you choose to become a Croatian / English / German teacher? How long have you been working in the profession? Did you teach Croatian/ English / German only in primary or in secondary schools? If yes, what are the similarities / differences?
2. What do you think what are your advantages in teaching, in what are you best as a teacher? Do you have any preferences regarding teaching units in language teaching, if so which? To which classes/grades did you teach Croatian / English / German - with whom do you prefer to work?

3. What is your biggest concern / what is the source of frustration in your work? Something in teaching, administration, space problem, etc.?
4. Do you attend congresses, do you conduct research?
5. What are your personal beliefs when it comes to teaching Croatian, English or German language? How would the language learning process, in your opinion, look like? What would you change, cancel, add? What are the main problems in working with students?
6. In your opinion what are the most effective ways of teaching languages in primary and/or secondary schools, depending were do you work?
7. How would you describe the way you teach the language?
8. What are your most important needs as teachers in language teaching?
9. How would you react to the integration of new methods and approaches to language teaching in general?
10. What is the role of technology in language teaching in yours expereince?

COMPREHENSION OF CORPUS LINGUISTICS

1. What first comes to your mind when you hear the term corpus linguistics?
2. What is your experience with corpus linguistics (use of corpus, search and analysis of search results using corpus tools):
    a) as a speaker of the mother tongue
    b) as a student of Croatian or some other language
        d) as a professor
3. In general, corpus tools represent a variety of ways corpus data can improve teaching and language adoption. Based on this definition, with which corpus tools are you familiar?
4. What do you think is the role of corpus tools in language teaching?
5. Are the corpus search results displayed to the user / teacher appropriately? What do you find problematic?
6. In your opinion, what is the attitude of administration in your institution towards the integration of corpus tools in curriculum?
7. Do think it is important to integrate educational course about the use of corpus tools into formal education of language teachers, or would it be sufficient only as additional education during professional development?
8. As a teacher, what do you think of the changes in the teaching process which would be cause by implementation of the corpus tools in teaching Croatian / English / German language? Do you think these changes would cause fear, overload, and dislike of teachers?

9. Do you think corpus tools should only be used by teachers or students (in a classroom/ at home)? Are the students motivated enough for such a task? And the teachers?
10. Which of the Croatian Computer Corps you would use to prepare teaching units and classes and why?

QUESTIONS RELATED TO RESEARCH

1. Do you have any questions about corpus methods and tools?
2. What questions do you have about this research?

ATTITUDE ABOUT TEACHING

(The goal is to identify the teacher's needs for a specific group of students and to identify which corpus and corpus tools the teacher would use to meet the teaching needs for that group / level of language learning).

1. What are the learning outcomes for classes you are teaching this school year ? Are they pre-defined with the program, can you independently define or modify them? What do you think is most important?
2. How do you operationalize these learning outcomes (activities, tasks, exams)? How is student progress evaluated: tests, grades, final grades?
3. How does your group of students look like (number of students, gender, age, student interest, what students are most likely to adopt)? Compared to your previous generations, what would you generally say about this one?
4. What do you think that are your strong sides as a teacher?
5. What are the biggest challenges in teaching this school year?
6. Are there specific problems / challenges regarding:
    a) the teaching materials (which materials you use and why, is there a need to upgrade material - more multimedia textbooks or interactive online exercises, tests?)
    b) specific classes
    c) inclusion / engagement of students in teaching
    d) class administration
    e) something else

IDENTIFICATION OF PERSONAL NEEDS FOR THE INCLUSION OF CORPUS TOOLS IN TEACHING PROCESS

1. In what ways would corpus tools be used to meet your needs and learning outcomes of the particular class?
2. Do you think that you would with the help of the corpora (i.e. the specific corpus tool) easily and quickly find appropriate examples and prepare a lesson for class? Can you list several concrete examples for the current class, but also for some that you have previously held depending on yours experience with corpora?

Development of a teaching unit plan that will include the use of corpus tools in language teaching.

THE SECOND PART OF INTERVIEW (HELD AFTER TEACHER'S USE OF CORPUS TOOLS FOR PREPARATION OF TEACHING MATERIALS FOR CLASS)

Structure and Description of Teaching Unit Prepared With Corpus Tools

1. What corpus did you use to prepare class?
2. What kind of teaching unit did you prepare with the help of the corpus?
3. In your opinion, what are the advantages of preparing corpus-based teaching materials and exercises?
4. In your opinion, what are the disadvantages of preparing corpus-based teaching materials and exercises?
5. What are your impressions of the teaching unite prepared with corpus tools?
6. Would you repeat this for the next unit? If yes, why? If not, why? If so, what would you change?
7. Do you think you will use again corpus tools? If yes, why? If not, why?
8. Which elements worked well and why?
9. Which elements did not work well and why?
10. Do you think you have achieved your goals for the teaching unit?
11. Do you think the students were satisfied with the teaching unit?

12. What do you think, did students better adopt presented materials in compareson to the previous class/grade?
13. Have you moved away from your curriculum? If so, how and why?
14. During the class (or while preparing the materials), have you encountered certain surprises?
15. What would you like to include in the teaching unit, and you did not?
16. How can corpus methodology help you to meet the needs of language learning with students?
17. After this experience, what do you think about certain corpus tools (concordance list, collocations, frequency, KWIC, morphosyntactic tags, CQL search) and what of the future role of corpus-based language teaching in your further work?
18. In your opinion, which corpus tools were of the greatest benefit to the preparation and implementation of the teaching unit and why?
19. Which corpus tools were of the least benefit to you and why?
20. What was your experience with preparation of class with the help of corpus tools compared to traditional preparation with the help of textbooks and manuals: simple and fast, effortless and demanding?
21. Do you think you could use direct corpora approach in your classroom with students? If so, for which students would be appropriate. If not, why? What are the limits and what are the advantages of using direct corpora approach in your classroom with students?
22. Do you have some thoughts and comments about the process itself?

APPENDIX B

Appendix B shows survey which was given to students from primary school who participated in this research and who were using DDL approach and corpus-based materials during the school lesson. Results of Appendix B are shown and interpreted in chapter 6.

SURVEY FOR STUDENTS AFTER DDL APPROACH USED IN THE CLASSROOM WITH COMPUTER CORPORA

1. Gender:
    a. Male
    b. Female

2. Fill in the age:
3. Rate your knowledge of Croatian:
    a. excellent
    b. very good
    c. good
    d. bad
4. How satisfied are you with todays presented curriculum in classroom?
    a. extremely satisfied
    b. very satisfied
    c. satisfied
    d. dissatisfied
5. Do you think that the lesson contributed to increasing your knowledge of the grammar of Croatian language?
    a. Yes
    b. No
6. Rate the degree of understanding of the presented material in this lesson in relation to previous classes:
    a. I completely understood lesson
    b. I understood lesson
    c. I did not understood lesson
    d. I do not see difference in connections to previous classes
7. In your opinion, the approach (the method of transferring knowledge and interaction in classroom) of language learning in today's classroom is:
    a. excellent
    b. very good
    c. good
    d. bad
8. In your opinion, the exercise you have previously solved is:
    a. completely understandable
    b. well understandable
    c. partly understandable
    d. not understandable
9. How satisfied are you with the exercises in today's class?
    a. extremely satisfied
    b. very satisfied
    c. satisfied
    d. dissatisfied

10. How satisfied are you with the current teaching materials you use in the process of learning Croatian language?
    a. extremely satisfied
    b. very satisfied
    c. satisfied
    d. dissatisfied
11. Do you think it would be easier to master the Croatian language if you are using computer and internet in the classroom?
    a. Yes
    b. No
12. In your opinion, which is the most effective way of learning Croatian language?
    a. Listening
    b. Writing
    c. Internet
    d. Communication
    e. Interactive computer programs
    f. All of the above
13. In which of listed below are you most interested when learning Croatian language:
    a. Writing essays
    b. Reading literature
    c. Reading about actual topics
    d. Solving tasks using internet
    e. Independently researching language using internet
    f. Solving tasks using computer applications programs
14. Would you use again corpus for learning Croatian language?
    a. Yes
    b. No
15. Do you think you could use corpus independently to learn Croatian language?
    a. Yes
    b. No

APPENDIX C

Appendix C shows teacher's AP corpus-based teaching unite (materials) which he prepared during this research for his students for learning Croatian as first language in primary school. Results of Appendix C are shown and interpreted in chapter 6.

LANGUAGE CORPORA

Grade: 8th
Subject: Croatian language and literacy
Theme of the class: Repetition of **idioms and word formation**
Time: two classes (90 minutes)
Work dynamic: Collaborative
Method: Project based

Introduction

Corpus is written or spoken language resource which is created and tagged for conducting language analysis. There are many types of corpora, for example general corpora which have hundreds of million words, but there are also a specialized corpora which are created for certain purpose and they are smaller.

A computer corpus is a computer-stored and searchable collection of text that represent a language for research purpose.

Link to corpus which we will use during the class:

1. Croatian National Corpus

   http://filip.ffzg.hr/cgi-bin/run.cgi/first_form

2. Croatian Web Corpus

   https://www.clarin.si/noske/run.cgi/first_form?corpname=hrwac;align

Tasks

1. TASK: During the class and resolving given tasks students will create presentation with their answers, they will incorporate images, screenshot and text in their presentation.
    a. One of the 4 ways of word formation is borrowing words from a different languages (taking words from a foreign language: hrv. *kompjuter* / eng. *computer*). Students will use corpora to search for synonyms in Croatian language and their variants from different languages. It is a general rule not to use foreign words unless absolutely necessary, because of the lack of Croatian terms.
2. TASK: You need to choose few pairs of given synonyms and look for them in corpora. Based on the results you need to investigate which word has a higher frequency in language use.
    a. barcode – crtični kod
    b. computer – računalo
    c. educational – obrazovni
    d. laptop – prijenosno računalo
    e. event – događanje
    f. experiment – pokus
    g. screen - zaslon
        i. Homonyms - words which have same spelling but different meaning depending on context in which they are used, for example word wheel (kola) have several different meaning:
        ii. a circular object connected at the centre to a bar, used for making vehicles or parts of machines move
        iii. type of dance in which participants (dancers) form a circle
        iv. to be connected or join on the base of similar characteristics
        v. name of Croatian literary magazine
        vi. sequence of sport competitions in certain time period
        vii. transport vehicle (car, coaches, animal drawn vehicles)
3. TASK: Using corpora you will search for the word sat (eng. *hour*) and from results you will write different meaning of the word.
4. TASK: Students will search word *veselo (eng. happily) and misleći (eng. think)* in corpora. For every word they must provide example (form corpora) how this word is used and how does it changes depending on context.
    a. Words can be expended with use of prefixes and/or suffixes .

5. TASK: Students will search for the root of the word in the corpus (root: -pis - search type: character) and look for examples of prefix, suffix, and formation by stacking within word families.
   a. **Idioms implies that expressions are related to at least two full meaningful words. The layout of the components always remains the same.**
6. TASK: Students will search corpora with the given parts of unusual idioms to see how their whole meaning and to see how their meaning is changing depending on the context in which they are showing up (examples: hrv. *nešto je trulo…* eng. *something is rotten …*).

Evaluation

Presenting the final work done by students.

Related Readings

To continue IGI Global's long-standing tradition of advancing innovation through emerging research, please find below a compiled list of recommended IGI Global book chapters and journal articles in the areas of language learning, curriculum design, and computer science. These related readings will provide additional information and guidance to further enrich your knowledge and assist you with your own research.

Abbadi, S. (2016). Globalization and Possibilities for Intercultural Awareness: Multimodal Arabic Culture Portfolios at a Catholic University. In C. Wang & L. Winstead (Eds.), *Handbook of Research on Foreign Language Education in the Digital Age* (pp. 277–294). Hershey, PA: IGI Global. doi:10.4018/978-1-5225-0177-0.ch013

Ahluwalia, G., & Gupta, D. (2017). Impact of Technology-Enhanced Language Learning on the Writing Skills of Engineering Students: A Case Study. In D. Tafazoli & M. Romero (Eds.), *Multiculturalism and Technology-Enhanced Language Learning* (pp. 33–56). Hershey, PA: IGI Global. doi:10.4018/978-1-5225-1882-2.ch003

Akayoglu, S., & Seferoglu, G. (2017). Social Presence Functions in Task-Based Language Activities in a Virtual Classroom in Second Life. In D. Tafazoli & M. Romero (Eds.), *Multiculturalism and Technology-Enhanced Language Learning* (pp. 181–198). Hershey, PA: IGI Global. doi:10.4018/978-1-5225-1882-2.ch011

Andrawiss-Dlamini, H. M., & Puntil, D. (2018). Open Up the Classroom: The Use of Film Excerpts and Video Clips in Lower Levels Language Courses. In C. Xiang (Ed.), *Cases on Audio-Visual Media in Language Education* (pp. 22–46). Hershey, PA: IGI Global. doi:10.4018/978-1-5225-2724-4.ch002

Anwaruddin, S. M. (2018). Beyond Determinism and Instrumentalism: Re-Conceptualizing Technology for CALL. In J. Perren, K. Kelch, J. Byun, S. Cervantes, & S. Safavi (Eds.), *Applications of CALL Theory in ESL and EFL Environments* (pp. 22–35). Hershey, PA: IGI Global. doi:10.4018/978-1-5225-2933-0.ch002

Ashtari, N. (2018). Mixed Reality Environments in Teaching and Learning English. In D. Tafazoli, M. Gomez Parra, & C. Huertas-Abril (Eds.), *Cross-Cultural Perspectives on Technology-Enhanced Language Learning* (pp. 187–202). Hershey, PA: IGI Global. doi:10.4018/978-1-5225-5463-9.ch011

Awada, G. M., Diab, H. B., & Faour, K. H. (2018). Effect of GI and Glogster on Improving the Intercultural Communication Skills in Higher Education. In D. Tafazoli, M. Gomez Parra, & C. Huertas-Abril (Eds.), *Cross-Cultural Perspectives on Technology-Enhanced Language Learning* (pp. 130–158). Hershey, PA: IGI Global. doi:10.4018/978-1-5225-5463-9.ch008

Azad, M. (2017). Dynamic Assessment and Multi-Media Language Instruction. In D. Tafazoli & M. Romero (Eds.), *Multiculturalism and Technology-Enhanced Language Learning* (pp. 230–251). Hershey, PA: IGI Global. doi:10.4018/978-1-5225-1882-2.ch014

Balchin, K., & Wild, C. (2018). It's All in the Numbers: Enhancing Technology Use in Urban and Rural Environments. In D. Tafazoli, M. Gomez Parra, & C. Huertas-Abril (Eds.), *Cross-Cultural Perspectives on Technology-Enhanced Language Learning* (pp. 203–221). Hershey, PA: IGI Global. doi:10.4018/978-1-5225-5463-9.ch012

Bañares-Marivela, E., & Rayón-Rumayor, L. (2017). Multimodal Narratives and iPad in Second Language Teaching. In D. Tafazoli & M. Romero (Eds.), *Multiculturalism and Technology-Enhanced Language Learning* (pp. 57–79). Hershey, PA: IGI Global. doi:10.4018/978-1-5225-1882-2.ch004

Barnes, M. (2017). Encouraging Communication through the Use of Educational Social Media Tools. In D. Tafazoli & M. Romero (Eds.), *Multiculturalism and Technology-Enhanced Language Learning* (pp. 1–12). Hershey, PA: IGI Global. doi:10.4018/978-1-5225-1882-2.ch001

Barrons, K. P. (2017). Flipped Instructional Technology: Developing MIS Competencies Applying Enterprise Resource Planning Software. In J. Loucky & J. Ware (Eds.), *Flipped Instruction Methods and Digital Technologies in the Language Learning Classroom* (pp. 183–195). Hershey, PA: IGI Global. doi:10.4018/978-1-5225-0824-3.ch008

Bekleyen, N., & Çelik, S. (2017). Attitudes of Adult EFL Learners towards Preparing for a Language Test via CALL. In D. Tafazoli & M. Romero (Eds.), *Multiculturalism and Technology-Enhanced Language Learning* (pp. 214–229). Hershey, PA: IGI Global. doi:10.4018/978-1-5225-1882-2.ch013

Blattner, G., Dalola, A., & Lomicka, L. (2016). Mind Your Hashtags: A Sociopragmatic Study of Student Interpretations of French Native Speakers' Tweets. In C. Wang & L. Winstead (Eds.), *Handbook of Research on Foreign Language Education in the Digital Age* (pp. 33–58). Hershey, PA: IGI Global. doi:10.4018/978-1-5225-0177-0.ch003

Bobkina, J., & Romero, E. D. (2018). Multimodal Listening Through Movie Trailers: Towards a Framework for Classroom Implementation. In C. Xiang (Ed.), *Cases on Audio-Visual Media in Language Education* (pp. 69–92). Hershey, PA: IGI Global. doi:10.4018/978-1-5225-2724-4.ch004

Bodah, E. T., Alldredge, J. M., Bodah, B. W., Neckel, A., & Goellner, E. (2016). Challenges and Perspectives of Language Education Technology in Brazil: From Confronting Native Language Loss to Implementing EFL Classes. In C. Wang & L. Winstead (Eds.), *Handbook of Research on Foreign Language Education in the Digital Age* (pp. 59–82). Hershey, PA: IGI Global. doi:10.4018/978-1-5225-0177-0.ch004

Bourgoin, R. C. (2016). French Immersion "So Why Would You do Something Like That to a Child?": Issues of Advocacy, Accessibility, and Inclusion. *International Journal of Bias, Identity and Diversities in Education, 1*(1), 42–58. doi:10.4018/IJBIDE.2016010104

Brown, D. (2016). Motivation and Learning Outcomes in Reciprocal SCMC Language-Learning. *International Journal of Computer-Assisted Language Learning and Teaching, 6*(2), 19–34. doi:10.4018/IJCALLT.2016040102

Burgo, C. (2016). Teaching Spanish in the Digital Age: A Flipped Classroom or Just Hybrid? In C. Wang & L. Winstead (Eds.), *Handbook of Research on Foreign Language Education in the Digital Age* (pp. 83–103). Hershey, PA: IGI Global. doi:10.4018/978-1-5225-0177-0.ch005

Carter, B., He, M., & Kawasaki, T. (2018). Using YouTube and WeChat to Promote Communicative and Intercultural Competence in Japanese and Mandarin. In C. Xiang (Ed.), *Cases on Audio-Visual Media in Language Education* (pp. 219–239). Hershey, PA: IGI Global. doi:10.4018/978-1-5225-2724-4.ch009

Cho, H. (2018). The Pitfalls and Promises of Electronic Portfolio Assessment With Secondary English Language Learners. In J. Perren, K. Kelch, J. Byun, S. Cervantes, & S. Safavi (Eds.), *Applications of CALL Theory in ESL and EFL Environments* (pp. 111–130). Hershey, PA: IGI Global. doi:10.4018/978-1-5225-2933-0.ch007

Cimermanova, I. (2017). Computer-Assisted Learning in Slovakia. In D. Tafazoli & M. Romero (Eds.), *Multiculturalism and Technology-Enhanced Language Learning* (pp. 252–270). Hershey, PA: IGI Global. doi:10.4018/978-1-5225-1882-2.ch015

Dalton, G., & Devitt, A. (2016). Gaeilge Gaming: Assessing how games can help children to learn Irish. *International Journal of Game-Based Learning*, *6*(4), 22–38. doi:10.4018/IJGBL.2016100102

Dinh, H. (2018). Teachers' Uses and Beliefs in the Integration of YouTube Videos Into English Language Teaching: A Comparison Between ESL and EFL Contexts. In J. Perren, K. Kelch, J. Byun, S. Cervantes, & S. Safavi (Eds.), *Applications of CALL Theory in ESL and EFL Environments* (pp. 94–110). Hershey, PA: IGI Global. doi:10.4018/978-1-5225-2933-0.ch006

Dixon, D. H., & Christison, M. (2018). The Usefulness of Massive Multiplayer Online Role Playing Games (MMORPGs) as Tools for Promoting Second Language Acquisition. In J. Perren, K. Kelch, J. Byun, S. Cervantes, & S. Safavi (Eds.), *Applications of CALL Theory in ESL and EFL Environments* (pp. 244–268). Hershey, PA: IGI Global. doi:10.4018/978-1-5225-2933-0.ch014

Dixon, T., & Christison, M. (2018). Teaching English Grammar in a Hybrid Academic ESL Course. In J. Perren, K. Kelch, J. Byun, S. Cervantes, & S. Safavi (Eds.), *Applications of CALL Theory in ESL and EFL Environments* (pp. 149–169). Hershey, PA: IGI Global. doi:10.4018/978-1-5225-2933-0.ch009

du Plessis, J. (2016). Reflection: How Now Shapes the Future – Emerging Trends from the LCTL Trenches. In C. Wang & L. Winstead (Eds.), *Handbook of Research on Foreign Language Education in the Digital Age* (pp. 1–8). Hershey, PA: IGI Global. doi:10.4018/978-1-5225-0177-0.ch001

Durand, S. (2018). Embracing Computer Corpora in the Language Learning Classroom and Using It in Your Classroom. In J. Perren, K. Kelch, J. Byun, S. Cervantes, & S. Safavi (Eds.), *Applications of CALL Theory in ESL and EFL Environments* (pp. 131–148). Hershey, PA: IGI Global. doi:10.4018/978-1-5225-2933-0.ch008

Foley-Ryan, M. M. (2018). Using News Reports in Language Education. In C. Xiang (Ed.), *Cases on Audio-Visual Media in Language Education* (pp. 47–68). Hershey, PA: IGI Global. doi:10.4018/978-1-5225-2724-4.ch003

Forsythe, E. (2017). Integrating Recent CALL Innovations into Flipped Instruction. In J. Loucky & J. Ware (Eds.), *Flipped Instruction Methods and Digital Technologies in the Language Learning Classroom* (pp. 270–277). Hershey, PA: IGI Global. doi:10.4018/978-1-5225-0824-3.ch012

Forsythe, E. (2017). Pedagogical Rationale for Flipped Learning and Digital Technology in Second Language Acquisition. In J. Loucky & J. Ware (Eds.), *Flipped Instruction Methods and Digital Technologies in the Language Learning Classroom* (pp. 1–20). Hershey, PA: IGI Global. doi:10.4018/978-1-5225-0824-3.ch001

Fuchs, C. (2016). The Structural and Dialogic Aspects of Language Massive Open Online Courses (LMOOCs): A Case Study. In C. Wang & L. Winstead (Eds.), *Handbook of Research on Foreign Language Education in the Digital Age* (pp. 10–32). Hershey, PA: IGI Global. doi:10.4018/978-1-5225-0177-0.ch002

Gabaudan, O. R. (2017). Students as Producers of Digital Audio-Visual Clips in Preparation for a Study Abroad Period: Collaboration for Independent Language Learning. In D. Tafazoli & M. Romero (Eds.), *Multiculturalism and Technology-Enhanced Language Learning* (pp. 97–115). Hershey, PA: IGI Global. doi:10.4018/978-1-5225-1882-2.ch006

Galvez, H. (2017). Flipped Instruction for Language Learning. In J. Loucky & J. Ware (Eds.), *Flipped Instruction Methods and Digital Technologies in the Language Learning Classroom* (pp. 91–107). Hershey, PA: IGI Global. doi:10.4018/978-1-5225-0824-3.ch004

Garnes-Tarazona, I. (2018). Exploring Socio-Cultural Elements in Three Commercial English Language Learning Apps. *International Journal of Computer-Assisted Language Learning and Teaching*, *8*(1), 65–82. doi:10.4018/IJCALLT.2018010105

Gasmi, A. A., & Thomas, M. (2017). Academic Writing in the Flipped EFL Classroom: A Case Study on Student Engagement in Oman. In J. Loucky & J. Ware (Eds.), *Flipped Instruction Methods and Digital Technologies in the Language Learning Classroom* (pp. 232–251). Hershey, PA: IGI Global. doi:10.4018/978-1-5225-0824-3.ch010

Gremler, C., & Wielander, E. (2018). The Benefits of Student-Led Video Production in the Language for Business Classroom. In C. Xiang (Ed.), *Cases on Audio-Visual Media in Language Education* (pp. 155–193). Hershey, PA: IGI Global. doi:10.4018/978-1-5225-2724-4.ch007

Heirati, J. K., Azadsarv, M., & Golzari, A. (2017). Technology-Enhanced Vocabulary Development through Semantic Network Development Model vs. Syntactic Structure Development Model. In D. Tafazoli & M. Romero (Eds.), *Multiculturalism and Technology-Enhanced Language Learning* (pp. 199–213). Hershey, PA: IGI Global. doi:10.4018/978-1-5225-1882-2.ch012

Ibrahim, K. H. (2018). The Foreign Language Learning Potential of Video Games: FL Games as Cross-Cultural Texts, Narratives, and Artifacts. In D. Tafazoli, M. Gomez Parra, & C. Huertas-Abril (Eds.), *Cross-Cultural Perspectives on Technology-Enhanced Language Learning* (pp. 159–171). Hershey, PA: IGI Global. doi:10.4018/978-1-5225-5463-9.ch009

Johnston, K. P., & Lawrence, G. (2018). A Theoretically Informed Approach to Collaborative Writing in EAP Contexts Using Web-Based Technologies. In J. Perren, K. Kelch, J. Byun, S. Cervantes, & S. Safavi (Eds.), *Applications of CALL Theory in ESL and EFL Environments* (pp. 1–21). Hershey, PA: IGI Global. doi:10.4018/978-1-5225-2933-0.ch001

Kan, Q., & Tang, J. (2018). Researching Mobile-Assisted English Language Learning Among Adult Distance Learners in China: Emerging Practices and Learner Perception of Teacher Role. *International Journal of Computer-Assisted Language Learning and Teaching*, *8*(3), 1–28. doi:10.4018/IJCALLT.2018070101

Kasemsap, K. (2017). Mastering Technology-Enhanced Language Learning, Computer-Assisted Language Learning, and Mobile-Assisted Language Learning. In D. Tafazoli & M. Romero (Eds.), *Multiculturalism and Technology-Enhanced Language Learning* (pp. 157–180). Hershey, PA: IGI Global. doi:10.4018/978-1-5225-1882-2.ch010

Katrnakova, H. (2018). Integration of Videoconferencing in ESP and EAP Courses: Focus on Community of Practice Interaction. In C. Xiang (Ed.), *Cases on Audio-Visual Media in Language Education* (pp. 283–303). Hershey, PA: IGI Global. doi:10.4018/978-1-5225-2724-4.ch012

Kirk, S., & Casenove, D. (2017). Flipping the Academic Writing Classroom. In J. Loucky & J. Ware (Eds.), *Flipped Instruction Methods and Digital Technologies in the Language Learning Classroom* (pp. 196–231). Hershey, PA: IGI Global. doi:10.4018/978-1-5225-0824-3.ch009

Kızıl, A. Ş., & Kilimci, A. (2017). Teaching Collocations through Web-Based Concordancing: A Corpus Informed Quasi-Experimental Study. In D. Tafazoli & M. Romero (Eds.), *Multiculturalism and Technology-Enhanced Language Learning* (pp. 142–156). Hershey, PA: IGI Global. doi:10.4018/978-1-5225-1882-2.ch009

Kostka, I., & Marshall, H. W. (2018). Flipped Learning in TESOL: Past, Present, and Future. In J. Perren, K. Kelch, J. Byun, S. Cervantes, & S. Safavi (Eds.), *Applications of CALL Theory in ESL and EFL Environments* (pp. 223–243). Hershey, PA: IGI Global. doi:10.4018/978-1-5225-2933-0.ch013

Lawrence, G., & Ahmed, F. (2018). Pedagogical Insights into Hyper-Immersive Virtual World Language Learning Environments. *International Journal of Computer-Assisted Language Learning and Teaching*, *8*(1), 1–14. doi:10.4018/IJCALLT.2018010101

Lawrence, G., & Spector-Cohen, E. (2018). Examining International Telecollaboration in Language Teacher Education. In D. Tafazoli, M. Gomez Parra, & C. Huertas-Abril (Eds.), *Cross-Cultural Perspectives on Technology-Enhanced Language Learning* (pp. 322–345). Hershey, PA: IGI Global. doi:10.4018/978-1-5225-5463-9.ch018

Le, N., & Dinh, H. (2018). Augmented Reality: A Brief Introduction, Its Potentials, and Implications in Language Education. In J. Perren, K. Kelch, J. Byun, S. Cervantes, & S. Safavi (Eds.), *Applications of CALL Theory in ESL and EFL Environments* (pp. 291–309). Hershey, PA: IGI Global. doi:10.4018/978-1-5225-2933-0.ch016

Lee, L. (2018). Using Telecollaboration 2.0 to Build Intercultural Communicative Competence: A Spanish-American Exchange. In D. Tafazoli, M. Gomez Parra, & C. Huertas-Abril (Eds.), *Cross-Cultural Perspectives on Technology-Enhanced Language Learning* (pp. 303–321). Hershey, PA: IGI Global. doi:10.4018/978-1-5225-5463-9.ch017

Legutko, A. (2016). Yiddish in the 21st Century: New Media to the Rescue of Endangered Languages. In C. Wang & L. Winstead (Eds.), *Handbook of Research on Foreign Language Education in the Digital Age* (pp. 236–252). Hershey, PA: IGI Global. doi:10.4018/978-1-5225-0177-0.ch011

Levy, T., & Cohen, L. J. (2017). Teaching English for Academic Purposes through the Use of Digital Tools. In J. Loucky & J. Ware (Eds.), *Flipped Instruction Methods and Digital Technologies in the Language Learning Classroom* (pp. 21–63). Hershey, PA: IGI Global. doi:10.4018/978-1-5225-0824-3.ch002

Lewis, T. N. (2016). Creating a Micro-Immersion Environment Through Telecollaboration. In C. Wang & L. Winstead (Eds.), *Handbook of Research on Foreign Language Education in the Digital Age* (pp. 144–169). Hershey, PA: IGI Global. doi:10.4018/978-1-5225-0177-0.ch007

Li, B., Yao, S., & Hong, W. (2016). Beginning Chinese as a Foreign Language Online Course Design: Utilizing Multiple Digital Modes and Assessments. In C. Wang & L. Winstead (Eds.), *Handbook of Research on Foreign Language Education in the Digital Age* (pp. 104–142). Hershey, PA: IGI Global. doi:10.4018/978-1-5225-0177-0.ch006

Lim, B., & Pyun, D. O. (2016). Korean Foreign Language Learning: Videoconferencing with Native Speakers. In C. Wang & L. Winstead (Eds.), *Handbook of Research on Foreign Language Education in the Digital Age* (pp. 253–276). Hershey, PA: IGI Global. doi:10.4018/978-1-5225-0177-0.ch012

Liontas, J. I. (2018). Understanding Idiomaticity in CALL. In J. Perren, K. Kelch, J. Byun, S. Cervantes, & S. Safavi (Eds.), *Applications of CALL Theory in ESL and EFL Environments* (pp. 36–58). Hershey, PA: IGI Global. doi:10.4018/978-1-5225-2933-0.ch003

Liu, H., Tao, W., & Cain, W. (2016). Investigating Mobile Assisted English Foreign Language Learning and Teaching in China: Issues, Attitudes and Perceptions. In C. Wang & L. Winstead (Eds.), *Handbook of Research on Foreign Language Education in the Digital Age* (pp. 315–333). Hershey, PA: IGI Global. doi:10.4018/978-1-5225-0177-0.ch015

Llull, J., Palacios, A., & Ulkuniemi, S. (2018). Fostering Intercultural Competence Through Art and ICT Among University Students in Spain and Finland. In D. Tafazoli, M. Gomez Parra, & C. Huertas-Abril (Eds.), *Cross-Cultural Perspectives on Technology-Enhanced Language Learning* (pp. 237–262). Hershey, PA: IGI Global. doi:10.4018/978-1-5225-5463-9.ch014

Loucky, J. P. (2017). Motivating and Empowering Students' Language Learning in Flipped Integrated English Classes. In J. Loucky & J. Ware (Eds.), *Flipped Instruction Methods and Digital Technologies in the Language Learning Classroom* (pp. 108–138). Hershey, PA: IGI Global. doi:10.4018/978-1-5225-0824-3.ch005

Loucky, J. P. (2017). Studies of Flipping Classes with Asian Students. In J. Loucky & J. Ware (Eds.), *Flipped Instruction Methods and Digital Technologies in the Language Learning Classroom* (pp. 64–90). Hershey, PA: IGI Global. doi:10.4018/978-1-5225-0824-3.ch003

Loucky, J. P. (2017). Testing a CALL Effectiveness Model: Online Media Can Open New Learning Possibilities. In J. Loucky & J. Ware (Eds.), *Flipped Instruction Methods and Digital Technologies in the Language Learning Classroom* (pp. 252–269). Hershey, PA: IGI Global. doi:10.4018/978-1-5225-0824-3.ch011

Luan, D. (2018). Exploring Intercultural Communication Through the Act of Translation in Subtitling. In C. Xiang (Ed.), *Cases on Audio-Visual Media in Language Education* (pp. 261–281). Hershey, PA: IGI Global. doi:10.4018/978-1-5225-2724-4.ch011

Martínez-Carrasco, R. (2018). Collaborative Writing 2.0: Socializing Critical, Cross-Cultural Agents Through Online, Project-Based Methodology. In D. Tafazoli, M. Gomez Parra, & C. Huertas-Abril (Eds.), *Cross-Cultural Perspectives on Technology-Enhanced Language Learning* (pp. 283–302). Hershey, PA: IGI Global. doi:10.4018/978-1-5225-5463-9.ch016

Mary, L., & Young, A. (2016). The Role of Multi-Media in Expanding Pre-Service Teachers' Understanding of Culturally and Linguistically Diverse Classrooms and Furthering Their Professional Identities. In C. Wang & L. Winstead (Eds.), *Handbook of Research on Foreign Language Education in the Digital Age* (pp. 296–314). Hershey, PA: IGI Global. doi:10.4018/978-1-5225-0177-0.ch014

Melo-Pfeifer, S. (2016). Translanguaging in Multilingual Chat Interaction: Opportunities for Intercomprehension between Romance Languages. In C. Wang & L. Winstead (Eds.), *Handbook of Research on Foreign Language Education in the Digital Age* (pp. 188–207). Hershey, PA: IGI Global. doi:10.4018/978-1-5225-0177-0.ch009

Mihăeş, L. C. (2018). Technology-Integrated Teaching and Assessment: ESP at the University of Bucharest. In J. Perren, K. Kelch, J. Byun, S. Cervantes, & S. Safavi (Eds.), *Applications of CALL Theory in ESL and EFL Environments* (pp. 187–205). Hershey, PA: IGI Global. doi:10.4018/978-1-5225-2933-0.ch011

Mohammadi, E., & Shirkamar, Z. S. (2018). Mobile-Assisted Language Learning: Challenges and Setbacks in Developing Countries. In D. Tafazoli, M. Gomez Parra, & C. Huertas-Abril (Eds.), *Cross-Cultural Perspectives on Technology-Enhanced Language Learning* (pp. 172–186). Hershey, PA: IGI Global. doi:10.4018/978-1-5225-5463-9.ch010

Monfared, A., Cervantes, S. E., Lee, S. M., & Jackson, M. (2018). Establishing a Praxis Between SLA Theory and CALL-Based Practices. In J. Perren, K. Kelch, J. Byun, S. Cervantes, & S. Safavi (Eds.), *Applications of CALL Theory in ESL and EFL Environments* (pp. 59–79). Hershey, PA: IGI Global. doi:10.4018/978-1-5225-2933-0.ch004

Morgana, V., & Shrestha, P. N. (2018). Investigating Students' and Teachers' Perceptions of Using the iPad in an Italian English as a Foreign Language Classroom. *International Journal of Computer-Assisted Language Learning and Teaching*, *8*(3), 29–49. doi:10.4018/IJCALLT.2018070102

Murtiningsih, S. R., & Rahmawati, F. (2018). A CALL-Mediated Course to Enhance EFL Pre-Service Teachers' Engagement. In J. Perren, K. Kelch, J. Byun, S. Cervantes, & S. Safavi (Eds.), *Applications of CALL Theory in ESL and EFL Environments* (pp. 170–186). Hershey, PA: IGI Global. doi:10.4018/978-1-5225-2933-0.ch010

Naidoo, V. (2017). Challenges Facing E-Learning. In D. Tafazoli & M. Romero (Eds.), *Multiculturalism and Technology-Enhanced Language Learning* (pp. 271–288). Hershey, PA: IGI Global. doi:10.4018/978-1-5225-1882-2.ch016

Newcombe, J., & Brick, B. (2017). Blending Video Games Into Language Learning. *International Journal of Computer-Assisted Language Learning and Teaching*, 7(4), 75–89. doi:10.4018/IJCALLT.2017100106

Olesova, L., & de Oliveira, L. (2018). Using Feedback in ESL and EFL Asynchronous Online Environments. In J. Perren, K. Kelch, J. Byun, S. Cervantes, & S. Safavi (Eds.), *Applications of CALL Theory in ESL and EFL Environments* (pp. 206–222). Hershey, PA: IGI Global. doi:10.4018/978-1-5225-2933-0.ch012

Pan, F. (2018). Short Video Production for Language Learning and Assessment. In C. Xiang (Ed.), *Cases on Audio-Visual Media in Language Education* (pp. 194–217). Hershey, PA: IGI Global. doi:10.4018/978-1-5225-2724-4.ch008

Piri, S., & Riahi, S. (2018). Cross-Cultural Perspectives on Technology-Enhanced Language Learning: A Review of Research. In D. Tafazoli, M. Gomez Parra, & C. Huertas-Abril (Eds.), *Cross-Cultural Perspectives on Technology-Enhanced Language Learning* (pp. 1–15). Hershey, PA: IGI Global. doi:10.4018/978-1-5225-5463-9.ch001

Przymus, S. D., & Smith, A. R. (2018). Eres un Gamer?: Engaging Transnational Children in Game-Ecology Language and Identity Socialization Within the EFL Environment. In J. Perren, K. Kelch, J. Byun, S. Cervantes, & S. Safavi (Eds.), *Applications of CALL Theory in ESL and EFL Environments* (pp. 269–290). Hershey, PA: IGI Global. doi:10.4018/978-1-5225-2933-0.ch015

Ramírez-Verdugo, M. D., & García de la Vega, A. (2018). A Conceptual Reference Framework for Sustainability Education in Multilingual and Cross-Cultural Settings: Applied Technology, Transmedia, and Digital Storytelling. In D. Tafazoli, M. Gomez Parra, & C. Huertas-Abril (Eds.), *Cross-Cultural Perspectives on Technology-Enhanced Language Learning* (pp. 222–236). Hershey, PA: IGI Global. doi:10.4018/978-1-5225-5463-9.ch013

Rao, Y., Wang, C., & Bender, J. (2016). French-Chinese Dialogical Interaction via Web Collaborative Blog-Writing: Code-Switching to Extend Online Tandem Language Learning. In C. Wang & L. Winstead (Eds.), *Handbook of Research on Foreign Language Education in the Digital Age* (pp. 208–234). Hershey, PA: IGI Global. doi:10.4018/978-1-5225-0177-0.ch010

Reitz, L., Sohny, A., & Lochmann, G. (2016). VR-Based Gamification of Communication Training and Oral Examination in a Second Language. *International Journal of Game-Based Learning*, *6*(2), 46–61. doi:10.4018/IJGBL.2016040104

Roberto, J. A. (2018). Cross-Cultural Languages Behind Technology-Enhanced Language Learning. In D. Tafazoli, M. Gomez Parra, & C. Huertas-Abril (Eds.), *Cross-Cultural Perspectives on Technology-Enhanced Language Learning* (pp. 16–46). Hershey, PA: IGI Global. doi:10.4018/978-1-5225-5463-9.ch002

Rosen, L. B., Maeda, M., & Roberts, N. (2017). Gain Time and Differentiate to Meet Student Needs in University Learning Environments: A Flipped Learning Approach. In J. Loucky & J. Ware (Eds.), *Flipped Instruction Methods and Digital Technologies in the Language Learning Classroom* (pp. 159–182). Hershey, PA: IGI Global. doi:10.4018/978-1-5225-0824-3.ch007

Sadeghi, A. R., & Ghorbani, S. (2017). The Impact of TED-Vodcast on Iranian EFL Learners' Academic Oral Proficiency. In D. Tafazoli & M. Romero (Eds.), *Multiculturalism and Technology-Enhanced Language Learning* (pp. 80–96). Hershey, PA: IGI Global. doi:10.4018/978-1-5225-1882-2.ch005

Sadoux, M. (2018). Life-Long Language Learning Strategies for a Brave New Digital World: Collaborative Design and Delivery of an Online Module. In C. Xiang (Ed.), *Cases on Audio-Visual Media in Language Education* (pp. 350–377). Hershey, PA: IGI Global. doi:10.4018/978-1-5225-2724-4.ch015

Sahragard, R., & Meihami, H. (2017). A Sociocultural Perspective into Intercultural Competence and Computer-Assisted Language Learning: Intercultural Competence and Computer-Assisted Language Learning. In D. Tafazoli & M. Romero (Eds.), *Multiculturalism and Technology-Enhanced Language Learning* (pp. 130–141). Hershey, PA: IGI Global. doi:10.4018/978-1-5225-1882-2.ch008

Saito, R., Thor, M. H., & Inose, H. (2018). Developing Intercultural Competence and Language Skills Through International Online Collaborative Learning. In C. Xiang (Ed.), *Cases on Audio-Visual Media in Language Education* (pp. 304–327). Hershey, PA: IGI Global. doi:10.4018/978-1-5225-2724-4.ch013

Santamaría-García, C. (2018). Connected Learners: Online and Off-Line Learning With a Focus on Politeness Intercultural Competences. In D. Tafazoli, M. Gomez Parra, & C. Huertas-Abril (Eds.), *Cross-Cultural Perspectives on Technology-Enhanced Language Learning* (pp. 83–99). Hershey, PA: IGI Global. doi:10.4018/978-1-5225-5463-9.ch005

Shahrokhi, M., & Taheri, S. (2016). The Impact of Blog Peer Feedback on Improving Iranian English Foreign Language Students' Writing. In C. Wang & L. Winstead (Eds.), *Handbook of Research on Foreign Language Education in the Digital Age* (pp. 365–386). Hershey, PA: IGI Global. doi:10.4018/978-1-5225-0177-0.ch017

Shiau, H., & Xiang, C. H. (2018). Learning English With Texting on Social Media: The Case of Taiwanese ESL Students in the U.S. In C. Xiang (Ed.), *Cases on Audio-Visual Media in Language Education* (pp. 240–260). Hershey, PA: IGI Global. doi:10.4018/978-1-5225-2724-4.ch010

Shin, D. (2018). Contextual Factors of Online Teacher Education in TESOL: An Activity Theory Perspective. In J. Perren, K. Kelch, J. Byun, S. Cervantes, & S. Safavi (Eds.), *Applications of CALL Theory in ESL and EFL Environments* (pp. 80–93). Hershey, PA: IGI Global. doi:10.4018/978-1-5225-2933-0.ch005

Smith, A. E., & O'Brien, D. (2018). Use of Videos in Teaching and Learning: Creating Language Video Resources for British Sign Language (BSL). In C. Xiang (Ed.), *Cases on Audio-Visual Media in Language Education* (pp. 1–21). Hershey, PA: IGI Global. doi:10.4018/978-1-5225-2724-4.ch001

Solmaz, O. (2018). Social Networking Sites: Cross-Cultural Perspectives, Implications, and Applicable Frameworks for L2 Teaching and Learning. In D. Tafazoli, M. Gomez Parra, & C. Huertas-Abril (Eds.), *Cross-Cultural Perspectives on Technology-Enhanced Language Learning* (pp. 118–129). Hershey, PA: IGI Global. doi:10.4018/978-1-5225-5463-9.ch007

Stannard, R., & Mann, S. (2018). Using Screen Capture Feedback to Establish Social Presence and Increase Student Engagement: A Genuine Innovation in Feedback. In C. Xiang (Ed.), *Cases on Audio-Visual Media in Language Education* (pp. 93–116). Hershey, PA: IGI Global. doi:10.4018/978-1-5225-2724-4.ch005

Stepanek, L., & Arriaga, C. G. (2018). Video Summaries of Academic Texts. In C. Xiang (Ed.), *Cases on Audio-Visual Media in Language Education* (pp. 328–349). Hershey, PA: IGI Global. doi:10.4018/978-1-5225-2724-4.ch014

Teng, F. (2017). A New Era of Applying CALL to Enhance EFL Learners' Lexical Knowledge. In J. Loucky & J. Ware (Eds.), *Flipped Instruction Methods and Digital Technologies in the Language Learning Classroom* (pp. 139–158). Hershey, PA: IGI Global. doi:10.4018/978-1-5225-0824-3.ch006

Vinagre, M. (2016). Developing Key Competences for Life-Long Learning through Virtual Collaboration: Teaching ICT in English as a Medium of Instruction. In C. Wang & L. Winstead (Eds.), *Handbook of Research on Foreign Language Education in the Digital Age* (pp. 170–187). Hershey, PA: IGI Global. doi:10.4018/978-1-5225-0177-0.ch008

Vurdien, R. (2017). Mobile Assisted Vocabulary Acquisition and Wikis to Enhance Writing Skills. *International Journal of Computer-Assisted Language Learning and Teaching*, *7*(2), 1–21. doi:10.4018/IJCALLT.2017040101

Vurdien, R., & Puranen, P. (2016). A Spanish-Finnish Telecollaboration to Develop Intercultural Competence and Learner Autonomy. *International Journal of Computer-Assisted Language Learning and Teaching*, *6*(3), 36–53. doi:10.4018/IJCALLT.2016070103

Vurdien, R., & Puranen, P. (2018). Intercultural Learning via Videoconferencing: Students' Attitudes and Experiences. In D. Tafazoli, M. Gomez Parra, & C. Huertas-Abril (Eds.), *Cross-Cultural Perspectives on Technology-Enhanced Language Learning* (pp. 264–282). Hershey, PA: IGI Global. doi:10.4018/978-1-5225-5463-9.ch015

Wang, A. (2018). Issues of Cross-Cultural Communications in a Globalizing Era. In D. Tafazoli, M. Gomez Parra, & C. Huertas-Abril (Eds.), *Cross-Cultural Perspectives on Technology-Enhanced Language Learning* (pp. 100–116). Hershey, PA: IGI Global. doi:10.4018/978-1-5225-5463-9.ch006

Werner, V., Lehl, M., & Walton, J. (2017). Pop Lyrics and Mobile Language Learning: Prospects and Challenges. *International Journal of Mobile and Blended Learning*, *9*(4), 33–48. doi:10.4018/IJMBL.2017100103

White, J. R. (2018). Marking Community Identity Through Languaging: Authentic Norms in TELL. In D. Tafazoli, M. Gomez Parra, & C. Huertas-Abril (Eds.), *Cross-Cultural Perspectives on Technology-Enhanced Language Learning* (pp. 47–67). Hershey, PA: IGI Global. doi:10.4018/978-1-5225-5463-9.ch003

Winstead, L. (2016). Mexican Heritage ELL and Native English Speaker Interaction: A Case Study of Tandem Language Learning Strategies. In C. Wang & L. Winstead (Eds.), *Handbook of Research on Foreign Language Education in the Digital Age* (pp. 334–364). Hershey, PA: IGI Global. doi:10.4018/978-1-5225-0177-0.ch016

Wu, P., & Marek, M. (2016). Incorporating LINE Smartphone Affordances: Cross-Cultural Collaboration, Willingness to Communicate, and Language Learning. *International Journal of Computer-Assisted Language Learning and Teaching*, *6*(2), 56–73. doi:10.4018/IJCALLT.2016040104

Xiang, C. H., & Moon, D. (2018). "Current Affairs in Mandarin": A Student-Led TV Talk Show at LSE. In C. Xiang (Ed.), *Cases on Audio-Visual Media in Language Education* (pp. 118–154). Hershey, PA: IGI Global. doi:10.4018/978-1-5225-2724-4.ch006

Yang, P. (2017). English Journal Writing on Moodle for EFL College Learners: An Investigation of English Self-Efficacy and Writing Performance. In D. Tafazoli & M. Romero (Eds.), *Multiculturalism and Technology-Enhanced Language Learning* (pp. 13–32). Hershey, PA: IGI Global. doi:10.4018/978-1-5225-1882-2.ch002

Yeromin, M., & Charskykh, I. (2017). Use of the Codes of Audio-Visual Media: Strengthening the Sub-Lingual International Communication in Higher Education. In D. Tafazoli & M. Romero (Eds.), *Multiculturalism and Technology-Enhanced Language Learning* (pp. 116–128). Hershey, PA: IGI Global. doi:10.4018/978-1-5225-1882-2.ch007

Yeromin, M. B., & Charskykh, I. (2018). Universal and Specific Codes of Cultural Context in Audio-Visual Media: Collision and Mutual Enrichment in International Technology-Enhanced Language Learning. In D. Tafazoli, M. Gomez Parra, & C. Huertas-Abril (Eds.), *Cross-Cultural Perspectives on Technology-Enhanced Language Learning* (pp. 68–82). Hershey, PA: IGI Global. doi:10.4018/978-1-5225-5463-9.ch004

Zhang, S. (2016). A Blended Chinese-as-a-Foreign-Language Short Course: Design and Perceptions. *International Journal of Computer-Assisted Language Learning and Teaching*, *6*(2), 35–55. doi:10.4018/IJCALLT.2016040103

Zhao, K. (2016). Enhancing Metacognitive Language Learning Strategy Use and Business Language Proficiency in Technology-Enhanced Collaborative Learning Environment. *International Journal of Computer-Assisted Language Learning and Teaching*, *6*(3), 68–78. doi:10.4018/IJCALLT.2016070105

About the Author

Kristina Posavec, originally from Zagreb, Croatia, has 12 years of experience in ICT education, primarily in long life adult education and university level education. Kristina currently works in Croatia as a lecturer of Computer Science at Faculty of Education and Rehabilitation, University of Zagreb and as IT project manager at University Computing Centre in Zagreb. She is actively participating in IT projects from HORIZON2020 (European Union scientific projects) were she is organizing, communicating, educating and writing about project activities and new technologies. In her line of work, she is closely working with primary and secondary schools, universities, professors, researchers and academia. She is actively involved in research projects, writing and reviewing scientific and research articles and presenting outcomes of the projects and researches on local and international conferences. Her main research interests are use of ICT in education, computer corpora, technology for language learning, assistive technologies, open science, digital competences, gamification, mobile learning, mixed and extended reality (VR and AR) used in education.

Index

www.ingramcontent.com/pod-product-compliance
Lightning Source LLC
LaVergne TN
LVHW081324300926
849161LV00008B/1867
* 9 7 8 1 7 9 9 8 3 6 8 0 3 *